WORLD WAR II
REMEMBERED

WORLD WAR II
REMEMBERED

by Residents of
Kendal at Hanover

∼

Clinton C. Gardner
Managing Editor

Editors
Jane Atwood Barlow
Robert W. Christie
Elinor Clark Horne
Mary Mecklin Jenkins
James E. Sheridan
Robert P. Stambaugh

KENDAL AT HANOVER RESIDENTS ASSOCIATION
Hanover, New Hampshire

Published by Kendal at Hanover Residents Association

Distributed by University Press of New England
One Court Street, Suite 250
Lebanon, NH 03766
www.upne.com

Manufactured in the United States of America
Designed by Linnea Spelman
Typeset in Minion Pro by Linnea Spelman

For permission to reproduce any of the material in this book, contact:
Clinton Gardner, Editor
Kendal at Hanover
80 Lyme Rd. # 263
Hanover, NH 03755
603-643-2335
clintgardnervt@gmail.com

Library of Congress Control Number: 2012931275
ISBN 978-0-9799970-0-6

Cover photograph "USS Shaw exploding during the Japanese attack on Pearl Harbor December 7, 1941" reproduced with permission from the National Archives.

Unless otherwise noted, all photographs are courtesy of the authors and their families. Photographs and maps from other sources are duly credited.

CONTENTS

The Pacific Theater and Far East

Stateside Service

Wartime in Europe and South America

Home Front

Post-War Service

Epilogue

ACKNOWLEDGMENTS

CHANCES ARE, MOST OF US WHO REMEMBER the events of December 7, 1941—and remember what we did during the next four years—won't be here a decade from now. Prompted by that realization, seven of us in the Kendal at Hanover retirement community (where we live among some 400 friends) decided to gather and publish the memoirs presented in this book.

At a meeting with prospective authors in February 2010, it became apparent that our book should include not only combat stories but also recollections of stateside service, life on the home front, and experiences while growing up in wartime Europe. Throughout the past year and a half our contributors worked with us to polish their essays and search old albums for wartime photos.

We also learned of Kendalites who had died in recent years but who had left written or recorded stories of wartime service. Their families went to great lengths to find the recordings and photos needed.

Cooperation in this endeavor has come from many sources.

First of all, we express deep gratitude to our 56 authors and their families who contributed the memoirs.

Next, we acknowledge, with special thanks, what we learned from the editors of a similar work, *Our Great War*, published in the fall of 2008 by residents of the Wake Robin retirement community in Shelburne, Vermont. In fact, it was after we learned of their book that we decided to produce one of our own. Our interest led Clint Gardner, early in 2010, to get in touch with Wake Robin resident Louise Ransom, the instigator of *Our Great War*, who told him just how they had gone about it, from recording memoirs when authors were not comfortable with writing, to ensuring stylistic consistency. For example, is this a book about WW II or WWII? We chose the first.

Recently a third New England retirement community, RiverWoods at Exeter, New Hampshire, published *The War We Knew*, their own collection of wartime memoirs, much like Wake Robin's *Our Great War*. This fine book includes maps and timelines, features which we ourselves had been planning for the present work—as the reader will soon see.

We also extend our thanks to several particular members of our Kendal community.

Edie Gieg's recordings of oral histories told by Bill Hotaling and Ed Scheu resulted in lively stories.

Corinne Johnson and Augusta Prince, two other Kendalites, were good enough to type up memoirs submitted as recordings or longhand manuscripts.

Dick Powell, as President of the Kendal at Hanover Residents Association last year, invited us to present our plans for the book to a meeting of the Association's Council. With his enthusiastic backing, the Council agreed that the Association would become the book's publisher.

We also offer our thanks to long-time memoir-writing instructor Joe Medlicott, for generously contributing our Introduction. We regret that the book's ground rules—only Kendalites as authors—prevented us from inviting him to contribute a story about his own European combat service, as a paratrooper with the 82nd Airborne Division.

While most of the photographs appearing in these pages were contributed by the authors themselves, a number of them came from other sources. The cover photo, for example, is from the United States National Archives. Other photos and maps are attributed below the image itself. The History Place web site (www.historyplace.com) helped us not only with their fine map of the Pacific Theater but also with facts for our Timeline. Similarly, the Matterhorn Travel web site (www.matterhorntravel.com) provided excellent maps for D-Day and the Battle of the Bulge.

Finally, we express our gratitude to the book's designer, Linnea Spelman. Patiently and with a sure eye, she has guided us through the production tasks so effectively as to enable us to bring out the book some weeks before its formal publication date of December 7, 2011—the 70th anniversary of Pearl Harbor.

It would delight us if our book, and similar collections, encouraged others of our generational peers to preserve their stories of WW II, as we have done here. All too soon the War will have no survivors.

—The Editors

INTRODUCTION

A DECORATED SOLDIER-COMPANION OF MINE was once asked by his grandson, "Were you a hero in the War, Granddad?" My friend answered, "No, but I served with a company of heroes."

"Hero" is an ambiguous word. But those who read the experiences written by the men and women in *World War II Remembered* will understand more fully the meaning of that word. There are 56 recollections of war in this remarkable book. Each account is a highly personal remembrance of life and death in a war fought 70 years ago in all corners of the globe. Each hero here captures the terror, the drama, the blood, and the boredom of war as they knew it. Each memory is a straightforward account of never-to-be-forgotten experiences. Each is a candid assessment of what it meant to serve.

Included in the collection is a vignette of a teenage girl who saved her allowance to buy chickens to supply food for the war effort. There is the tale of a physician who spent the entire War as a prisoner of the Japanese and received a medal for his extraordinary efforts in tending his fellow prisoners. There is a memoir by an Air Corps navigator who led his squadron over the wrong German target, bombed the wrong town, and yet destroyed an enemy armored division below. There is the story of an infantry non-com who never quite learned to sight his rifle but who effectively sprayed the enemy with machine-gun fire. There is the account of a man who, because of his deep-seated moral conscience, refused to fight; instead, he served "stateside" as a Conscientious Objector, a medical orderly, and a guinea pig in the Army's efforts to discover and fight infectious diseases among combat troops. And there are grainy photos here of men and women, many in uniform, that enrich each narrative. They are youthful, serious, focused, and intense as they carried the burdens of war. One photo shows a small squad of GIs on a barren German hillside; three of them were killed just days after the picture was snapped—portraits of young men forever frozen in time.

What stands out so clearly in these "remembrances of things past" is the unmistakable ring of authenticity in every account, a rare quality in the literature of war. Even after 70 years, every recollection remains vivid. Time has done little to dim those parlous times and recollections; they add depth and breadth to tales of wartime and to the significance of experiences lived in service.

There are no Hollywood heroics told in this collection. The cost of war is woven into the fabric of every tale, of every remembrance. Each writer "tells it like it was"—tells tales spun from the enormity of war at home and abroad. Like many such collections of experiences lived in times of terrible stress, *World War II Remembered* stands as a valuable historical document; each vignette answers the question asked by the grandson of my wartime companion. From every tale of high dramas and bitter consequences, from every tale of service rendered in places less dangerous than the front lines, what emerges is a chronicle of enormous sacrifice on the part of a great nation engaged in a great war.

Those who have contributed their remembrances here can be proud to share them with their sons and daughters, their husbands, wives, friends, and grandchildren who might ask what they did in the War—and if they were heroes. *World War II Remembered* is an exceptional human document—a legacy of greatness to be treasured for a very long time.

Joe Medlicott
Emeritus Professor of English, University of Connecticut.
Instructor of English, Deerfield Academy.
Teacher of memoir writing at The Institute for Lifelong Education at Dartmouth.
In World War II served as paratrooper with the 82nd Airborne Division.

World War II Timeline

Pre-War

1918   *November 11.* World War I ends, leaving Germany in a disastrous economic situation.

1933   Adolf Hitler takes power and sets out to establish a German empire in Europe. Persecution of Jews begins.

1937   Japan invades China.

1938   *September.* Germany seizes part of Czechoslovakia. Neville Chamberlain, Prime Minister of England, appeases Hitler at Munich. Nazi persecution of Jews intensifies.

War

1939   *September 1.* Germany invades Poland from the west.

September 3. Great Britain and France declare war on Germany, followed by Australia, Canada, and most of the British Commonwealth countries.

September 17. Soviet Union, under Joseph Stalin, invades Poland from the east.

1939–40 Germany conducts a series of *Blitzkriegs* (lightning wars) and overcomes Belgium, Denmark, Finland, France, Holland, and Norway.

1940   Britain, led by Prime Minister Winston Churchill, stands alone and undergoes bombing of both industrial and civilian targets.

1941   *June 22.* Germany breaks her nonaggression pact and attacks the Soviet Union.

December 7. Japanese attack Pearl Harbor in Hawaii and destroy much of the United States Pacific fleet.

December 8. The United States, led by President Franklin D. Roosevelt, declares war on Japan.

December 11. The United States declares war on Germany, Italy, and other Axis countries.

1942   The United States converts factories to produce planes and ships; conscripts young men into the armed forces; organizes auxiliary services for women.

Early. Japanese attack islands in Pacific and U.S. ships.

March. United States begins interning Japanese Americans.

June 4–5. The United States defeats Japanese navy at Midway.

August 7. The United States Marines attack Guadalcanal.

Summer. British and American victories in North Africa. The Soviet Union mounts heroic defense of Leningrad (St. Petersburg) and Stalingrad.

Nazis begin systematic extermination of Jews at death camps. The United States attacks Japanese-occupied territory in China from India by flying over the Himalayas.

1943   *July-September.* British, Canadian, and American troops invade Sicily, then southern Italy; Italy surrenders, but fighting continues as Allies battle north.

1944   *June 6.* D-Day. The Allies launch a major invasion of Normandy in France.

Summer. The United States invades Guam (*July 19*) and Leyte, Philippines (*October 20*).

August 25. Paris is liberated by the Allies.

December 16. The Germans launch a major counteroffensive ("The Battle of the Bulge") in the Ardennes Forest near the German-Belgian border.

1945   *February.* U.S. forces invade Iwo Jima; then, in April, Okinawa.

April 12. Roosevelt dies. Vice-President Harry Truman becomes President.

April 30. Hitler commits suicide.

May 8. V-E Day. The War in Europe ends with Germany's unconditional surrender.

August. The United States drops nuclear bombs on the Japanese cities of Hiroshima (*Aug. 6*) and Nagasaki (*Aug. 9*).

August 15. V-J Day. Japan surrenders, ending the deadliest conflict in human history, with well over 50 million fatalities.

The European Theater

EUROPEAN THEATER MAPS

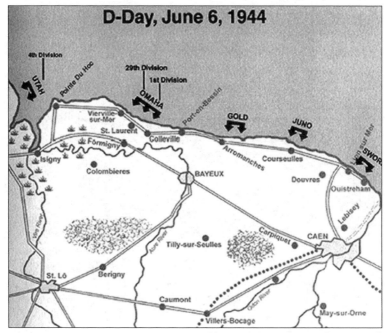

(Map courtesy of Matterhorn Travel)

1. D-Day, June 6, 1944

THREE OF OUR EUROPEAN THEATER AUTHORS describe what it was like to participate in the D-Day invasion of Normandy:

- **Francis Dymnicki**'s B-26 Marauder bomber attacked the big coastal guns to the west of Vierville on Omaha Beach.
- **Clint Gardner**, with the 29th Infantry Division, landed at 9:00 a.m. on the beach just in front of Vierville, "Omaha Dog Green."
- **Ed Scheu**'s Landing Craft Infantry (LCI) landed British troops at nearby Gold Beach.

In the weeks after D-Day, until July 19 the Germans prevented the American troops from taking the strategic city of Saint-Lô, shown lower left. Soon thereafter the American and British armies broke through the German lines—and the Americans reached Paris on August 25th.

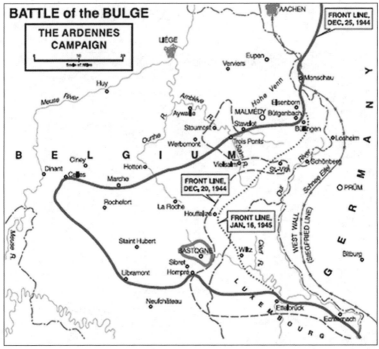

(Map courtesy of Matterhorn Travel)

2. The Battle of the Bulge, December 16, 1944–January 26, 1945

SEVEN OF OUR EUROPEAN THEATER AUTHORS describe their experiences during this critical battle. Four of them were wounded.

- **Bob Christie** was wounded while serving as a tank platoon leader in the Third Armored Division.
- **Francis Dymnicki**'s B-26 bomber flew so low that he was wounded by German flak.
- **John Fagan**, 75th Infantry Division, was seriously wounded at St. Vith on January 26.
- **Clint Gardner** was wounded at Malmedy on December 30.
- **Bill Hotaling** was captured near St. Vith in the first days of the Bulge.
- **Malcolm McLane** had his P-47 Thunderbolt shot down over the Bulge on December 23.
- **Bob Stambaugh**'s 36th Armored Infantry regiment was actively engaged in Bulge combat.

THE CAGE

~

Robert L. Allen
U.S. Army

Sergeant Robert Allen, a medic in the 86th Company of the 10th Mountain Division, was wounded in Italy on January 6, 1945. After several months in the hospital, he was discharged, placed on limited duty, and assigned to the Medical Division of the Disciplinary Training Center near Pisa.

ONE NIGHT IN MAY OF 1945 we saw flakes of blue light coming from the stockade at the Disciplinary Training Center. Acetylene torches, someone said; later we heard that they were reinforcing a cage to hold Ezra Pound. (The American poet had made broadcasts from Italy to American audiences and to American troops deploring the war between Italy and the United States. The U.S. government indicted him for acts of treason.)

The Disciplinary Training Center (DTC) spread over a broad field a few miles north of Pisa on the road to Viareggio. The ugly barbed-wire stockade held back the slime and filth of the whole Mediterranean

Theater of Operations: convicted rapists, murderers, and traitors who had been members of our armed forces. Each "trainee" was on his way to a federal prison in the United States—unless he could "soldier out" of the DTC.

By following a fantastic routine, accepting cruelty in the extreme, and turning himself into a "GI" automaton, a trainee could have his federal prison term canceled and be returned to duty. This took a lot of guts or a lot of hate, and not all men could do it. One afternoon some of them tried to run away, but businesslike short bursts from an automatic rifle in a guard tower chopped them down. (I rode to the hospital with two of them and watched helplessly while they bled to death.) Some had a try at suicide and others poured lye on their feet to earn a trip to the hospital in Pisa.

Inside the stockade there was a secondary enclosure for the Medical and Dental sections, two mess halls, several areas where the trainees pitched their pup tents, and solitary confinement and death cells. The solitary cells, "boxes," were seven-foot concrete cubes with peepholes in their steel doors. To be "boxed" meant two weeks on bread and water with a blanket and a bucket. The death cells were wire cages about ten feet square at the base and seven feet high. Condemned prisoners, later to be hanged at Aversa, paced the cages.

The jailers at the DTC (the Headquarters Company, Provost, Guard, and Medical sections) lived in pyramidal tents outside the stockade. We had our own mess hall, recreation hall, and stables (the colonel liked to ride). The Provost Section men had the most to do with the prisoners. Their whim was law to the trainees and their job was to assure that life as a trainee was tougher than life at the front. It was interesting to observe how quickly many of the new men in the Provost section learned to enjoy their work.

The Provost boys were in charge of Ezra Pound.

A Frustrated Old Man

The morning after we had seen the acetylene torches, all DTC personnel were ordered to keep clear of Pound; no one was to speak to him. I recognized him easily by the beard and the glasses. His molting, amber Vandyke was not the red beard that once bounded through the salons and cafés of London and Paris. The Ezra Pound in the cage was a frustrated old man who had never received the recognition he desired—recognition that came to a number of his associates.

He wore an Army fatigue uniform, unbuttoned at the neck. He walked back and forth on the concrete floor, making no effort to look outside. His trousers hung loose and his shoes were unlaced. (Belts and shoelaces were always taken from men in the cages.) A special guard stood outside his cage, which, at night, was brightly lighted. Everyone looked at him. The trainees marching by or working the area considered Pound with awe, taking the reinforced cage as evidence that he was a particularly tough customer.

The United States authorities had taken him into custody at Rapallo, where he made his home, and brought him directly to the DTC. The weeks in the cage were hard on Pound. As shelter, a piece of tarpaper was thrown over the top. Also, he had a pup tent, which—quite ingeniously—he pitched in several different ways. Later he told me of spending hours watching wasps construct a nest and of his fascination with the work of an ant colony. He was permitted books and writing materials but refused a typewriter because, he said, the "damned dust would ruin it." His daily exercises caused quite a stir. He would engage in imaginary tennis matches, making graceful, looping forehands and backhands. He assumed fencing stances and danced nimbly about the cage, shadow-boxing.

"What's he training for?" one of the trainees asked me.

Through his antics he became a camp character, and after a while he exchanged a few clandestine words each day with the trainees who brought his food. Because the dust and harsh sun in the cage inflamed his eyes, he was transferred to a tent within the Medical Compound. His furniture was an Army cot and a small wooden packing crate; later a second packing crate and a table were added.

During the first week or so in the Medical Compound he kept to himself in his tent. His food, eaten from an Army mess kit, was handed to him through the Medical Compound fence. He soon stripped off his Army fatigue clothes and spent the warm summer days comfortably attired only in Army olive drab underwear, a fatigue cap, and GI shoes and socks.

He found an old broom handle that became a tennis racquet, a billiard cue, a rapier, a baseball bat to hit small stones, and a stick which he swung out smartly to match his long stride. His constitutionals wore a circular path in the compound grass.

It was arranged for Pound to come on sick call after the trainees and to receive treatment, if necessary, in the evenings. Foot baths and eye drops were the most frequent prescriptions on his card. Far from being reticent in talking about his case, he seemed anxious to discuss the charges against him, and we in the Medical Section were a good audience. He claimed that he would never be brought to trial because he "had too much on several people in Washington" for the Government to allow him to testify in court. He admitted that he had made broadcasts from Rome, but said that they were in no way treasonable and that he had never supported the Fascists. His connection with Mussolini was brushed off lightly with a laugh. He said that he had seen "Muss" (or "Ben") once and then they had talked only for a short time about nonpolitical matters. It was clear that Mussolini had not given him the time or attention he thought his economic theories warranted. After his evening treatment, he would stride to the door of our prefab, put his crumpled Army fatigue hat onto the back of his head, tuck his stick under his arm, and wave an appreciative and smiling good night.

Pound's Psychiatrist

Pound's conduct was a welcome topic of conversation at the DTC. His sanity was questioned not only by trainees but also, eventually, by the camp psychiatrist. Stories about Pound's interview with the psychiatrist flew around the camp: a trainee working with the psychiatrist had told a friend about it. Pound, always spoken of as "Ezra," became sort of a hero among the trainees when word was spread that he had "made a dummy of the psychiatrist"—that he had turned questions around so that even the psychiatrist became confused. In the end, the unofficial opinion of the psychiatrist was that Ezra Pound was sane, although perhaps "a little exotic," as one of my friends put it.

Throughout the summer of 1945 Pound was in excellent spirits. He was granted permission to use the dispensary typewriter in the evening, and it was not unusual to see him typing a letter to some trainee's girl or mother, with the trainee dictating at his shoulder and Pound interpreting for him.

After taps when all trainees were in their tents, Pound worked on his *Cantos* and Chinese translations. The constant clanging and banging of the typewriter, which he punched angrily with his index fingers, were always accompanied by a high-pitched humming sound he made as the carriage raced the bell. He swore well and profusely over typing errors.

During the late evenings, the only person with him was the Charge of Quarters (CQ), and often, after typing, Pound would let down completely to rant and rave about the "dunghill usurers" and "usurping cutthroats." Among others, he damned Mussolini ("the crude peasant"), Hitler, FDR, Churchill, and Henry Morgenthau. His green eyes snapped as he tapped his glasses on the desk and shouted that the American people had been swindled on monetary exchanges. He insisted that wars could be avoided if the true nature of money were understood. "When," he would ask, "will the United States return to Constitutional government?"

The rainy, gray fall weather came and Pound's tent was anything but comfortable. His request for more blankets was delayed for a week while an officious corporal pondered the matter.

He became extremely depressed. One evening I borrowed a book of Chinese translations from him. "Please, don't lose it and return it in the morning," he said. "It's my very blood and bone." He told us that when he was picked up in May, he had expected to be flown directly to Washington. Even when the vehicle carrying him stopped at the DTC, he thought that his visit would end as soon as a plane was readied at Pisa airfield. Then, in that cold, wet fall, with no indication of when the occupation of Italy would be terminated, he almost despaired of ever leaving Pisa.

He read voraciously—novels, magazines, everything that was given to him. The Mediterranean edition of *The Stars and Stripes* and the overseas editions of *Time* and *Newsweek* were his sources of news. Early in November *The Stars and Stripes* carried a story that six Italian radio technicians were to be flown to Washington to testify at a grand-jury investigations of his case. Pound knew that, in order to establish him as a traitor, the Justice Department would have to produce at least two witnesses who had seen him commit a treasonous act. At first he made light of the whole story and asserted that no one had ever seen him broadcast. He said that the six technicians were obviously impostors "just making the flight to get some decent food."

His last two weeks at the DTC were the most difficult for him. His tone of conversation changed, and occasionally he spoke of himself in the past tense. Several times he said, "If I go down, someone must carry on."

One evening after taps in the middle of November, Pound was sitting in the dispensary reading Joseph E. Davies' *Mission to Moscow.* The CQ sat at the desk next to him. From time to time Pound commented on the book. Suddenly the door opened and two young lieutenants entered. They told Pound that he would be flown to Washington in one hour and to get his personal effects together. They turned and left. Pound handed the book to the CQ and asked him to thank all the medical personnel for their kindness. He then walked to the door of the prefab, turned, and with a half-smile, put both hands around his neck to form a noose and jerked up his chin.

At his trial in Washington, D.C., Ezra Pound was declared insane by a board of psychiatrists and was committed to St. Elizabeth's Hospital.

The preceding account was published as a letter in Esquire *magazine, February 1958. Ezra Pound was released after 12 years and returned to Italy, where he died in 1972.*

Bob worked in the Public Relations Department of Dartmouth College in the 1950s and became Assistant Secretary of the College. In 1960 he and his family moved to Lincoln, Massachusetts. He worked for the Kendall Company in Boston and later became Vice President of the Kendall Foundation in Boston. He and his wife Carol retired to Castine, Maine, and in 2005 moved to Kendal at Hanover.

THE WRONG TOWN

~

James Wheeler Ashley
U.S. Army Air Force

As remembered by his wife Joan

JIM ASHLEY HAD KNEE REPLACEMENT IN 2002. All went well, but by the end of the second day, he was becoming agitated about his confinement and announced he was going to get up. Of course I told him no, but he wasn't listening. It was time for me to leave. I went to the nursing station and told them that he was acting strangely, and just might really try to get out of bed. I was waved off by the male nurse with an, "Oh no, don't you worry!" The phone rang when I got back to our Norwich house. Jim had gotten out of bed and fallen. I rushed back. He seemed sobered by his adventure but sure he was OK. Since Jim had proved to be unreliable, a sitter or minder was called. She came at 11:00 p.m. and I went home. The next morning I hurried back; I knew the shift changed at 7:00 a.m. and I wondered who was minding Jim now.

Opening the door, I found a nice-looking man about Jim's own age. They were deep in conversation. I sat in the corner and knitted. World

War II. "What were you in?" "Army Air Force." "Army Air Force." "Where were you stationed? " "Toward the end of the war, in France." "Me too." "What position were you in?" "Pilot." "Navigator." "What did you fly?" "B-26; we called it the Baltimore Whore because, with its short wings, it had no visible means of support." "So did we." They yarned away, having the best time with old memories.

Then the other guy, the pilot, whose name was Ken Magner, said "There is one mission I will never forget, December 23, 1944." Silence. Jim's eyes widened and with a sharp intake of breath, he said, "I was on that one too!" They were staring at each other and I had goose bumps.

Evidently Jim's group had gone in first over the German rail yard and identified the target; then Jim, as lead navigator, gave the signal to drop the bombs, after which his plane peeled off and set out for home base. Their attack, however, stirred up a vigorous German antiaircraft defense, and Ken's group, arriving at the target a bit later, suffered enormous damage; about half of the group's planes were lost. And all the while it went on, Jim listened to it on his plane's radio.

To think that in a hospital tucked away in mid-New Hampshire 58 years later, two old veterans would be talking about the very same mission over Germany, reliving the fear and the horror! The room had gone silent as they both remembered. After he was released from the hospital, it was discovered that Jim would have to return for more surgery on his knee as a result of his Type-A certainty that walking to the bathroom was a cinch. In the meantime, the story about Ken and Jim had gotten around the hospital, and a man from radiology asked Jim if he could do a videotape of him describing all his wartime adventures. Ken too. They both said yes, and it is that tape of Jim from which I have taken the following story.

It started off as a routine mission to bomb a railroad on the border of Belgium and Germany. Jim, lead navigator again, with map in hand, spied the target and so signaled. All 36 planes in the group dropped their bombs. As they turned away from the target, Jim realized with a numbing chill of horror that the town they had bombed was not their assigned target. They had bombed the wrong town! It was a quiet flight back to their base in France. They immediately reported their mistake to the Colonel. Although it had been Jim's call, the entire crew of his plane—five men—were held responsible. The Colonel ordered them to be confined to their tents while he looked into the matter. It was a sober afternoon as the five of them contemplated a possible court-martial.

The hours wore on. Finally the MPs drove up again in a jeep and took them to headquarters. The Colonel shouted at them, "You are the luckiest sons-of-bitches I ever knew!" The report had gone through all the levels of SHAEF (Supreme Headquarters Allied Expeditionary Force) to the top, the Canadian General Dempsey at that time. Then the word traveled back down the pyramid to the Colonel's desk. A German panzer division had moved into the town shortly before Jim's group arrived overhead. That division had therefore been the accidental target of the American attack, and was destroyed. General Dempsey's note read, "Best job of strategic bombing I ever saw."

Instead of court-martials, all five of the crew received the Distinguished Flying Cross.

In addition to that Distinguished Flying Cross, by the War's end, when Jim had flown 40 missions, he was awarded the Air Medal, seven Oak Leaf Clusters, and five battle stars.

Jim was born in 1923 and grew up in La Grange, Illinois. After a short stint at Fordham University, he was called into the Cadet Program, in which he had enlisted after Pearl Harbor. The Bomb ended the War before Jim could transfer to Japan, and he was discharged almost immediately. He talked his way into Northwestern Law School (without finishing his undergraduate degree). He married and had five children. Jim practiced law at McDermott, Will & Emery in Chicago until his retirement. In 1975, he married Joan Crawford and in 1988 they moved to Vershire, Vermont. Later they lived in Norwich, Vermont, and in 2006 they moved to Kendal at Hanover, where Jim died in 2007.

On Death, Hunting, and Killing

~

Robert W. Christie, M.D.
U.S. Army

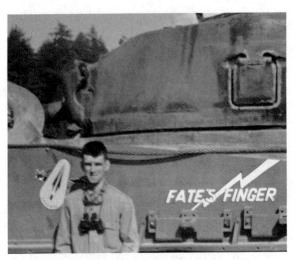

Bob next to his M4A3 Sherman tank, 'Fate's Finger,'
at War's end, May, 1945, near the Elbe River

Y MEMORIES FROM WORLD WAR II were published in 2001 as *Fate's Finger*, a memoir partially fictionalized for reasons explained in its preface. In the book, my *alter ego*, Morrie Shapiro, depicts my personal experiences to the extent that I wished them to be known.

Therefore, rather than relating even more War stories here, I have chosen three poems that express my feelings about my service in the European Theater of Operations as a platoon leader and eventually company commander in a medium tank company of the 33rd Armored Regiment of the Third Armored Division, First Army.

The first poem consists of the lyrics from a song by an unknown author. I heard it sung occasionally in the battalion during intervals between action, as memorialized in Chapter 14 of *Fate's Finger*. The last two poems are my own.

I. Experiential Advice

This poem's lyrics are a parody of the folk song "The Wabash Cannon Ball," occasionally sung to a guitar. The Colonel referred to was Lt. Col. William Lovelady, Second Battalion commander in the 33rd Armored Regiment of the Third Armored Division. He was a personally fearless and militarily aggressive commander. In combat, he could be seen standing on the back of his tank, smoking his pipe while issuing commands. Everyone in his battalion felt that they were personally violating one of *Murphy's Laws of Combat*: "Never follow a guy braver than yourself."

My initial assignment to the Third Armored was to the Second Battalion of the 33rd AR during the German Ardennes offensive, commonly called "The Battle of the Bulge." After returning to the Division from a hospital in Liege, Belgium, I was reassigned to Company F in the Third Battalion as a tank platoon leader.

THE TENNESSEE CANNONBALL
(Author unknown)

Said the Colonel to the General
"I'm from Soddy, Tennessee
And I've taken the Second Battalion
Clear into Germany.

"I'm Commander of the Task Force
Of B and D and E
And I will take them deeper in
If they will follow me."

Said the General to the Colonel
In a loud and rasping voice,
"Just order them to go on in
They have no other choice."

Said the General to the Colonel
"If you take them 'cross the bar,
I'll write you up for a DSC
And another Silver Star."

"There's nothing there to stop you
But a little small arms fire."
(If an 88's a "small arm"
Then I'm a goddam liar.)

"Oh, shoot, shoot, shoot, keep rollin' boys
There's nothing up ahead."
Twenty minutes later
The whole Task Force was dead.

So you tankers just remember
While you burn that gasoline
Remember what the Colonel said
And what the Colonel's seen.

And if you want to draw Old Fogey pay
And see your folks next fall
Stay thirty miles behind the tanks
Of the Tennessee Cannonball!

II. Faith in God

This poem reflects my reaction to the irony, indeed my perception of the hypocrisy, inherent in expressions of our often-professed devotion to biblical scripture as a bulwark of our Christian faith and love in times of stress when the chips are down, and particularly when *"Gott [ist] mit uns!"* The poem is structured to show the realistic progression of apprehension, surprise, fear, acknowledgment, response, control, rage, and relief in combat.

TANK!
A Reading from Psalm 55, Holy Bible (NRSV)
(Verses 1–6; 15; 23.)

1. Give ear to my prayer, O God
do not hide yourself from my
supplication

God, help me! I'm scared!

2. Attend to me, and answer me;
I am troubled in my complaint.
I am distraught

Jesus, a Mark V......!

3. by the noise of
the enemy,
because of the clamor of the
wicked.

The sonofabitch sees us...

For they bring trouble upon me,
and in anger they cherish
enmity against me.

The eighty-eight's swinging towards us...

4. My heart is in anguish within me,
the terrors of death have fallen upon me.

*"Gunner! Tank! AP! Crosshairs on turret cross...
Traverse right....Steaddddy ...... On!"*

5. Fear and trembling come upon me,
and horror overwhelms me.

My heart's thumping, I'm shaking. Christ!

6. And I say "Oh that I had wings like a dove!
I would fly away and be at rest;

Settle down, man. You're on your own.

15. Let death come upon them;
let them go down alive to
Sheol;
for evil is in their homes
and in their hearts.

Okay, Smitty, let's get him.... Now....! FIRE!
Bow gun! Cut the fuckers down if any bail out!

23. But you, O God, will cast them down
into the lowest pit;
The bloodthirsty and treacherous
shall not live out half their days.
But I will trust in you.

Christ, we got the bastards! We're alive!
Thanks be to you, O God of love!
Selah.

III. Existential Guilt

This last poem expresses the feelings of guilt I have had since returning from the War— long after. I finally realized I was experiencing what theologian Martin Buber has characterized as *existential guilt*: that is, guilt related to harm actually done to others. The poem arose out of somewhere deep in memory some fifty years later. Perhaps this is a World War II analog of what is presently called "post-traumatic stress syndrome" in service personnel returning from combat. I have wondered if my choice of medicine as a life's work was an unconscious attempt to expiate such guilt.

HUNTER

I am not a hunter.
I am a killer.
Once you have killed
you are a killer,
not a hunter.

I hunted bullfrogs with a BB gun.
I got 'em.
I once shot at a dragonfly in flight.
A big one.
Nailed him.

When I got a .22 I went for squirrels.
And chipmunks.
Got a lot of them.
Skun a red squirrel out once.
Stretched it on a frame of sticks I made myself
and stretched the pelt tight with fishing line.
I was proud.
Kept it for years.

Caught fish too.
Sunfish to salmon.
That is not called hunting.
It has a different name:
Fishing.
Why?
Because you catch it by deception
and then kill it?

I bought a shotgun.
Good for partridge.
At least I ate them.

The U.S. Army gave me a Garand.
Govt. Issue: M-1.
I was a good shot.
Expert Marksman the medal said.

Then they gave me the 76 mm cannon
and three machine guns
attached to 'Fate's Finger':
Medium tank, an M4A3.

I hunted people with it.
Some I never saw.
Shot them with HEs,
high explosive shells,
in houses in bleak wrecked towns
two thousand yards away.

Women, kids, old people, enemy soldiers?
Who knows?
They could never lay it on me.
Two thousand yards away, right?

I hunted big cats:
panzers, Tigers and Panthers
while they were hunting me.
The hunter-killer game.
I got all of them first.
APs.
Armor Piercing.
Expert Marksman, right?
Wrong.
Lucky bastard.

When I came home
I bought a thirty-ought-six,
bolt-action, an old friend.
Still-hunted white-tail deer,
but only bucks.
One shot, neck or heart.
Chivalrous chauvinist.
Their antlers hang in my camp.
Thank God
they couldn't hunt me.

I am not a hunter.
I am a killer.
I always will be.

I was only a hunter
until that first frog.
Now I hunt only for truth.
I can't kill that.

Bob is a retired pathologist who enlisted while still a student at Norwich University, the country's oldest private military college, shortly after Pearl Harbor. He emerged from the Army forty months later after having served as a tank company commander with the Third Armored Division during the War in Europe, and later in the Constabulary, the post-combat occupation force in Germany. He was awarded a Bronze Star and three Battle Stars (Ardennes, Rhineland, Central Germany). His war stories, first as a tank platoon leader and later as company commander, are recorded in a published memoir, Fate's Finger *(Xlibris, 2001, ISBN 1-4010-2914-0). Bob and his wife Connie came to Kendal at Hanover in 2008.*

Coming in Low under the Clouds

~

Francis Dymnicki
U.S. Army Air Force

With his B-26 crew, Francis stands second from right

I ENLISTED IN THE ARMY AIR FORCE IN 1943. My first assignment was for training at an Air Force radio school in Sioux Falls, South Dakota. Radio school was distinguished by the fact that the field was on a 24-hour schedule, with reveille (wake-up call) at 12 midnight. Keeping awake during classes was difficult, and if you were caught dozing three times you were forced to finish the class standing up. Getting proper sleep was equally difficult when those in the barracks had days off and made a lot of noise carousing around.

When I was able to take Morse code 20 words per minute, I was shipped out to gunnery school in Laredo, Texas, a desolate area next to the Mexican border. At gunnery school, along with weapon disassembling and reassembling, which had to be done blindfolded, there was shooting of all kinds, all day and every day: skeet shooting, shooting from a truck as it traveled a circuitous route, and machine-gun shooting, as an actual rear gunner from A-6 aircraft, where you were in an open cockpit behind the pilot, an experience similar to that of a World War I gunner.

That course completed, I was shipped to Barksdale Field, Louisiana, for assignment as a crew member on a B-26 Marauder bomber. There were six men to a crew: pilot, co-pilot, bombardier, navigator, engineer, and a radioman who also served as a waist gunner—all good men. They came from various parts of the country.

The B-26 was a medium bomber used in both the European and the Pacific Theaters. It had the best mission-survival experience of any of the combat aircraft, but it required an experienced pilot to get it off and back onto the ground in one piece. It was considered to be a "hot ship" and, as with many other types of World War II aircraft, was often referred to as "the flying prostitute" because it was said that it had no visible means of air support. It made up for this apparent lack of support by its speed. B-17s took off at 70 miles per hour, but B-26s had to get up to 120 m.p.h., which made it difficult to control on take-off and landing. At Tampa Bay airfield, where the runway ran to the water's edge, the story was, "two a day at Tampa Bay." High attrition during training at Barksdale was due to the fact that green pilots were at the controls, which greatly contributed to the frequency of crashes.

From Barksdale to Stone

When we finished training at Barksdale Field, we were deemed qualified to fly to Europe. We were picked up by Air Transport in Homestead Field, Florida. Our first leg was to Cuba, where I picked up a case of bourbon for the munificent sum of $32. My idea was that we could celebrate successful landings each step of the way—which would take us to Brazil, then over the Atlantic to Africa, and finally up the coast to England.

From Cuba, the next destination was Recife, Brazil, located where the South American continent projects farthest east into the Atlantic Ocean. We slept under netting and were too exhausted to do more than tumble into bed at night.

After Brazil, the next leg of the journey was to the island of Ascension—a tiny speck of land close to Africa. It was a hairy trip, and although we had gas tanks in the bomb bay where we would have carried bombs on a combat mission, the possibility of running out of gas while over the Atlantic was worrisome. But we had a good navigator and we made it.

After flying to Liberia and Morocco, we reached our final destination. It was night when we landed at an Air Force base in Stone, southern England. Stone was a large munitions depot staffed mostly by women. Great Britain was drafting women into military service and placing them anywhere they were needed for the war effort.

My bombardier crewmate and I thought we would investigate Stone and found our way to a hall full of dancers—90% of them women; in a minute it seemed that the whole dance floor's occupants started towards us. We looked at one another, recognized that we were hopelessly outnumbered, and rather than jeopardize British-American relations, beat a hasty retreat. England was obviously going to be a pleasant destination—although we soon learned of the jealousy of British servicemen, who said that American GIs were "over-paid, over-sexed, and over here"!

At our new base we were assigned to groups and squadrons. The men were glad to see us: we were the first replacements their outfits had received since they had arrived there. The length of their tours of duty before rotation had kept being extended. Tour length started at 25 missions, then went to 30 missions, then 40, and by the time I finished it was 65 missions. B-17 crews flew only 35 missions before rotation back to the United States, but their missions were longer than ours and they traveled greater distances. There was competition between us, and they railed against what they considered unfairness. We countered that they spent a lot of time over "Splasher 17" (Atlantic Ocean) and climbed to a safer 30,000-foot altitude, which took a lot of non-combat time.

Good guys, though.

We flew day-missions that focused mostly on bombing bridges that crossed the Seine. All the bridges (some seemed to be over cow paths) were soon down—from Paris to the Atlantic. This was to prevent the Germans from moving easily to counter the invasion that was expected to come. On some of our missions I was surprised to discover what an important part train traffic played in the War.

As D-Day approached, we would drop altitude making our way home, and we could see troops loading onto barges. Some of those poor guys stayed on their craft for two or three days before D-Day, appearing to be headed for Calais in France so that the Germans would think that Calais was where the invasion would be. This was part of an elaborate effort to make the enemy think that General Patton would lead the invasion. It was believed that the German high command considered Patton to be the best general the Allies had and that they feared him the most; where he went was where the invasion would begin.

D-Day eve, the officers of our squadron came into our barracks and told us to get some early rest because big things were about to happen. And happen they did. Reveille was 12 midnight, and as we made our way to the briefing room we could see every plane that could fly being prepared and painted with identification stripes. Our group soon took off, and we found the skies around us over the English Channel loaded with airplanes scrambling into position. It was D-Day, and below us was a wide panorama of ships of all sizes and shapes, all headed in the same direction. It had to be seen to be believed.

B-26 Marauder bombers, as painted for D-Day

Our assigned target that eventful day was the big coastal guns on the bluffs overlooking the beaches in Normandy. Below us our U.S. Navy's guns were blasting away, and it was obvious that the invasion was really under way. We were only over our target for two or three minutes, and after bomb release we banked sharply and headed home unscathed.

That same afternoon we prepared for another mission. Because of the extended daylight hours at Britain's latitudes, we could fly until almost 10:30 p.m., and therefore very often flew two missions a day.

Our second mission on D-Day afternoon was with Col. Vance, the commander of the group; his presence was considered to be a great honor. Col. Vance had been on Corregidor with General MacArthur, and a story associated with him was that when MacArthur's staff flew from Corregidor, to make weight for Vance on the overloaded plane a hundred pounds of gold bullion had to be tossed out, making him worth his weight in gold. Col. Vance hated the Japanese and believed that the European Theatre was a sideshow in comparison to the war in the Pacific. The slogans in our group during that period were "Take a chance over France with Col. Vance" and "Two a day over the Pas de Calais."

This afternoon mission was to bomb a marshalling railroad yard in Amiens, a town known to have a beautiful cathedral. I remember that the weather on D-Day was terrible, with a ceiling of about 1,000 to 1500 feet. We normally flew at 12,000 feet. Altitude was of course important because the accuracy of the flak thrown up was much lower at higher altitudes: for every 1,000 feet of altitude the flak lost one foot of accuracy, so the level we came in at on a bombing run made a huge difference in the amount of danger from enemy ground fire. On this day, though, we had to fly so low that I could actually see their guys in foxholes aiming their rifles at us.

The usual routine in a bombing run over target was to follow guidance by the lead plane's bombardier. When he released his bombs, it was the signal for all the 36 planes in the group to follow suit. We hit our target that afternoon, destroying a German panzer division on its way to the invasion scene. Fortunately, all of our planes came home safely, although a few airmen were wounded by ground fire. We were put in for a Presidential Citation for accomplishing this dangerous mission; unfortunately, a few missions later, we dropped bombs on our own troops, so no citation.

My job on the B-26 was to maintain radio contact with our base. As we approached enemy territory, I left the radio and became the waist gunner, manning two .50-caliber machine guns, one on each side of the plane. My job also was to go through the bomb bay and pull the pins from the bombs, thereby arming them before they were dropped.

When the flak got heavy, the guys would yell, "Nick, pull in the gun!" so they could bail out quickly if we were badly hit; the parachutes we wore were chest 'chutes that required lots of clearance for a quick exit.

Piccadilly

For relief from stress we sometimes had 48-hour passes, usually every ten days. Those times, we took off for London—where most of us headed straight for Piccadilly Circus and its many "ladies of the night." There we were, young American flyboys on leave, many of us virgins, dickering with professionals for a new adventure and rite of passage in a city far from home. I remember one song that was popular with the Brits at the time. Here I'm including only the second verse of "The Piccadilly Hymn," as the other verses are unprintable:

> I don't want to be a sojer,
> I don't want to go to war;
> > Just want to hang around
> > Piccadilly Underground
> Livin' off the earnin's
> Of an 'igh-clas leidy ...

Being a well-brought-up American boy, of course, for my entertainment I headed for the British Museum, with its magnificent sculpture, Parthenon friezes, and great paintings.

After the encirclement of the enemy and subsequent breakthrough in Falaise in northern France, we flew further beyond the front. Our outfit bombed targets in France, and then in Germany. The 9th Air Force was a tactical outfit (as compared with a strategic B-17 unit) that supported troops and focused on targets of opportunity. This tactical function was distinct from the strategic function of the B-17s, so we moved from our airfield in England to a decrepit French airfield near Pontoise, but this was not at all bad. Now when we had a pass, we could get to Paris instead of London.

The Battle of the Bulge

The big event, of course, was the Battle of the Bulge. The Germans had assembled 1,000 tanks and some crack troops with the hope of dividing the American and British forces and then carrying on to the North Sea. The Germans were blessed by bad weather because the flight ceiling, averaging about 1200 feet, severely limited Allied tactical air support to ground troops. The situation became increasingly dire, so we were ordered to fly whatever the ceiling, meaning we had to go in to bomb enemy tanks. We did this in three-ship flights at low altitude and so were vulnerable to enemy ground fire. My leg caught some of the flak they threw at us, but we were able to get back to the field, where I received medical care and thus survived the ordeal.

The weather cleared, and General Patton was anxious to cut off the Germans from behind their advance, so the Air Force was able to start bombing again. War, of course, is a matter of luck and opportunity; we needed both so that generals like Patton could take advantage of the situation.

Eventually, when the War ended in Europe five months later, we went back to England and got on a troop ship that took us back to the United States. The ship I was on was crammed with freed American P.O.Ws, whose pockets were loaded with back pay, and card and dice games took place all over the ship. I recall that $24,000 was in the pot in one of the crap games—far, far out of my league.

I finally saw the Statue of Liberty and was discharged shortly thereafter, having flown 65 missions and earned five battle stars and a Purple Heart.

A native of New York City, Francis was educated there in public elementary schools, Stuyvesant High School, and New York University. After the War he worked as a lithographic printer and helped establish a large printing company. A volunteer in the New York Botanical Garden for many years, he developed a special interest in ferns. He is a gardener and raises orchids. Francis came to Kendal at Hanover in 1996.

MEETING THE ENEMY

~

Kingsley Ervin
U.S. Army

FIFTEEN OF US WERE SITTING IN THE BACK OF THE GMC, on wooden benches along either side of the truck bed. Heaped in the middle lay our duffle bags, along with the equipment needed in a fire-direction center. There seemed little danger of enemy fire. We had taken off our helmets in the early spring cool of April. Even the canvas cover over our heads had been rolled back.

The truck moved slowly, in convoy, along unfamiliar German roads. After the collapse of the Remagen counteroffensive, we had crossed the Rhine, our division still attached to Patton's Third Army. In theory we were chasing the retreating enemy. But enemies were hard to find: a few straggling groups of soldiers, adolescents or older men from the *Heimwehr*, pathetic local defense groups. We would round them up, and they would be sent off with the troops assigned to collect prisoners. We drove into small villages where no inhabitants appeared, and frightened shopkeepers tending empty shelves could tell us little. Only rarely had we had to set up the howitzer attack that was our battalion's mission, to provide close covering fire for the 89th Infantry Division as it moved across a battle line.

On this afternoon we were driving through a thin woods when the trucks stopped before wooden gates, tall and protected by barbed wire. Carbines ready, we got out and approached the gates warily. But we saw that they were open, and we entered a large yard with buildings beyond.

All around the yard were huddled shapes. It did not take us long to see they were bodies, clothed in striped, filthy pajama-like garments. The heads were shaved, the faces gaunt. A few were lying face up, staring at the sky. As we entered further we could see more bodies, some piled in heaps. The buildings seemed mainly empty, though a few shapes lay about on the floors. Everywhere was a cold, sweetish, rotten smell, distantly of sweat and dirt, but somehow abstracted and sinister.

An officer came up. We went to hear what he had to say. "The SS shot them all before they took off." From what? None of us had heard of forced labor camps. No one knew what to do.

Then we noticed that some of the bodies were still alive. An arm moved, a head turned slowly. We went over and looked. One or two of us knelt down to see whether we could help.

Our Battalion Commander's Order

More trucks stopped, and a call came to fall in—to assemble in some sort of military formation. We did this casually, but waited in lines to listen. The battalion commander, a tall, thin Texan, spoke to us.

"No one touches any of these bodies. We don't know what diseases they may have, and we can't risk anyone getting infected."

Silence. A hand went up. "Sir, some of them are alive."

"I know. But we have to wait for medical units. I don't want any of you men catching anything. That's an order. Leave them alone."

We were ordered to fall out. Quietly we discussed what we'd seen. I said bitterly, "He's a good Christian, a Baptist. He preaches to us about it. What kind of Christianity is this?"

No one said anything. We were mute with horror. We had seen battle, with plenty of wounded. We knew the faint sweetness of damp plaster dust covering rounded shapes in a bombed stairwell. But the silent, stench-filled emptiness of the big camp was a new experience.

A few of us wandered again to the buildings, wooden barracks-like places, some with tiers of bunks, some with tables. We saw only scattered bodies, some buckets, odd tools.

Jeeps and trucks pulled up. There was active discussion among the officers. Some had gone into the small town nearby; one group returned with a couple of men, German civilians. One was said to be the mayor of the town. He was taken to look around, and seemed surprised. There was talk of forcing the inhabitants to dig a grave for the bodies.

Then we were called together. We piled in our truck and drove off to our assigned quarters, a small hotel where the tables of a fire-direction center could be arranged. We slept in rooms upstairs. Life went on, in the way of pursuing armies—field kitchens, meals in mess kits, short stops for instructions or regrouping.

We talked later about the death camp. Another battalion had found a much bigger one nearby, at Buchenwald (ours was near the small village of Ohrdruf). Our captain said Ohrdruf had been for Gypsy and Ukrainian laborers, who were forced by the camp authorities to work as long as they could in local factories and fields, then shot. Before long, *The Stars and Stripes* began to give detailed accounts of the camps being discovered. The extent of the forced-labor program was only beginning to be known. News of the plan to destroy Jews had hardly started to reach us.

Soldiers in a war take short views. I was a twenty-year-old PFC, a literary aesthete drafted from college less than two years earlier. Most of us wanted only to do, or to appear to do, the job we had been trained for, to follow orders, and contrive whatever creature comforts we could manage. The big picture and political principles belonged to another order of life.

Still, the image of the Ohrdruf camp remained the most searing memory the War had left me. In retrospect, my own circumstances negotiated its significance. The Army, and the War itself, came to seem enormous systems that shrank individuals to anonymity and irresponsible opportunism. It was easier to scorn the military setting that framed my response than it was to examine and judge the culture that had created the camps. My memory became a tool of shallow self-pity; it was years before I realized that the colonel was right in recognizing his formal obligation to keep his soldiers healthy and effective. His devotion to his task was echoed years later by Eichmann, on trial in Jerusalem. By then it had become clearer that any huge system, its power unchallengeable, will not destroy human response: it will isolate and shrink it. We admire the system's power and efficiency, and feel safe when we identify the power as ours. Quietly our "humanity" becomes private, and our protests largely rhetorical.

And through all this framing of experience, the memory of the first encounter simply lives on, a buried land mine. Last week, seeing the film *The Reader*, I sobbed with horror at the shots of fingers clutching barbed wire, and the crowded straw-filled bunks of the camp, though they had little to do with the story. Our lives rest invisibly on the undiminished power of such images. Our understanding may frame them. It can do nothing to dim them.

Shortly after the end of the War, Kingsley joined the young founders of the Salzburg Seminar and spent several years in Europe developing that institution. He later taught in schools in New York City and Greece before becoming headmaster of Grace Church School in 1977, a position he held for the next nineteen years. He and his wife, Schatzi, entered Kendal at Hanover in 2003. Schatzi died in 2008. Kingsley wrote the above article a few months before his own death in December 2009.

Limited Service

John Fagan
U.S. Army

I JOINED THE 75TH INFANTRY DIVISION while it was on Louisiana Maneuvers in the spring of 1944. It was a drastic change from St. John's University in Brooklyn, where I had spent the previous three months in the Army Specialized Training Program (ASTP). When that program ended, I wondered what assignment I would get: when I had been inducted at Fort Dix, I had been classified "limited service" because of poor vision in my right eye that made me ineligible for flight duty.

The Infantry proved to be a more democratic army than I expected. Captain Walsh and the other officers of "C" company shared the same living conditions as the enlisted men. We all walked through the mud, slept in pup tents, ate the same food, and swatted the same insects. The many former ASTP men who arrived when I did provided great company and I was soon thoroughly enjoying the experience. Four of us— Bob Doyle, Bob Millspaugh, Wendell Underwood, and I—were all in the same squad and came to be close buddies. The shared experiences on maneuvers soon bonded the approximately 180 men of "C" Company.

One such experience was the crossing of the Sabine River, which runs between Louisiana and Texas. We approached the river on a training maneuver at approximately 4 a.m. in total darkness. A pontoon bridge was in place over the river but it was barely visible to those of us running in the dark. As our company was crossing the river, the spacing between men became too tight. The walkway sank below the surface of the water and several of us were swept into the fast flow. I dropped my rifle, helmet, field pack, and cartridge belt into the water and managed to reach one of the pontoons and pull myself back onto the bridge. Bob Doyle escaped from the river in a similar manner. A third man was not so fortunate. He was swept downstream while making a loud cry—and was lost.

Shortly after maneuvers we were moved to Camp Breckenridge, Kentucky, for additional training. Here we gained practice with weapons, and some of us were assigned specific tasks. During rifle range practice, for example, Underwood and Millspaugh both earned "expert" ratings. As a result, Underwood became the squad scout and was given a rifle with a telescopic sight; a scout normally walked in advance of the squad, alert to any sign of the enemy. Millspaugh became the Browning Automatic Rifle (BAR) man, the only man in the squad with an automatic rifle. Two other guys, Mallory and Russo, became a "bazooka" team. I expected to become a mortar man or machine gunner so I could sight with either eye; however, my superior officers lacked my insight and instead promoted me to Sergeant. The classification of "limited service" had vanished, and I learned to fire from the hip.

From Wales to Belgium

The move overseas that October was aboard the transport ship *Brazil*. We were in the center of the convoy enjoying moonlight nights on deck despite tight bunk space below. After arriving overseas, we spent a month in the town of Porthcawl located on the south coast of Wales. Soon after that we left for France, where we were loaded onto a 2.5-ton truck and transported to Belgium. I remember the night they loaded the platoon of 40 men onto the truck at 10:00 p.m. We all had full field packs and rifles as we squeezed aboard. My position as Sergeant of the 3rd squad made me the last to board. I found space sitting next to

Sergeant Smith on the roof of the cab with my feet dangling into the crowded open-top truck. We both did our best to maintain our balance there as the truck proceeded in a convoy without headlights. It soon began to rain, and we had to sit in a cold puddle on this December night. It was around 2:00 a.m. when we finally stopped and could download. The driver poured gasoline from a GI can into depressions in the frozen ground and lit it, and we all circled these fires and tried to thaw out. I managed to open the pasteboard container on a K ration—with my teeth, because my fingers were frozen.

Another memorable ride was aboard a half-track, a vehicle with wheels on the front and caterpillar tracks on the back. Our company was being moved to a forward area so that we could be placed somewhere in action, when the column was attacked by a German plane and pelted by machine-gun fire. We quickly jumped from the vehicle and scattered off the roadway. Bob Millspaugh, carrying the BAR and a heavy cartridge belt, suffered a bad ankle sprain when he hit the ground. The sprain made it impossible for him to continue on foot and we were forced to leave him behind. He was later captured by the Germans.

We gradually became accustomed to living in the field. There seemed to be constant snowfall, and we learned how to distinguish the sound of outgoing from incoming artillery so that we knew when to take cover. Artillery shelling was almost constant and the trees were gradually reduced to large sticks. We learned to avoid all buildings because if one fired from a building, the whole building then would become a clear target. And we learned to always—but always—dig a foxhole, no matter how frozen the earth might be and to cover it with logs whenever possible.

Our infantry company was teamed with troops from the 3rd Armored Division, and we gradually pushed forward along very rural roads through a forested area. The Germans wore white winter uniforms, making them hard to see in the snow, especially when trying to infiltrate our defensive positions as we moved forward. We did not have white coverings, winterized boots, or other winter accessories. We were in rural terrain littered with dead soldiers, both German and American, disabled tanks, and dead farm animals killed by flying shrapnel. We received a copy of the U.S. Army weekly paper, *Yank*, where we learned that we were in a battle called "The Bulge" and faced crack German SS and Panzer Divisions.

December 24, 1944

Of course the ultimate moment of truth is first combat. Ours came on December 24, 1944. It was late in the day and we moved forward without much understanding of the situation. The 1st and 2nd platoons were committed before us, and we listened to small-arms fire as each platoon engaged the enemy. Our move into action entailed a circling movement to the right in order to approach the enemy flank. When the enemy machine guns turned to us, our bazooka team responded. The Germans directed a withering fire at us. The noise was deafening. Very few soldiers from the 3rd platoon returned from that fight. The night passed before seven of us, out of 40, found our way to the rest of "C" Company. Underwood and I resumed our contacts and shared a foxhole. Our friend Bob Doyle and the rest of the 3rd squad were missing.

We had lost so many men that we had to pause in our advance for three or four weeks, until the company received some replacements. By this time I had earned my fourth stripe, making me a Staff Sergeant. I was given 11 new men (a whole squad); I met them in a barn, where we could have a light and I could get their names on an envelope. I deployed them two to a site with instructions to dig in. I spent the balance of the night moving from site to site to keep in contact with them. Underwood was also assigned some new men and assigned to another platoon as a squad leader. The replacements we received were drawn from various units and lacked prior infantry training, but they were not far behind us in combat experience. By this time, we were capturing German troops that had perhaps been forced into service, as they were quick to surrender. It was clear the fight was changing and both sides were being forced to use inadequately trained men.

On January 26, 1945, we moved forward in an attack on St. Vith. My squad led the company attack across an open field with approximately eight inches of fresh snow on the ground. As we entered the woods on the far side, a machine gun opened fire and one of my men fell. I turned and yelled to the men, "Get down!"—and with that I was struck in the head and went down. I lay watching the snow turn red, contemplating my fate.

It was 50 years later that I attended a reunion of the 75th Infantry Division in Atlanta and learned what had happened after I fell. I had been struck in the head by a German bullet. Sergeant Tony Spermul had carried me to the rear and received the Silver Star for his action. Later, I was seen walking without my helmet but with an egg-like protrusion on the side of my head. I also learned that Sylvester Lombardo transported me to First Aid on the hood of the company jeep. The upshot was that I was awarded a Combat Infantryman Badge, a Bronze Star, a Purple Heart, and a medical discharge. My friends Bob Doyle and Bob Millspaugh were found in a prisoner-of-war camp and had survived their stay in the military.

John received a Bachelor's degree in Mechanical Engineering from Newark College of Engineering in 1949. He worked for many years in the development of military ordnance in The Picatinny Arsenal, the Army's principal center for research and development of various weapons systems. Subsequently, he was manager for infantry munitions at the Army Munitions Command, and later worked in several commercial fields. He married in 1952 and had four children and four grandsons. His wife died in 1988, and in 1990 he married May Blatz. They entered Kendal at Hanover in 2004. Throughout his life, John has enjoyed woodworking and carving, photography, and bird watching.

Three Unlikely Wounds

Clinton Gardner
U.S. Army

Clint, by one of his 90 mm guns,
Spa, Belgium, October 1944

D-Day, June 6, 1944

OMAHA BEACH. 5:30 A.M. PEERING SOUTH THROUGH THE DARKNESS of mist and clouds, waiting patiently for the first sights and sounds, the twenty of us lining the rails of our little LCT (Landing Craft Tank) were suddenly rewarded. The whole horizon, three miles away, began to pulse with bright flashes like heat lightning. Seconds later we heard the thunder: battleships like the old *USS Texas*, and B-17 bombers, were pulverizing Rommel's wall. Soon engineers would land in the surf to blow up his mined obstacles. Our LCT was loaded with four ammunition trucks, so we'd blow up too if we were hit just right.

I was an advance scout for B Battery of the 110th Antiaircraft Artillery Battalion; as a first lieutenant, my mission was to stake out our position near the beachside town of Vierville—and then lead the battery to it on D-Day afternoon. With three other lieutenants, from Batteries

A, C, and D, I was landing in Normandy with infantry from the 116th Regiment of the First Army's 29th Division.

9:00 a.m. Now it was our turn. Only a half-mile away, the 100-foot cliff above the beach suddenly emerged from mist of low clouds and smoke of gunfire. Machine-gun bullets splashed the water around us and clanked on our ship's metal sides. We maneuvered between two still-mined obstacles, then grated to a halt on the sand. Our commander shouted, "The ramp is down!" and we jumped off into two feet of water, lowered our heads, and waded 40 feet to shore, with the ammo trucks unloading behind us.

The beach was strewn with hundreds of bodies. With its camouflage net still neatly in place, that pillbox, which we knew would be to the right of the beach exit road, was spitting fire on us, and the huge concrete barrier that stretched across the exit road was equally untouched. What we'd been told would be "the most concentrated air bombardment in history" had completely missed its target!

I dashed across 30 feet of sand to take cover in tall beach grass on an embankment where infantry soldiers were busy digging foxholes, then dug my own fast. It looked like the 116th hadn't captured any part of that cliff, just 200 yards away.

I soon realized that our Dog Green sector of Omaha Beach was turning into a disaster. Nothing was going as planned. You couldn't have made a movie out of this; nobody would believe it. There must have been a thousand soldiers in our sector, but no one was in charge, no one knew what was going on.

For hours we watched mortars blow up our boats just as they touched shore, and saw high-velocity shells tear apart our armored cars.

By late afternoon, we'd been trapped on the beach for almost 11 hours. Up and down the beach, a quarter mile each way, I could see hundreds of foxholes, with helmeted heads of soldiers popping out of them, like curious prairie dogs. The fire from that German pillbox on the exit road was now only sporadic. Still, it was instant and deadly whenever we presented a target.

5:00 p.m. As I started to enlarge my foxhole, I heard a thundering blast and realized that the engineers might finally have blown up that concrete barrier which blocked the exit road. Crouching above my foxhole, I looked through the rising dust and saw that they'd succeeded. The barrier was gone! We might soon be off Omaha Dog Green.

Suddenly I heard a sharp explosion just in front of me. My head snapped back as if hit by a sledgehammer, and a curtain of warm blood poured over my forehead, closing my eyes. My whole body shivered into shock. My God, I thought, what's happened? There was a loud ringing sound in my head, and I felt unsteady.

Not knowing whether I'd last another minute, I found myself standing up.

Then, ever so slowly, like an automaton, raising my right arm, my right hand found a gaping hole in my helmet. Feeling past sharp metal curls, my fingers continued downward, through sticky remnants of hair, to touch the soft, wet surface of my brain.

Still moving at half speed, I did the same thing with my left hand. Incredibly, both hands fitted together through my helmet, as my fingers explored that warm mush inside my skull.

Why could I think? How long would I breathe?

I swept the blood from my eyes, using my fingers like windshield wipers.

Peering through the thick dust of mortars exploding all around, in a nearby trench I saw Lieutenants Knollman and Phillips, the scouts from A and C batteries.

As I stumbled down into their trench, they stared back at me aghast, and I could see my impending death reflected in their widening eyes.

I was a red statue, about to fall.

I tried to speak to Knollman, but no words came out. I expected to die in a matter of minutes, maybe seconds. But then, as seconds became minutes, incredibly I failed to die.

Instead, I felt a surge of determination to live. My body's shivering slowed. Returning my hands to the helmet, I found it would not come off; those metal curls must have clamped it into my scalp. I opened the first-aid kit mounted on my belt, took out the sulfa powder, and poured it into the hole, then gently stuffed all the kit's gauze bandaging down into the wound.

Strangely, I felt no pain at all; I thought it must be shock.

Yet I continued to bleed profusely and realized I might soon faint.

So I found those pressure points by my ears and pressed them about two minutes. That slowed the bleeding.

I tried speaking to Knollman again, and now words came out, but they...were...at...half...speed, sounding like a run-down turntable.

As all this was happening, there were the first signs of movement off the beach. I saw all those prairie dogs getting up out of their foxholes and heading toward the now-open road that led up to Vierville.

What was left of our armored cars formed a protective vanguard for the infantry as they headed inland. I wanted to walk, to follow them, but I could barely stand. It would be safer in Vierville or even just below the cliff, since those German mortars, with their high, arching trajectories, couldn't hit me again over there. Knollman and Phillips followed after the infantry, saying they'd send medics back for me—if they found any. That seemed unlikely, since we had seen a boatload of medics and ambulances blown to smithereens about noon.

Fearing I'd pass out and be left exposed to more fire, I began to despair. There were at least ten others wounded and dying in our trench.

Then, out of the blue, a British army captain appeared. With his men, he moved all of us to the base of the cliff, where we'd be much safer. God bless the British! They were better soldiers than we were.

For the next few hours I passed in and out of consciousness. I think it was about 9:00 p.m., after a 16-hour day, when I went to sleep.

Omaha Beach, June 7

The next morning, D+1, I choked down K rations with my water. Some medics came by and told us they'd move us off the beach as soon as their outfit could set up a field hospital near Vierville.

Now our beachhead looked entirely different, with orderly movement of trucks and troops—under very little enemy fire. I felt unexpectedly refreshed, savoring the sight of success, where on D-Day I saw mostly failure. I began to think I'd survive after all.

Finally, about 4:00 p.m., the medics arrived, and helped several of us into their jeep. As they drove us up the Vierville draw, we passed many grotesquely sprawled bodies—ours and theirs. We continued about a mile inland to the 29th Division hospital, a huge canvas tent, perhaps a hundred feet on each side.

The doctor, a captain, removed the bandage from my helmet hole.

"You're lucky, Lieutenant," he said. "That mortar fragment just ploughed through your scalp, right down to your skull, but the bone isn't fractured at all, just scarred."

He explained to me that the mush which I thought was my brain was actually the half inch of flesh we have above the skull. He gave me a local anesthetic, since their morphine had been lost in landing. While the captain held my head still, two majors twisted and jerked my helmet for several minutes before it finally unhooked from my scalp. Not a comfortable process, but very little pain. They showed me the helmet. The hole was as big as I'd thought it was.

The doctors dressed the wound with a huge white gauze bandage, covering my head. Meanwhile, sniper bullets were zipping through the top of the tent. One of the majors said, "This is quite a contrast with my practice in Miami." After an hour of attention, I was put on a stretcher to wait for a truck down to the beach, then a boat back to England.

A shot of morphine on that boat started me drifting off to sleep—as I thought about my unlikely survival. If I had raised my head just one inch higher, at 5:00 p.m. on D-Day, my skull would have been split wide open—and I'd certainly not have lived to tell this story.

I kept my helmet with me—and at the army hospital in Salisbury, England, a British captain from the Imperial War Museum came to visit me. He said they wanted to acquire it, since its hole was the largest they had seen for a survivor in either World War I or II. Instead of donating it to them, I sent it home. After only three weeks in the hospital, I was back in Normandy on July 10. There I became Executive Officer of the 110th's A Battery.

Malmedy, Belgium—December 21, 1944

"Hold at any cost" was the order the 110th received December 16, as a column of 40 German Tiger tanks, painted proudly with the white

U.S. Army star, came rumbling toward our positions, where we were defending the Belgian towns of Spa and Malmedy. Suddenly, we were the ones on the defensive. Behind the tanks were at least 15 German divisions, led by SS troops, in a completely unexpected and massive counterattack.

Just south of us, about 15 miles away, we'd heard an SS division had taken St. Vith and sliced through the green troops of our 106th and 99th Divisions, capturing at least five thousand and probably killing a lot more. Their goal was evidently Antwerp, which would have split the U.S. and British armies and deprived us of our main supply port.

But von Rundstedt's offensive had not been able to get beyond the outskirts of Malmedy, which is on the main road to Antwerp. The sixteen 90-millimeter guns of our battalion were now deployed as tank destroyers on that road, and we were right at the front with infantry of the 30th Division. Our position was critical to containing this attack, since we were on a ridge which anchored the northern flank of our defense line.

Of course we realized that von Rundstedt's tactics could change at any moment—and I'd be the first to know. That was because my command post, "Red 3," was a half mile in front of our guns. The idea was that, if I saw tanks clanking toward us, I'd telephone the guns and give them the time needed to get fully manned. The SS evidently knew we were there, since during the night, they fired rockets at the brick farmhouse where four of us from A Battery were billeted with a seven-man infantry squad. They hadn't killed anybody, but they *had* succeeded in removing our bathroom wall!

Malmedy, December 30, 1944

Around 12:45 p.m., as Corporal Cohen, Corporal Stein, Private Reinart, and I were getting chow ready, we heard bombs dropping. I looked out the window and saw that it was our own bombers, B-24s! The windows shook and the house rocked. We put on our helmets. I rang the phone to our main command post and reported, "We are being bombed near Red 3."

Sergeant Loftus, infantry, had just stepped into the room but, hearing the bombs, he left again, following Private Reinart, who was on his way out to see what was happening. I had just finished saying "Red 3," and Loftus and Reinart had been out of the room only a second or so, when a terrific explosion flattened the house to the ground. The ceiling and walls fell in on us. The bomb had fallen squarely on the center of the house, about 15 feet from us.

We were all buried in blackness and debris. Seriously doubting whether I would live, I decided to examine myself and see. I rose up, heaving about a hundred pounds of rubbish off my back, and saw light. The ceiling was about a foot over my head as I knelt there, and I could see through it: the second story had been blown away.

From a heap of rubbish, dirt, bricks, and plaster in front of me came groans and cries from Cohen and Stein. They were buried under hundreds of pounds of the rubbish and several beams. Reinart could not be heard. I thought he might be dead or unconscious. I started digging frantically with my bare hands.

Both buried men kept calling for air. Stein repeated over and over, "Get it off my head." I was afraid they might be seriously injured— arms or legs or ribs crushed. I was dazed and shocked, and my arms and hands were bleeding badly, so I probably wasn't removing as much rock and dirt as I could have, but nobody else was around. Behind me, as I frantically scratched at the dirt, I saw a man standing up, dazed, streaked with blood, clothes torn. Then I saw that his arm, his right arm, had been blown off at the shoulder.

I yelled to him that I needed help. He didn't reply. I didn't see him again; somebody must have helped him away.

Seconds seemed like minutes. Nobody came to help us. They must have been dazed. Finally some infantrymen showed up; one turned a fire extinguisher on our overturned stove, another got beside me and worked on Cohen. He was visible after about five minutes' digging. Just his helmet, face, and shoulder could be seen in the rubble, like a chick hatching from its shell. Soon I removed a brick that revealed Stein's helmet with a big beam resting on it. We lifted the beam off, then I let somebody relieve me from digging. I staggered out and went to sit down in a jeep. On my way I passed a soldier lying on the ground, dead, his face bloody and battered. I didn't recognize him at the time, but he was our friend Loftus, who had left the room with Reinart. Reinart, I learned, was in good shape. He had been blown out through the hallway and out the front door and been knocked unconscious. His leg was severely bruised.

Soon Stein was led out to the jeep, his head bruised and slightly cut. Then Cohen came out smiling and walking by himself. We all were dazed and shocked. I was the least injured, with only glass cuts on my arms and hands.

But others in the house had not been so lucky. Besides Loftus, who had been killed in the room next to us, Sergeant Greenwood of the infantry had been killed in the room beyond that, but only 15 feet from where we had been. Four of the civilians in the house, on the cellar stairs or in the cellar, were killed: a man, a woman, and two children. Within 20 feet of us six people had died, and four had been seriously wounded. It might just as well have been us.

When I went back to the house a few days later, I stood where the front door had blown out, only a few feet from where we'd been buried:

Buchenwald, Weimar—April 23, 1945

As our jeep pulled up to the concentration camp's main gate, we were startled by the scene in front of us. Clustering around the gate, like young animals testing their ability to leave their place of birth, were hundreds of humanlike apparitions. Scraps of dirty clothing failed to conceal the condition of their bodies.

We were instantly surrounded by this swarm of skeletons draped in yellowing flesh. They shuffled, hobbled, and stumbled toward us, try-ing to smile, but their lips would not turn up. Their eyes were glassy and bulbous, buried deep behind cheekbones that almost broke through tight-stretched parchment skin. Their voices cackled as they intro-duced themselves in German, Russian, French, and countless other languages we could not recognize. Nervously, excitedly, they cried out: "*Sprechen sie Deutsch?* . . . *Ich Russich* . . . *Polski* . . . *Czech* . . . *Italiani.*" And a few in English: "I am a Spanish Loyalist . . ." "I am a German political prisoner . . ." "I have been here nine years."

They were men as tall as we, but with only half as much flesh. Most were dressed in the camp uniform with vertical blue-and-white stripes. But many had already found something to replace part of this despised garment. Some had put on pieces of Russian, French, or Polish army uniforms. Others wore bits of civilian clothing. Several had tied rags on their feet for want of shoes.

As Captain Peter Ball, our team's leader, and I got out of the jeep, we saw two men standing quietly to the right of the main gate. They came forward and introduced themselves. First, Hans Eiden, the camp's "senior" inmate, the *Lagerältester.* He was perhaps 45 years old, with sad eyes and a sunken face. Then Walter Bartel, Eiden's deputy, several years younger, ruddy and roundish: he looked like he'd taken advantage of his position to get enough food. They told us they were both political prisoners, German Communists. Neither of them spoke English, but my German had become quite serviceable. That was fortu-nate, because Captain Ball spoke not a word of it.

What had brought me to Buchenwald? Well, in early March, First Army had put out a desperate call for officers to volunteer for military government. Since the 110th had already reached the Rhine at Rema-gen, and it was clear the War would soon be over, I responded to that call. Overnight I became Executive Officer of a military government team, one headed by Captain Ball and one that was soon informed we'd be in charge of Buchenwald upon its liberation.

But it turned out that, contrary to the announced strategy, it was actually Third Army that took Weimar and liberated the camp. Gen-eral Patton had gotten his troops there on April 11; in a typical Patton maneuver, he'd outflanked General Bradley's First Army! Thus, today, his Third Army officers were turning camp administration over to us.

I told Eiden and Bartel that we'd meet with them after lunch to discuss the immediate tasks that lay ahead of us. Then our jeep led the little convoy of trucks, which contained our team of four officers and six enlisted men, a quarter mile south to the four handsome houses where we'd live. They looked like a group of alpine lodges. The largest, where the former SS commander, *Obersturmbannführer* Herman Pister, had lived, was where Peter and I would be.

Patton's Orders

At lunch a Third Army officer, Lt. Stanley Kaufmann, briefed us on what had happened since their April 11 arrival. Some 20,000 prisoners were here that day, many of them only half alive. Over 300 bodies were piled in the crematorium's yard—and over two hundred more lay in or near camp buildings. General Patton, along with Generals Eisenhower and Bradley, had seen Buchenwald on April 13; Patton was so shocked that he gave orders that everything should stay just as it was for a week. Thus the world, via the press, could see the unspeakable scene. This was the first large concentration camp to be liberated, so photographers and correspondents had descended upon it immediately.

Almost every nation in Europe was represented in the camp. There were 4,000 Russians, 2,900 French, 3,100 Poles, 2,100 Germans, and 2,000 Czechs, plus hundreds of Belgians, Dutch, Austrians, Yugoslavs, Spaniards, and Italians; finally, some Greeks, Norwegians, Danes, and Swedes. Among these nationalities were about 2,000 Jews.

Third Army had set up a hospital in 12 SS barracks buildings—and filled them with the 3,000 inmates who needed emergency care. Stanley said that over 50 were still dying daily, and that Third Army was behind on burying them.

When we met Eiden and Bartel after lunch, in our commandant's office, we started by discussing how to bury the remaining bodies in that yard and gather up all the other bodies still lying about the camp. I suggested that we might contact the mayor of Weimar and arrange for 400 able-bodied men to come up to the camp daily and do the burial and other clean-up work. Eiden thought that was a great idea.

"Now could you give us a tour of the camp?" I asked him. Eiden suggested he begin by going over to the large camp map posted on the office wall. He pointed to a large rail yard in the lower right of the map.

"This tells you something about Buchenwald's purpose," he said. "We were not only a labor camp but one of the main 'switching centers' in the whole camp system. If the Gestapo arrested you in Paris or Berlin, you might well be sent here for your first processing. Over 240,000 were processed through here since the camp opened in 1937, almost all of them males. If you passed inspection for working, you might stay here or go to another work camp like Dachau. If you didn't pass the inspection—that is, you seemed too weak—or if you were Jewish, you'd often get on the rail line for Auschwitz. That was an extermination camp, a *Vernichtungslager*."

"A nice name," I commented. "A camp that turns you into 'nothing.' "

"Have you heard how many Auschwitz could gas in a day?" he asked.

"No," I replied.

"Over a thousand. We have learned a lot about Auschwitz because some of the former prisoners there were evacuated to Buchenwald this spring. The SS must have gassed over a million there, on a regular production line, with worker prisoners forced to pick up the bodies and burn them in the crematorium."

"My God!" I exclaimed, as a shiver ran through my body. "And did they gas anybody here?"

"No. Since we were a work camp, our crematorium was used primarily for those who died of beatings, disease, or starvation. We had only about 10,000 who were shot or tortured to death. Compared to those at Auschwitz, our crematorium is tiny. As you'll see, it has only three ovens; it could burn only 200 a day. All told, 51,000 died here, most of them in the 'Little Camp.' Incoming prisoners went there for processing, but only Jews ever stayed there. Little Camp inmates weren't on our regular work details. Sometimes there were two thousand in there, crowded on three-tiered shelves, with a death rate of about 50 a day. The SS allowed them very little food."

"So you did have a little extermination going on here too, didn't you?" I asked Eiden.

"Yes. For the Russians and the Jews, in a way, we did. But your press is starting to report about Buchenwald as if we were the worst concentration camp. Actually, once you know the whole story, I think you'll find that all the other camps were worse than this."

On that note, we stood up and began our tour of "the best" camp.

Our first stop was at the crematorium, a masonry building with a slanted tile roof. Its 30-foot smokestack rose like a grim monument, soaring above those flimsy one-story wooden buildings.

As we approached the crematorium, we were assaulted by an awful stench. Then we saw them. In two piles, like cords of wood, there were still over 100 emaciated bodies stacked against the building's wall. I looked quickly and then averted my eyes; it seemed indecent to stare at them. Inside were the three ovens, but downstairs there was something much more horrifying: a "strangulation room," with one access being a trap door from the outside. Offending prisoners were pushed through that door into this room, where they were immediately clubbed by sadistic SS guards, then hung on meat hooks until they strangled to death.

Leaving that horrendous room, we went on to the "experimental barracks," where Nazi "scientists" conducted quite unusual experiments on selected inmates. For example, to test how long it took for a person to die in cold water, ice was added to the water, ever so slowly. That way the stopwatch could catch the exact second the inmate died.

Then to the stable, where 7,000 Russian prisoners of war had been shot during one week. And on to other unexpected buildings: one was even a brothel for the prisoners!

Our last stop was at the entrance gate tower, from which we could view some of the 64 barracks:

Buchenwald, May 1, 1945

On this May Day, the prisoners put on a huge political demonstration, one that brought some 15,000 of them, with red flags waving, to fill most of roll-call plaza. Eiden and Bartel had given us no warning of this event, perhaps afraid we'd have forbidden it. All this revolutionary zeal had burst out of bodies that, two weeks ago, were scarcely able to move.

And on this day I became the commandant of Buchenwald, Herman Pister's successor! Well, actually I succeeded Peter because he had delegated this position to me. First Army had just made our team responsible for two more nearby concentration camps, Nordhausen and Ohrdruf (both much smaller and much worse than this), so Peter could be here only about a third of his time.

Finally, this day we could see the War in Europe was coming to an end. The Red Army had entered Berlin a few days earlier, and on April 27 our troops had linked up with the Russians at the Elbe.

With peace fast approaching, we began the first large bus transport of inmates back to their homelands. And the French began sending planes daily to an improvised airfield just outside of town. Those planes and our buses returned most of their compatriots.

Buchenwald, July 4, 1945

After V-E Day on May 8, we were able to establish regular truck convoys that took all West European prisoners back to their homelands. By early June we were left with only about 3,000 Poles and 4,000 Russians, for whom transport was more complicated. Still, during June, we managed to get almost all of them headed east.

Since Buchenwald is located in the East German zone that would be occupied by the Russians, I and the rest of our American team left the camp at noon. The night before, I had gone down to Weimar, where I met with the Red Army officers who would be taking over from us. We got along fine—and drank so much vodka that one of our Soviet friends, by way of celebration, fired off his revolver into the ceiling!

So far as I can tell, I have suffered no shell shock from my two unlikely wounds on Omaha Beach and at Malmedy, but now I suspect that I may never recover from the equally unlikely wound that Buchenwald has given me. Nor do I really want to recover from it. This third wound has begun to turn me into a citizen of Europe, with all its suffering—and hopefully into a citizen of that global community which must emerge after this War.

The preceding text has been drawn almost entirely from my wartime journal and letters to my parents, written in 1944-45. Those documents, segments of which I have used in a book, are now located in the Rauner library at Dartmouth—along with my fractured helmet.

After growing up in Larchmont, New York, Clint went on to Phillips Exeter and Dartmouth. He and his wife Libby met in Hanover in 1946. They lived in Berlin 1948–49, where he was Managing Editor of Die Neue Zeitung, *the U.S. Military Government newspaper. After that, they settled in Armonk, New York, and raised three children. In 1956 they founded Shopping International, a mail-order company, and soon moved it to Norwich, Vermont. Upon leaving the business world in 1979, Clint became the president of a citizens exchange project called US-USSR Bridges for Peace (1981–1994). He and Libby came to Kendal at Hanover in 2003.*

Captured in The Bulge

William Hotaling
U.S. Army

This memoir is adapted from a recording made by Edith Gieg

LET ME PREFACE THIS BY SAYING that I ain't no hero. I was lucky. Unlucky to get captured, but lucky to make it through.

I was inducted into the Army in 1943 as a buck private and spent time at Camp Upton, on Long Island, and Camp Stewart, in Georgia, before ending up in officers' training at Fort Benning, an infantry school. Right after I graduated in July 1944, Jean Perrine and I were married.

I was then sent to Camp Atterbury in Indiana to join the 106th Division. We trained that summer and were shipped overseas in the fall, crisscrossing the Atlantic because of the submarines.

We arrived in Scotland on November 2, 1944, went by train to Buford, in the Cotswolds, and trained there until late November, when we were shipped to Le Havre.

We were then taken by truck to a position in Eifel, near St. Vith, on the Belgian border, to relieve the tried and tested 2nd Division that had been there for some time—I as a mortar platoon leader in the heavy weapons company.

Though in a combat area, we had pretty lush quarters. One night my CO called me to come right away. I assumed there was a problem; instead, I found him in his pajamas and bathrobe, with a bottle of booze. He wanted me to make a fourth at bridge.

Our group was stationed on high ground and could watch fighter planes in dog fights. I think I fired the mortars only twice. The Germans had formerly occupied the same spot, so they were familiar with it and knew just how to attack us. And that they did—on December 16, in their huge counterattack (later called "the Battle of the Bulge"). After some days of fog and snow, the weather broke and the Germans came in with artillery. Our commander was killed. We were told to pack up and put what we could on our backs and set out on foot, walking all night through the woods. Our orders were to attack the nearby town of Schönberg in the morning.

The men behind us were badly shot up and one of them threw out a white flag, whereupon the Germans stopped firing. We were on high ground, and by the time the Germans had got back into their tanks, we had run off into the woods. About 100 of us were wandering around in there, far behind German lines, with the enemy shelling us. Finally, our command group sent a task force to talk to them, saying we wanted to send out our wounded over a road they controlled. The group reported back that our situation was hopeless and we should surrender before we were blown to pieces. The officers agreed—but first we stripped our weapons so they couldn't be fired.

The Battle of the Bulge resulted from a calculated risk on the part of the Americans. Normally a division protects about five miles of property, but we were protecting 27 miles, so the Germans were able to go right through us.

Surrendering

We surrendered to a sharp panzer division—real gentlemen, able to speak English. They separated the men and the officers. They remarked what a horrible war this was and, since it was just before Christmas, wouldn't it be great to be home. That ended abruptly, though, when they ordered, "Get moving." They double-timed us back from the front, a long day's walk. When I was captured I had been wearing overshoes and a trench coat with a liner, but one of the friendly Germans took them away from me, so all I had was the outer cover.

We were taken to a rail yard where they billeted us in 40-by-8 box-cars—meaning 40 men, or eight horses. The boxcar I was put in had horse manure at one end. It was so crowded that we had to take turns sitting and standing. In prison life, the ranking officer is the command-ing officer. Ours was a medical officer, and fortunately he could speak German. He said we'd walk instead of staying in the boxcars—so, the Germans walked us. One day we saw a B-24 hit by flak. The pilot came down in a parachute and landed just about 200 yards from where we were walking. He came over, delighted that we were Americans. All we said was, Buster, get in line because you're going with us. All we wanted to know from him was what he had had for breakfast that morning.

I don't know how many days we walked before we reached the first of the five prison camps I was assigned to. In prison camp you're interrogated, and in Army training we had been told to just give name, rank, and serial number; don't answer any other questions. We got away with it.

In the camps you registered and were interrogated and given a shower, and that was it. Not much food, but the Germans didn't have much either. In the first camp, they gave us turnip soup. I don't like turnip soup; never have, and never will. The Red Cross food packages were a godsend: one per man at first, later one to seven or eight.

After a few days, we were put back into boxcars and shipped to a POW Camp for officers in Schubin, Poland. The Americans had it well organized. Lots of spit and polish. You always had to salute the German colonel, and our colonel held inspections regularly. We were in Schubin about 10 days, until the Russians began to approach. The Germans were scared to death of the Russians, who were real tough characters at that time.

We started walking again—our longest walk, about 300 miles—to Hamburg. Bear in mind that this was January–February and the weather was much like it is in northern New England. Sometimes rainy, sometimes snowy. The prisoners were all officers—a full colonel was our top-ranking officer. Quite a guy. He carried a set of bagpipes; we all wondered about that, but we soon understood. Every night when we stopped, the command group would set up a perimeter guard and we would tune in BBC on the radio to get the latest war news while the Colonel played his bagpipes to drown out the radio. He never explained where the radio came from. Every morning, the Germans gave us a fabricated news report, but we waited for the true story on BBC.

It was interesting that the Colonel had bagpipes. Others had strange things, too. One night, a group wanted to paint a sign: somebody had a paint brush, somebody else had yellow paint and blue paint and a board, and they got the sign painted. One man was carrying a wood plane: why? Nobody knows. I carried an old pair of GI trousers. I tied the pant legs and put it around my neck to keep me warm, and I kept cans in the pant legs: I picked these up along the way so that I could make little cook stoves out of them. If I was in a farmyard, I could get snow and melt it, to get hot water for shaving or for something warm to drink. One time in Germany, on our way through a little town, the string came off the pant leg and the cans fell to the ground, helter-skelter. The townspeople laughed, but I didn't care: I went after my cans. All these odd collections helped me later when my boots were in bad shape and I found the wire and pliers I needed to make repairs.

As we traveled, we were billeted in many places. Barns were best; in the hayloft near the cattle you could be warm. Once we were billeted at a submarine base near the Baltic Sea, other times in churches or schools. Dysentery was prevalent. Once as I was walking along, a guy fell by the wayside and the Germans wouldn't let me touch him. I don't know what happened to him. No bathroom privileges: you had to use your pants.

A Postcard Home

Once, just before we were put into boxcars, they allowed us to send a postcard. All we could say was that we were well and had walked about 250 miles. I wrote mine on March 1, 1945; Jean received it April 1. She had been notified in December that I was missing in action, and only with the arrival of the postcard—when she recognized my lousy handwriting—did she learn that I was a prisoner of war.

In a bizarre incident that spring, General Patton sent about 200 men, some ten tanks, and ten or twelve half-tracks 40 miles into German territory to fight their way through to our camp. Our Lieutenant

Colonel Waters, who was Patton's son-in-law, went out to the troops with a white flag. He was shot, but survived. The U.S. soldiers took the camp, released us, and told us to find a buddy and head west. My buddy and I hitched a ride on one of the half-tracks, but we hadn't gone very far before the Germans arrived. We had no weapons, so we fled into nearby hills and, from a treetop, watched the firefight. The next morning we were recaptured and returned to the prison camp. We were not punished, but soon thereafter we were marched to Nuremberg and then to a camp outside Munich.

Within another three weeks the War ended, and Patton and Red Cross girls arrived. The girls asked us to identify ourselves and then brought us up to date on the latest movies and songs. They asked what else they could do for us, and one man called out, "Hey, come over here. I want to smell you."

We flew to Rheims on May 8, and soon thereafter we were on our way home. I had been in Europe exactly seven months—from November 2, 1944 to June 2, 1945.

Bill grew up in northern New York State, graduated from Dartmouth in 1941, and spent his career in sales with Bethlehem Steel. He and Jean lived in New Jersey, Missouri, and Ohio while raising their three sons. On retirement in 1983 they moved to Hanover, where Bill became a volunteer at the Dartmouth-Hitchcock Hospital, the Historical Society, and the Hood Museum, and found more time for skiing and canoeing. In 2002 Bill and Jean came to Kendal at Hanover. Jean died in 2007, Bill in 2009.

Coffee and Doughnuts, Anyone?

Pamela Symington Mayer
American Red Cross

IT WAS 1943. I WAS 23 YEARS OLD, newly graduated from college, still living with my family in midtown Manhattan with no idea what I wanted to do with my life. But of course, given what was going on in the wider world, it had to be war work.

After a brief stint with the Office of War Information, I was able to get a job with the overseas American Red Cross, and within a few months I had boarded a troopship and was on my way to England. It was a circuitous trip, dodging submarines, sharing a crowded ship— mostly with nurses, who had not much respect for Red Cross girls.

When we arrived in England in mid-January, I was posted to an airfield at Fulbeck, a small village near Nottingham in Lincolnshire. The job was to help establish and run a club for enlisted men who were part of the 9th Air Force Troop Carrier Command, exclusively dedicated to transporting and backing up the bombers and fighters that were flying missions across the English Channel each night. This information would have been strictly censored at the time: my parents never did know where I was writing from. Over the months that followed, I wrote countless letters to my parents sharing it all, and thirty years later I came across these letters in my father's desk. Here, I offer some extracts.

Recollections of Wartime Red Cross

FULBECK, JANUARY 13, 1944—At last more or less settled in one place. How I miss you all! I'm in something called an Aeroclub—at least that's what it's going to be. At the moment it's nothing but a couple of draughty rooms inside an unpainted Nissen hut. It's right on the airfield, in the midst of a lot of barracks and a lot of mud—an incredible amount of mud! It's strictly for enlisted men. Another girl and myself are supposed to set it up and run it, only we can't really start until the walls are painted, and they're still wet from being rained on before the roof went up. She hasn't arrived yet and I'm the only woman on the post ...

FULBECK, JANUARY 20, 1944—It's a huge challenge, not to mention a lot of pioneering: we make things up as we go along. There hasn't been any sort of Red Cross on the post until now—whatever we do is better than what existed before. I'm happy to say that the other girl is the "Club Director," which means she'll be doing the things I'm not much interested in (like keeping accounts, hiring help, requisitioning stuff), and my job will be to organize and keep running whatever goes on at the Club—anything from dances to debates to homemade concerts to ping pong tournaments (if we ever get a ping pong table). We've already got the most important thing, namely a fireplace—since right now there's nowhere else for the men to go in their spare time—or just to get warm. It's very cold outside.

FULBECK, FEBRUARY 5, 1944—This will probably be short. I've closed the Club and am waiting to hear the planes come in. The minute I hear the first one land, I'll go down to meet them. It's nice, almost the nicest thing I do, because they want so little, and it's so rewarding to give it to them—donuts, coffee, a smile to let them know that you're glad they made it back ... not much else. All day they're like any other soldiers, exhausting in their demands, but when they come in at night, after they've been flying, they're too tired to want anything—just to be acknowledged and appreciated, which is easy.

Fulbeck, February 20, 1944—It's later than I intended. There's no place warm enough to sit and write except the Club, and once there, a hundred things interrupt. Our furniture dribbles in, one chair at a time, and the staff's about half of what it should be. The place is huge—but getting more attractive every day. I spend a good deal of time getting to know the people in the village, and hoping they'll want to invite the soldiers into their homes. Sometimes it works and sometimes not—but I like spending time with them.

Wantage, Oxfordshire, August 2, 1944—We all know that the follow-up to the invasion will happen any day, and probably our group will go quite soon after. It's a very strange feeling. Apparently the 9th Air Force has made an agreement with the Red Cross, saying they'll transport Aeroclubs across the channel. And we'll be among the first, since we're part of an "Air Depot" group, rather than Troop Carrier. (This all may be censored out, but it's worth trying.) Anyway, once we get there, we'll be considered part of the 9th Air Force "Civil Affairs" outreach (rather than "Red Cross"), which means that along with organizing a Club, we'll be doing what we can to help France recover from years of occupation. Quite an assignment!

Laon (Northern France), Late August 1944—I wonder if my mail is getting through to you? I'm sure it must be. D-Day was three months ago, but we haven't gotten any mail yet. We're in a combat zone, the Front is fairly close, and moving ever closer to the German border. Our primary work is still to provide a homelike atmosphere for the enlisted men, but it's turned out to be much more than that. Fortunately my French is passable—which is one reason they assigned me to this group.

Laon, Early September 1944—At first we were living in pup tents (we're in a "combat zone," after all), and the central problem was how to stay reasonably clean. Dressing in them would have been a problem if we had ever undressed, but since we didn't, it hardly mattered. A few days into this, and then our chaplain blessedly arranged for us two women (Doris and me) to be housed in a nearby chateau. The owners are living in Paris, but there are caretakers living in the basement. We have two beautiful upstairs rooms, which would be luxurious if there were still running water—only there isn't. The very dear caretakers bring us some in pitchers, every morning.

Laon, October 6, 1944—The Club itself is an odd setup. The group we're serving is spread over a nine-mile area, with four assorted outfits; the "Club" will eventually consist of a very big hospital tent in each of them. You wouldn't believe how homelike a tent can look. So far only one of them is functioning, but it's really nice … books, soft chairs, a Victrola, pictures. All day we make donuts, with help from six refugee Polish girls. My days are divided about equally between the village, three miles away, and the Club. I've been assigned a monster truck (which I drive myself): it not only gets me around, but serves as a carrier for the mobile canteen, which gets put on the truck to do the rounds each evening.

Laon, October 7, 1944—This is almost too much of a job: just totally challenging. We open the Club at eight and stop at midnight, and all day there are a million unfinished things to do, both in the functioning big tent and in all the small auxiliary tents scattered around (wherever the mobile canteen makes its regular stops). We divide our time: each night one of us stays in the home tent while the other drives the truck around the countryside. You can't imagine what it's like … driving through complete blackness in a truck that breaks down every ten miles or so, but is still a blessing, over dirt roads filled with bomb craters and wrecked tanks, finally arriving in the midst of an apparently deserted and desolate little circle of tents … and then suddenly a host of shouting and waving boys, pouring out like ants from an anthill, wanting nothing in the world but a couple of donuts and a cup of coffee—and a girl who speaks American to them.

I love chugging through the French countryside, stopping whenever I can find an excuse to chat with the old people and the children who clatter after us in their sabots. Everywhere we go there are children, and everywhere we meet them they want to shake hands and talk. One day I ran into five young boys: they seemed about eight, but actually they're nearer to fourteen. They were lost and cold and miserable, no food for two days, no prospect of getting any. If they had families, they didn't know where they were; they were truly destitute. So I brought them back to the base and fed them, and the men found enough clothes to halfway cover them. That was three weeks ago and they've been with us ever since, helping out in all sorts of ways. The men very much like having them around, and so do I.

LAON, OCTOBER 25, 1944—We're settling down pretty well. Last night we had the first dance since we've been here … in a borrowed neighboring chateau … and it was a huge success, though haphazard in the extreme. The "nice girls" (i.e. the invited ones, whose families I've become friendly with) arrived in Army trucks along with chaperones—which included small brothers, grandmothers, several pets—and a good many uninvited who manage to slip in anyway, without chaperones. It was a huge scramble and the men loved it.

LAON, DECEMBER 24, 1944—Here, as you can imagine, things are pretty dramatic. The news is so very bad that no one thinks about much else …yet at the same time Christmas goes on.

The men are all restricted, have been for a week, and it's been clear and bitter cold …

I'll never forget Christmas Eve, 1944. Everyone that had anything to drink was drinking it, all three Clubs were very gay and very noisy because no one wanted to stop long enough to think. Then at midnight nearly everyone went to the midnight service. It was held in a bombed-out stable about a quarter of a mile from here, halfway out the airstrip. We walked out, wearing helmets, everyone but us carrying guns, not quite believing it was Christmas yet singing carols anyway. It was a breathless kind of feeling, the cold and the carols and the whole peculiar business of celebrating "peace on earth good will toward men" while the planes around us took off on their missions and the guns rattled when the guards called out to us as we passed.

Halfway through the service there was an alert. No one moved. Through the bombed ceiling we could see the stars, and occasionally the moving stars that were planes. Then the service went on; we sang "Silent Night, Holy Night," and the men's voices were unbelievably beautiful.

I left before it was over, walked back alone, and lit candles in the Club and started the fires. In one corner we had a most lovely tree, decorated with things the boys had made out in the shops: sheet-metal stars and shavings, and lights that one of them strung up from a wrecked plane. A couple of weeks ago I found a hand-carved exquisite little crèche. In front of it I lit the long-burning candle you sent, and across from it hung the Santa Claus poster we used to have when we were little. Truly, it was a lovely sight, with the candles and the silver sheen that only candles can give. From the beams hung holly and mistletoe and a kind of tinsel which the ack-ack units use to deflect radar. The whole place had a kind of glow when the men came back—everyone was sober and quiet and a little sad but not the kind of sadness that is bad.

The little group that usually gets together for a hot jitterbug session every night gravitated toward the piano. One of them had a violin, another a clarinet, and they played more carols, softly, a little wistfully, not as sure of themselves as when they play their jive, but still willing to try for the sake of the rest of us who were listening.

We stayed most of the night; no one wanted to be alone. It was a very curious sort of feeling ...

The next day, Christmas, was different altogether. Everyone was working as usual, but mostly everyone felt pretty happy. The weather was still cold but very beautiful. We had parties everywhere, and a lot of liquor from somewhere, and in between jobs the boys stopped in. Most of the morning I spent taking the truck around, handing out the inevitable coffee and donuts ... they never get tired of them. The only difference was that the donuts had jam and sugar and raisins.

Christmas night I managed to get four truckloads of girls onto the field—I'll never know how. By the time the provost marshal caught up with me, it was almost time to close anyway and it didn't matter. It was the gayest party we've had since we've been over here.

So really it's a good thing we're here, and most of the time I'm conscious of it and grateful for the opportunity. A lot of things have been happening lately to make me increasingly aware of our job and its possibilities and responsibilities—especially in a time like this, with the news, and Christmas, and the way things are in France.

I wouldn't be doing anything else for the world.

Pam spent her early years in New York City and then attended Radcliffe. Directly after the War, she married David Mayer and subsequently had four children. The family lived in The Netherlands while David was working for the Marshall Plan, then spent 30 years in the Washington, D.C., area. Here Pam earned a graduate degree in Adult Education, became deeply involved in the emerging Human Potential movement, and began her teaching work in earnest. The family retired to Newfane, Vermont, where Pam welcomed their six grandchildren; explored, with her students, the psychological and spiritual aspects of healing; and established a spiritual and educational healing program in the woods surrounding her garden. They entered Kendal at Hanover in 1991. David died in 2006 and Pam in 2011.

SHOT DOWN OVER THE BULGE

~

Malcolm McLane
U.S. Army Air Force

THIS STORY BEGINS ON SATURDAY, THE 16TH OF DECEMBER, 1944, the day the Germans jumped off across the Sauer River on their last desperate offensive into Luxembourg and Belgium. It was the beginning of the Battle of the Bulge.

I was a P-47 pilot in the 406th Fighter Group of the Ninth U.S. Air Force. We had provided air support missions for the D-Day landings in Normandy and then continued flying ground missions for Patton's Third Army across France. At the time of the Ardennes breakthrough, we were based at Field A-80, a dozen miles east of Reims. The famous 101st Airborne Division, veterans of parachute landings in Germany and Holland, were quartered in barracks on our field. They were regrouping for an early return to the States.

Our missions on Saturday, December 16th, were to hit German tank concentrations, but it was late Sunday before we realized the seriousness of the situation. The 101st Airborne had been alerted for active duty that evening, and all day Monday their reconnaissance pilots were dropping in at our Intelligence Room to get maps of the area, which was totally new to them.

On Monday, the 18th, I flew my last mission before the weather closed in solid on Tuesday. There was no flying through Friday, at a time when air support was so desperately needed to help break up the fast-moving German advance across northern Luxembourg and Belgium to Bastogne, Stavelot, Malmedy, and Liège.

After lunch on Tuesday, when I realized that there would be no more flying that day, I hitchhiked to Paris in the rain with a 48-hour pass through Thursday and another one lined up for Friday and Saturday. I procured a spare bed from the Air Force billeting officer, then had a great time with old friends in the city.

On Thursday I learned from other boys in the squadron who were also on pass in Paris that all leaves were cancelled and that there would be no truck out to the field on Saturday. Next morning, I caught a subway to the edge of town soon after lunch and eventually hopped a big truck to Reims and later to the field after dark.

Still no missions had been flown in four days, but "Stormy" the weatherman had hopes for the morrow. I read all the teletypes for the week, brushing up on the news, and put myself up on the squadron mission board to lead the cover flight on the morning mission.

December 23, 1944

Saturday, December 23, was definitely clear compared to the last four days and we knew there would be big things doing. We were up at seven, over to Group Intelligence for the briefing of flight leaders—and a few minutes for breakfast, then to the Squadron Briefing Room before piling into jeeps with the maps, 'chutes, and helmets. We finally arrived at the flight line with 30 minutes before take-off and setting course for Trier.

Our mission was to carry out an armed reconnaissance within the triangle of Trier-Bitburg-Bastogne, with special attention to be paid to German pontoon bridges across the Sauer. We had 12 ships in the squadron, each loaded with a 500-pound bomb under each wing and a cluster of fragmentation bombs on the belly rack.

Jonesy was leading the squadron as Red Flight Leader and I was leading Yellow Flight for top cover, four planes to a flight. The other four ships made up Blue Flight and were alongside Red Flight a couple of thousand feet below me. The two other squadrons in the group based on our field had similar missions, with one of them escorting C-47 cargo planes to Bastogne, to drop supplies to the now-encircled 101st Airborne Division.

We flew out over the World War I No-Man's Land from Reims to Verdun, across the Argonne Forest to the Meuse, and dead over Luxembourg to reach the Moselle at Trier. We circled the city just out of flak range as German 88's tried to reach us and we spotted supply trains in the valley east of the town.

(Courtesy of National Museum of the U.S. Air Force)

Malcolm's plane, the P-47 Thunderbolt

Jonesy started down with his flight while Blue Flight circled, and we covered them both at 8,000 feet. The bombs from the dive-bombing runs of Jonesy's flight had burst and he was about to go in on a strafing pass when I spotted "beaucoup bogies" to the northeast and several thousand feet above.

I started up in a wide, sweeping turn to gain altitude and to close our range sufficiently to identify them. They were headed our way, and when they dropped their external fuel tanks, I knew they were bandits. I called Jones on the radio and told him to forget the targets below and get on up: we were in for a fight. I told everyone in the squadron to jettison all bombs and external tanks not yet dropped, and as the first flight of Jerries headed down toward the boys on the deck, I started in to break up the enemy fighters directly ahead and slightly above me. There were at least eight to ten more, lazily circling well above us, making a total of at least 20.

I had the number four man of a Jerry flight in my sights and was about to fire, when a Messerschmitt 109 flashed by directly over my canopy, black crosses distinctly visible beneath each wing. Almost simultaneously, there was a loud bang and a flash of flame filled the cockpit. A 20-mm shell from one of his cannons had evidently made a direct hit on my main fuel tank directly beneath my seat and the tank had exploded. Reflex action made me close my eyes and my colored goggles were on my forehead. My oxygen mask covered most of my face.

Without needing to think or plan or decide what to do, my training, my experience, and my will to live made my right hand grab for the emergency canopy release directly overhead and my left hand for the safety belt release across my stomach. In a fraction of a second, the entire bubble canopy was gone and I was falling out of the cockpit, half pushed by fire and thrashing legs and half pulled by the 200-mile-an-hour slipstream.

As my mind started working again, I was falling clear of the plane and I reached for the ripcord on my chest. The blessed thing worked and it was the happiest moment of my life when I looked up and saw that great canopy overhead gently letting me down to earth. All too gently, however, because I soon realized the dogfight was still going on all around me, and Jerry planes filled the air. As I drifted downward for five minutes, my watch said 0945, nine months to the minute after I pulled out of the harbor in New York.

I had time to look the countryside over as I drifted down and saw that I would land in a hilly, snow-laden forest a dozen miles northeast of Trier and a few miles north of the Moselle River. I saw a couple of our P-47s shoot down at least one other Jerry plane and sweated out another ME-109 that looked as though he were contemplating making a pass at me. He circled at a hundred yards and held fire, and I breathed more easily. The earth came up gradually at first, but at the end of my fall, the trees seemed to rush at me and I slid down through some tall firs and touched the ground lightly as my parachute caught on the branches overhead.

My first instinct was to run, lest I be captured immediately, but I soon realized I was too deep in the forest to have been spotted. Heading west, I crossed several ravines until I met a main tributary to the Moselle River, with rail and road traffic paralleling the stream. Working south through the woods just out of sight, I reached the Moselle by the middle of the afternoon, but found it full of great blocks of ice in a rushing current. All roads and bridges were obviously well guarded, so I headed back north (again), hoping by nightfall to find a place to ford the smaller stream and work west.

It was dark by six o'clock and very cold, and I descended to the road to find a crossing. I was remembering that I was in Germany proper at the time, where there is no underground, and that I was behind the "Bulge." The Germans were making better time in their advance to the west than I was. During my search for a crossing, a German soldier hailed me and I knew my game was up. Frozen feet would have been the only gain in fording the stream, and 50 miles without food or shelter would have been impossible even if what was left of the *Wehrmacht* had not stood between me and the disorganized American lines.

Locked in a Farmhouse

The soldier took me in to the nearest village and turned me over to the officer in charge of the local garrison. He in turn searched me and asked a few questions and promised medical treatment for my eyes, which were now almost closed from swelling and were without eyebrows and eyelashes, probably from the fire in the cockpit.

In all my time in German military hands, I was never pushed around or mishandled. Mistreatment consisted entirely of inadequate food rations, bad living conditions, and illegal solitary confinement for interrogation purposes. That night I was locked and barred in a farmhouse room with a blanket and some straw on the floor. The lady of the house brought in a bit of hot milk soup and some cooked potatoes and cabbage, a definite boost to my morale.

The next morning they started me off on my German ration, which amounted to a sixth of a loaf of *kriegsbrot* (war bread) a day with an occasional chunk of ersatz baloney and a cup or two of burned-barley coffee.

That afternoon I was joined by an Armored Division lieutenant named Lutkehaus, who was particularly bitter about his nickname, "Lucky." From him I heard the first of an endless line of "horror stories," the individual POW's answer to the question of a fellow POW, "What the hell are you doing here?" This whole account is my "horror story."

Christmas Eve, "Lucky," eight GIs captured with him, and I were taken by a truck 20 miles to Wittlich. There was heavy bombing of the town that day by B-26s, making 2,000 homeless. We were taken to a great, heavily-barred county jail on the edge of town, where a thousand or more other newly captured Americans were awaiting transport out of the battle zone.

We spent four days there, sleeping on the floor most of the time and working on rubble heaps in town all one day, with the payment when we got back of a steel helmet full of hot cabbage water per seven men. One day the guard called for all Air Force personnel and three of us spoke up, with wonder in our minds and fear in our hearts. Actually it turned out to be a lucky break, for we joined a dozen other fliers and their five Luftwaffe guards and started off for the Interrogation Center near Frankfurt on our own. Catching trains and hiking, we reached Oberursel, near Frankfurt, just before New Year's Day.

There we were each popped into a little 8-by-10-foot cell. There was a wooden bed with a loosely filled sack of straw for a mattress, one blanket, a glazed window to let in light, and nothing else. The blackout shutters were closed from five in the afternoon until eight in the morning, leaving the room in total darkness for fifteen hours. The only break in the day came at mealtime, when guards opened your door long enough to push in two slices of bread and ersatz coffee for breakfast and supper and a bowl of grass-like soup for lunch.

The first interrogation was short, for everyone refused to give more than his name, rank, and serial number. After three days or so in solitary, each airman was taken to an interrogator's office. Cigarettes were offered, and the interrogator chatted along in perfect English, first joking and kidding, then threatening. Leading questions were asked, and every bit of information previously accumulated was used to make you think that there was no harm in talking. Eventually, if they became convinced you had no special information, they cleared you as a recognized POW and shipped you on to Dulagluft at Wetzlar, in a little over a week in my case.

In Wetzlar we were issued GI clothing brought in by the Red Cross and some toilet articles. We stayed there only one night before being piled into a troop train for a four-day ride to Stalagluft I, a prison camp for commissioned Allied airmen, 90 miles north of Berlin.

Stalagluft I

The camp was divided into four compounds of approximately 2,000 men in each. My compound had 10 barracks forming a rectangle where we stood roll call and played softball. A walk was soon worn down around the barracks, roughly 100 yards to a side. This, then, was where I was to sweat out the War with some 2,300 other "*Kriegies*" (from *Kriegsgefangene*, POW). My barracks had 10 rooms, 24 men to a 20-by-25-foot room. We divided into two shifts for eating purposes, each shift determining how to prepare and ration what food we got.

At first, Red Cross parcels were still arriving with some regularity, and this 11-pound food parcel issued each man every week was sufficient to carry a man along comfortably. But the arrival of new parcels soon ceased. For six weeks we lived solely on the German ration of a bowl of soup a day and a loaf of bread apiece each week. The coal ration diminished. There was little to do except talk and hope.

The one bright moment of the day was the *POW-WOW*, the secret newspaper with all the latest BBC news. Its source was always a mystery to us, but its value in morale was immeasurable. We all became ardent commentators on the news, and the pins in our maps were being moved constantly. The Russian drive from Warsaw started soon after I reached camp but ran out in February, just 90 miles away on the Oder River; Montgomery's drive in Holland came shortly after, though. Soon Patton was across the Rhine. And we knew it couldn't be more than a couple of months.

Holy Week, 1945, was the turning point for the *Kriegies* of Stalag I. News of Remagen came on the 23rd of March, followed by four days of the best weather in camp. We sunbathed all the time and those with energy enough got up ball games while the other 2,000 watched.

All through April we followed the news and made bets on when and how the end would come. By the end of the month we could hear the guns as the Russians moved over the Oder to Berlin and on toward the Western Allies.

Colonel Zemke's Gamble

On Sunday, April 29, there was a sudden flurry of air activity at the neighboring airfield, and on Monday reports came through that the Germans were evacuating the camp. The Germans were indeed leaving, but Colonel Zemke, the Senior Allied Officer in camp, refused to allow his men to be moved. It was a daring gamble for him to take. The German Commandant wished no blood on his hands, so he turned the camp over to the Americans and left with his men. We were free men—or were we?

We awoke on Tuesday, May 1, to find our own men had been appointed MPs in all the towers. We were now in No-Man's Land, with the unpredictable Russians rapidly advancing our way. Zemke sent out patrols that day to contact the Russians, and the first of their tanks reached the camp that night.

On Wednesday, as the main Russian tank force continued their dash westward to meet the Americans at Weimar, a strange, guerilla-like force spread over the land. We were hurriedly ordered to prepare to leave for Odessa! The Russian lieutenant colonel hardly realized the problem he had run up against, and Zemke, in order to prevent such a foolhardy move and to placate these wild Russians, let it be known that we might now bust out of camp. For a day or two there was little discipline left as many Americans joined the Russians in drunken, riotous looting of warehouses, farms, and stores in Barth.

Order was eventually restored as a General Borisoff arrived in the area to set up military law and the *Kriegies* trickled back into camp. Marshall Rokosovsky himself stopped by to see us on his way to meet Montgomery after the surrender at Luneburg Heath on Friday, May 5. The Russians did everything in their power to see that we were well fed and amused, but it was not in their power to get us out, which was our only desire. That was a job for Moscow to arrange, and they demanded complete passport information on every man to be repatriated, all in Russian.

In the meantime, we listened to BBC reports of V-E Day on May 8. And still we waited to leave. It was not until Sunday, May 13, that we were flown to France by Eighth Air Force B-17s. That night we ate at our first GI mess near Reims. The next morning we were flown to Le Havre, and our hopes for immediate shipment zoomed. For three weeks, however, I lay about the great tent city of Camp Lucky Strike, constantly being told that we would ship out in a few days.

Despairing of ever leaving that dusty camp of boredom, Camp Lucky Strike, I arranged to get orders to go to England for transport to the States, with a seven-day delay en route. I was able to visit my brother Charles in Frankfurt, had some Paris in the spring, and hit the beach at Bournemouth before going on to Glasgow. There, I boarded the Queen Elizabeth with a couple of hundred POWs and 15,000 GIs. Accommodations had improved over the trip out, for we were now only three bunks deep as opposed to the quadruple-deckers outbound. The trip was fast, however, and that's what counted most.

We docked in New York June 29, and I got home July 2, 1945, after 60 days of perpetual motion.

Malcolm was born in 1924 in Manchester, New Hampshire. He attended St. Paul's School, Dartmouth, and Harvard Law School. He also studied in Oxford, England, as a Rhodes Scholar. In 1948, he married Susan Neidlinger, daughter of Dartmouth's only Dean, Lloyd Neidlinger. They were married for 57 years and raised five children in Concord, New Hampshire, where Malcolm practiced law with the firm of Orr and Reno. He also served on many local and state boards, committees, and commissions. When his wife developed Alzheimer's, he and his daughter Ann Kuster wrote a book entitled The Last Dance: Facing Alzheimer's with Love and Laughter. *Malcolm died in 2008 after just three years at Kendal at Hanover.*

A Quartermaster on D-Day

Edward M. Scheu
U.S. Navy

*This memoir was transcribed from a recording
made by Edith Gieg*

WORLD WAR II REALLY SPLIT OUR FAMILY UP; we didn't get back together again until the end. Sadly, we lost my brother Don, the brother I was closest to, which was a real blow to me. But my brother Bob sort of moved in and filled the gap.

Much to the consternation of my father, when I came home for Christmas in 1942 after my first semester at Dartmouth, I announced that I had joined the Navy. Father was upset because he felt I should have tried to get into an officer training program. But I had three brothers all out there exposed "on the line," and I just couldn't stand not being there with them.

I went from Buffalo, I remember. I shipped out the day after Christmas, 1942, to Samson Naval Training Station, on the Finger Lakes in upstate New York. We were the first group to go in there, helping to build the facility. After I had been there for about three months, I was fortunate to be selected for Quartermaster School. This was right up my alley: it involved training in navigation and signaling, rather than dealing with stores and so on, as in the Army.

From Samson I went to my ship, an LCI (Landing Craft Infantry), which I picked up at the Quincy Yard in Boston. We took the ship on a shakedown cruise down the East Coast and up the Chesapeake to Solomon Island, a site for amphibious training. After training there for a number of months, I got promoted to Petty Officer Third Class—QM3. We left Solomon and headed for the North Atlantic, crossing by way of the Azores.

The fun thing for me was that we had a wonderful skipper who was an educator. He had been principal of a school in Philadelphia and was a great one for working with young people to improve whatever they were doing. We also had three officers none of whom knew the first thing about navigation. So, as an enlisted man, I ended up as the ship's navigator. And the skipper proudly defended that. He probably broke all kinds of regulations to do it but, being the kind of guy he was, he took me under his wing, and I became the navigator. All I can say is we hit the Azores right on the nose.

From there, we went up to England, where we joined a whole armada of ships practicing for the Normandy invasion.

As D-Day dawned, the weather was overcast, with a sort of on-and-off light rain but not too much wind, fortunately. So Eisenhower made the decision to go ahead with the invasion.

Landing Montgomery's Troops

Since ours was one of the 20 U.S. ships assigned to take Montgomery's First Army to the beachheads, we weren't part of the regular U.S. fleet. But that simply didn't matter. We were in the second wave to hit the beach at Gold, just down from Omaha.

We crossed the English Channel all night long, each ship following the one ahead. It was completely dark except for a little blue light on the stern of the boat ahead. All in all, there were about 3,000 ships, all—or the majority of them—going across the Channel at one time. Yet as far as I know, there were no accidents; you just had to be on your toes.

In the gray dawn, we could see hundreds and hundreds of ships massing along the French coast. We took our position. Loaded with troops from Southampton, England, we had about 170 men on board. The unique thing about my ship was its very shallow draft, so that we could run it right up on the beach and disgorge our infantrymen. The Germans were showing very strong activity against us, but those Brits were something. They had all been fighting in Africa; they were tough guys.

And they took the beach.

One of the great advantages was that the weather limited the German Luftwaffe, so that few German planes were raiding the beaches, though there were some the first night.

We were stuck on the beach: some damage to our ship had to be repaired. So, a whole bunch of us were issued rifles, and we went in and fought with the English soldiers. Of course we were a disaster: we didn't know the first thing about fighting on the land. And, frankly, we were scared to death. We did go in there with them, though, working our way inland for a short distance. But then the next morning we got orders to return to our ship, which by then had been repaired. And we hauled off the beach and headed back to England.

The most interesting thing for me on that trip back was that, besides being the navigator, I was the ship's doctor. Normally, this meant giving out a few things like aspirin; but on that trip I ended up taking close to 150 stitches, in maybe 15 or 20 different people. All the way across, I worked day and night to sew these boys up; we knew they wouldn't be getting to a hospital quick enough.

It wasn't all grim disaster, though. A fun thing happened there on the French coast. Alongside us was a British LCT that was damaged beyond repair, so the crew was abandoning it. Just before leaving for England, a couple of us snuck aboard that abandoned ship and found two big casks of rum. We took them back to Southampton because, of course, being in the U.S. Navy, we weren't supposed to have any alcohol. We cleaned out a couple of garbage cans, poured in the rum, added a big can of dry lemon, stirred it all up—and so, when we arrived in England, we were all set to throw a great big cocktail party for all the GIs waiting to go across the Channel to war.

But suddenly I noticed we were receiving a flashing light, indicating an incoming message. I left the cocktail party with a drink in my hand and jumped onto my ship, went up and got on the light, and started receiving the message. I heard somebody come up behind me, and without looking up, I handed him my drink. When I finished receiving the message, I turned around—and there stood an admiral, holding my drink. He said, "Here, sailor. I think you'd better take this ashore." We had some fun about that!

Landing American Troops and Supplies

After a couple of days there in England, we reloaded, this time with American GIs, and headed once again for the Normandy coast, where we disgorged them in the vicinity of Utah Beach, I believe.

From then on, we had the interesting duty of running barges. The big merchant ships would lay offshore of the D-Day beaches and load up the barges with matériel; then we'd tie our boat alongside the barge and run it like the devil toward the beach. Just before we hit, we'd cut the barge loose and it would run right up on the beach; then we'd back away and go back for another load. We kept that up for several weeks. I thought that whole French coast was going to sink, we had piled so much stuff there.

So: that was our major job after the invasion of Normandy.

One other aside. There was a terrific storm about five days after the initial assault, and it was a pretty wild time on the beachhead, trying to save ships, trying to save people. And the most interesting thing was that as we went alongside a floating dry dock to pick people up, one of them turned out to be *my brother Bob*! I had had a chance to see him in England before the invasion. He was the skipper of a little Coast Guard cutter on duty to pick up survivors—and now *we* picked *him* up! He stayed aboard for the rest of that day until we could get him back to his ship.

After that, we were assigned back to the East Coast of the United States, at Norfolk. But I loved the Navy at sea. So I applied for immediate sea duty, and was the last of the 500 stationed in Norfolk to end up with this assignment.

I wasn't doing exactly what I had wanted, though. I was promoted to first class quartermaster and started serving with Admiral Riley, a great guy, before he sailed for the Pacific. Then, left behind in Norfolk, I ended up training 90-day wonders—so called because they had had very little experience in navigation; they were young people like me, but with college degrees, who were made ensigns before they went to sea.

Well, I lost communications with my brother Bob. My older brother Bill mustered out of the Army because of the loss of a kidney. My third brother, Don, was on a submarine running patrols, and though we wrote to each other, I never saw him again. Back when I was in England, I had had an eerie premonition about him. One night while on watch up in the conning tower in a little harbor, Fowey Harbor, with our boatswain's mate, a fellow by the name of Stan, I suddenly just knew that something had happened to Don. At one point Stan went ashore, and Lord knows where he got it, but he brought back a bottle of Scotch, and we pretty much polished it off that night. All this time I just knew something had happened to Don. Spooky.

Sure enough, about a month later I got word from the Red Cross that Don was listed as missing. His submarine had, I believe, hit a mine off the coast of Formosa. There were no survivors.

Ed was born in Buffalo, New York, in 1924. He graduated from Nichols School, Dartmouth, and Tuck—the latter two after his naval service in WW II. His business career led him all over the globe, beginning at Scott Paper, and RJ Lipton, as president of Good Humor and Diamond Match companies, and finally as CEO of his own company, Atkins and Merrill (later Luminescent Systems). Ed's passions were friends, skiing, flying, and, most importantly, his family and sailing—preferably together. Ed and his wife Molly moved to Hanover in 1974, where he remained very active in the College, and with dog training, before and after his retirement. He and Molly entered Kendal at Hanover in 2001. Ed died in 2010.

The Bitter End

~

Robert P. Stambaugh
U.S. Army

WHEN THE WHOLE WORLD CHANGED on December 7, 1941, I was a senior in chemical engineering at Purdue University in Indiana and only five months away from graduation. I had already accepted a position at a Union Carbide Research and Development Facility in Bound Brook, New Jersey. Six days after graduating in June 1942, I reported to the Lab and was assigned to the group working on developing plastic materials to replace natural rubber, which was not available. As casualties mounted in both Europe and the Pacific, I was drafted into active military service.

At the same time that I was going through basic training in the heat of Camp Wheeler in Georgia, the Third Armored Division, which I was destined to join four months later, was landing on the beaches of Normandy on D-Day+15.

This memoir is about one of the several dramatic adventures that I experienced during that awful period. Like many other WW II survivors, I have buried these things deeply in my memory and have not allowed them to surface for more than 60 years. Now in our waning years, many of the forbidden memories are bubbling up and we want to talk about them. The incident described here took place during the very last days of the War in Europe. It happened on the Mulde River in Central Germany on April 11, 1945.

The Beginning

The Third Armored Division was a very large fighting force of over 15,000 men. It contained all the elements needed to operate as an independent unit. After regrouping on the plains above Omaha Beach, the Division had been immediately committed to action at St. Lô, and then through the murderous hedgerows of Normandy. Over the following months, it continued the attack through Northern France, Luxembourg, and Belgium and then breached the formidable defenses of the Siegfried Line at the German border. When the little German town of Eupen was captured, it was the first time since the days of Napoleon that German territory had been occupied by a foreign army. The offensive continued against fierce resistance, capturing the city of Aachen and then the town of Stolberg.

In Stolberg, the Third Armored finally got relief from its five months of continuous combat. It was replaced by the 104th ("Timberwolf") Infantry Division and placed on reserve status to rebuild its strength. Replacements of every kind came pouring into the town, including new tanks and personnel. I was one of those replacements. I became a member of the second platoon of Fox Company of the 36th Armored Infantry Regiment. It was early November of 1944, the time when my war really began. I had missed the first half of the War in Europe but certainly was not going to miss the second half, which was about to begin.

At first, life in Stolberg was really pretty good. Each squad had "requisitioned" its own house, and hot meals were picked up from a central field kitchen set up in the town square. Morale was further raised when all troops were served an old-fashioned Thanksgiving dinner, complete with turkey and all the trimmings. Many of the veterans from the battles in France were given passes to Paris or Holland. However, there were plenty of reminders that a war was still going on. There were occasional rounds of incoming artillery, and a small German reconnaissance plane dubbed "Bed-check Charlie" flew over every night at about ten o'clock. It was also necessary to maintain the security of our area by manning two-man foxholes around our perimeter, with an hour on and an hour off for each partner. The tanks and infantry spent many hours in the fields around Stolberg in training for the functioning of an armored division.

It was during one of these exercises that a jeep came speeding across the fields with a loud speaker ordering immediate return to quarters. We were moving out—not toward Berlin, as planned, but back the way we had come. The Germans had mounted an all-out surprise attack into Belgium.

The date was December 16, 1944, and the "Battle of the Bulge" had begun.

The Ardennes Campaign, as it is properly called, lasted for only about 40 days, but it seemed like forever. We were actively engaged for all but a few of those days. The weather was so awful and the activity so chaotic that it still remains a blur in my memory. There was no separation between eating and sleeping and freezing and just staying alive for days on end. Everyone had some level of frostbite, from frozen fingers and toes to trench foot. A dry pair of wool socks was worth a fortune. By the time it quieted down in late-January, we were exhausted, but now we also had to contend with a sea of war prisoners.

Moving East

When we got back into Germany, things improved rapidly as rain and mud replaced the snow and ice. We resumed our advance and were soon in a long column of tanks and half-tracks moving triumphantly down a main boulevard in the city of Cologne, all the way to the beautiful cathedral sitting on the banks of the Rhine. Downtown Cologne was a graveyard of bombed-out and burned buildings, but the cathedral seemed miraculously spared. It was assumed by all that getting an armored division across the Rhine River would be a major endeavor. However, an infantry division to the south, by a streak of good luck, had gotten units across the Rhine bridge at Remagen before the Germans could blow it up. They had held the far bank while other Allied troops, including the Third Armored, quickly surged across on a hurriedly constructed pontoon bridge. The breakthrough had now been made, and the Third Armored Division did what it was designed to do. We attacked at full speed in all directions, just as our cavalry predecessors had done in days of old.

Advancing as much as 100 miles on some days, we knew we were approaching the final phase of the War. At least once along the way, we outran our fuel supply and the whole armada stopped and formed a defensive position until the supply trains arrived the next morning. A major battle then developed at the city of Paderborn, a large industrial hub, which was also the headquarters for the elite Nazi SS Divisions. It was in the action at Paderborn that the Commanding General of the Third Armored Division, Major General Maurice Rose, who had been captured in a surprise encounter with a German tank, while surrendering, was shot down in cold blood by a German soldier. It was also where I was wounded by shrapnel from a German bazooka shell; it hit one of our tanks while we were clearing a nearby village, house to house. I couldn't walk and was evacuated to a field hospital. I was not seriously wounded and was able to return to duty in a few days after treatment and the removal of the shrapnel fragments.

The Last Battle

The final strategic operation, which sealed the fate of the Third Reich, then occurred. The U.S. First Army, including the Third Armored Division, curled north from Paderborn and met up with the U.S. Ninth Army coming from the north to encircle the "Ruhr Pocket." The Ruhr is the large industrial area containing many of the factories which produced Germany's war matériel. Included in the trap were 335,000 German war prisoners.

By the early days of April in 1945, the spirits of those of us in the Third Armored were greatly lifted by the first warm days of spring and the knowledge that the outcome of the War in Europe was now certain and not very far away. It remained necessary only to advance to the Elbe River and to make contact with the Russians. We were advancing briskly again with the tanks of the 32nd and 33rd Armored Regiments in the lead. We, the soldiers of the 36th Armored Infantry, were riding on the rear decks of the tanks or in our accompanying half-tracks. Resistance was sporadic but sometimes very intensive, as some Germans were continuing to fight delaying actions. A common enemy tactic was to set up an ambush by hiding tanks behind houses and barns in small peaceful-looking villages. Deadly encounters often would follow, and soldiers on both sides were still being killed. Unlike earlier advances, most of the civilians were now back in their homes, and many were waving white cloths of surrender and even cheering us on. We later learned that not all were that happy to see us but were terribly afraid of the Russians: they were urging us to keep going all the way to Moscow.

The mission of our division was to take the city of Dessau on the Elbe River but then to stop. We were told that an agreement had been reached at Yalta by the Big Three (Britain, the United States, and the Soviet Union) to cease all operations at the Elbe River. After a brief celebration, all parties were to withdraw a short distance in order to avoid the possibility of unpleasant incidents.

At the Mulde

On April 11, our lead elements had reached the Mulde, a small river some 100 feet wide, that joined the Elbe about ten miles farther on. We were not surprised to find that the metal-framed bridge had been almost completely destroyed by the retreating enemy. Standard practice in situations like this was for the infantry to get across the river and set up defensive positions along the other bank. The tanks, with their infantry protection, would be positioned on the heights above the river to control the area. The Division Engineering Battalion, which always followed closely behind, would be called forward to build a temporary bridge and the advance would continue.

Our Second Platoon of Fox Company was riding the lead tanks as we approached the river. We were sent forward on foot, and gingerly picked our way across the river, through the twisted metal girders, and then deployed both ways on the opposite shore. There was no enemy resistance, but the sharp and shifting metal parts of the bridge made crossing very slow and dangerous. There was a flood plain about 100 feet back from the river bank and beyond it a flood-control dike about 10 feet high. We were pleasantly surprised to find that the Germans had abandoned some good two-man foxholes in the flats, about 100 feet apart. We promptly put them to our own use and settled down to wait for the division engineers who would build a new bridge.

There were at first no signs of life from the other side of the dike, but we gradually heard German voices and knew something was going on. My partner, Max Britton, and I went on watch, with one of us trying to get some sleep while the other stayed awake, an hour on and an hour off. As it grew darker, the noise became much louder and more raucous. There were now a lot more of them, and they were obviously having some kind of drunken party. We had no choice but to sweat it out in the foxholes until help came our way.

Suddenly, in the middle of the night, a dozen or more uniformed Germans came screaming over the top of the dike and down upon us. When we saw them firing guns point blank into the foxhole next to ours, we took off for the river and plunged in. I don't remember any shots being fired at us. As I entered the cold water, I dropped my rifle and helmet, but I was still heavy with clothes and equipment. Near the middle of the river, my feet lost contact with the bottom. I was sure I was going to drown. After a few endless moments, my feet touched again. I was finally able to move slowly on to the other bank, where I collapsed. I can't remember whether Max was with me. The men with the tanks above must have witnessed or heard the event and come down to help us.

The next thing I remembered was waking up between clean white sheets in a hospital. I was in Nordhausen, and I remember being told I had slept for two days. In WW II, this total exhaustion was called "battle fatigue" and it was quite common. The remedy was doses of huge blue pills known as "Blue 88s." I think they were large doses of phenobarbital, and they usually restored the patient to normal health.

While I had been sleeping, the engineering battalion had indeed built the bridge, and on April 15 the Third Armored Division crossed the Mulde. They entered Dessau and met the Russians a few days later. I was released from the hospital with a fresh new uniform and a great feeling of relief. It turned out to be May 8, V-E Day. We celebrated with a glass of orange juice and a small portion of medical alcohol doled out by the medics to all patients. A few days later, I caught up with Fox Company and learned that my partner Max Britton had made it back, but I also received the sad but not unexpected news that two other members of our squad had not. They must have been among the very last American soldiers killed in action during the war in Europe.

Bob's squad at a break on the autobahn about three weeks before end of the War in Europe. Bob is at left. Moe Fink (without helmet) was killed on patrol by a German machine gun a few days after this. The two men on his left were both killed in their foxhole on the bank of the Mulde River, just days before the War ended, as described in this memoir.

Trained as a chemical engineer at Purdue, Bob had a 40-year career with Union Carbide in technical and management positions, including General Manager of Carbide's Parma Technical Center and corporate head of recruiting. He was married to Roberta "Bobby" Walker, his college sweetheart, for 65 years. They had four children, now all with families. Retiring from New Canaan, Connecticut, to Vermont in 1982, Bob served as a director and president of the Quechee Lakes Landowners Association. He and Bobby moved to Kendal at Hanover in 1996, where Bobby died in 2007.

The Pacific Theater and Far East

PACIFIC THEATER AND FAR EAST MAP

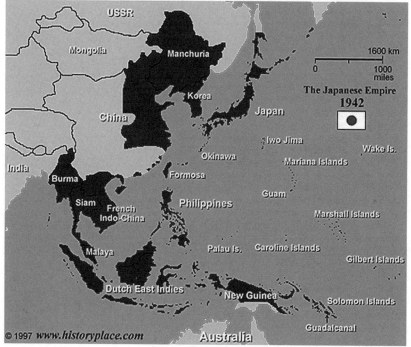

(Map courtesy of The History Place, Historyplace.com)

Pacific Theater and Far East Authors

TEN OF OUR PACIFIC-FAR EAST AUTHORS describe action on the islands or countries shown above and on the next page (in a closeup view). One author was at the Aleutian Islands, to the northeast of the map area:

- **Frank Browning** describes his flights from eastern Burma to China—and a wrong-destination landing in India.
- **Sam Doak** reports how his destroyer sank at the eastern end of New Guinea. Later he was at Guam, Guadalcanal, the Philippines, and Okinawa.
- **Robert Encherman** saw service in the Aleutian Islands.
- **George Harris** tells of tigers at Assam in northeastern India.
- **John Hennessey** was at Luzon in the Philippines when the atomic bombs were dropped.

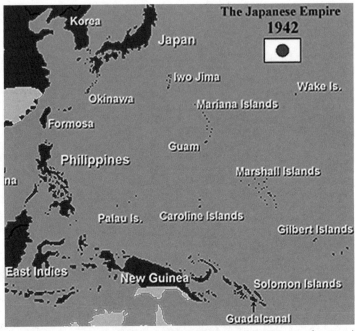

(Map courtesy of The History Place, Historyplace.com)

- **Alan Horton** sailed to the Philippines, then on to Okinawa and Tokyo Bay.
- **James Keeley** was a prisoner in the Philippines, then later in Japan.
- **Robert Stanton** was stationed at Luzon in the Philippines.
- **William Tate**'s voyages took him to New Guinea, Australia, the Philippines, Borneo in the Dutch East Indies, and Nagasaki, Japan.
- **Arthur Turner** flew combat missions above Guadalcanal, the Gilbert Islands, Marshall Islands, and Solomon Islands.
- **John Weeks** reports adventures at Milne Bay, Papua, New Guinea.

OVER THE HUMP

Frank Browning
U.S. Army Air Force

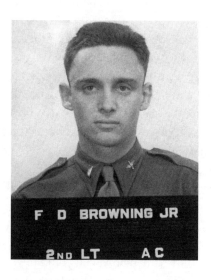

T HIS IS A NAVIGATION STORY. As I think about it now, it seems hard to believe, but it did happen this way, in May of 1945.

I had come to China earlier by navigating a new B-25 bomber with a full crew of six, 14,045 miles from West Palm Beach, Florida, to join the 490th Bomb Squadron at a small airstrip called Warazup on the Burma Road. The squadron was camped in a small clearing in the jungle. When we reported in, our pilot casually said, "We just heard the squadron is moving to China." The commanding officer was most upset. No one but he was supposed to know about it; it was a military secret, serious business. Who told us? "Oh, we heard it on the radio from a Japanese station while flying in."

That ended the conversation. The squadron was indeed moving to China, as the Japanese knew.

An Air Force freight unit called Combat Cargo was transporting the squadron's crew men, equipment, and supplies from the base at Warazup to a new base the Chinese had built for us at a town in China called Hanchung (Nancheng). Many flights were required through the always bad weather over the Hump. Once I was on a night flight that was caught in a bad storm; the plane was collecting heavy ice on the wings and propellers. The pilot ordered us to jettison all the cargo in order to stay airborne, and we made an emergency landing at a small Chinese air strip—not our own—far short of our destination.

We were now stranded on this remote air strip, with an airplane that had been damaged in landing, waiting for transportation. During our wait, one of the pilots came looking for me. He had found out that there was a B-25 waiting to be taken to Calcutta in India. He had volunteered to be the pilot but needed a navigator. Did I want to come? Of course I did. Calcutta was great compared to north China. We knew that Calcutta had good places to stay, elegant restaurants, theaters, and even Coke machines. Sure, I would go.

From China back to India was also on the route known as the Hump. It crossed over the Himalayan Mountains, the tallest in the world. Actually, they were too high for planes to fly over: you flew around the highest parts, but it was tricky because it meant flying a longer distance. The weather was always bad, usually requiring instrument flying, with clouds above and below; you could never see how close you were to danger. Many airplanes were lost flying over the Hump.

We had trouble leaving—bad weather—but finally it improved enough for takeoff, and we were cleared to Calcutta. Just the two of us, no other crew. Right after takeoff we were in the clouds, but this was normal. What wasn't normal was that soon our compass, an electronic type, started to act up and to turn in circles, plus we had trouble with the electrical system and the radio going on and off. Where there should have been an emergency compass on the panel, there was only a hole; someone had removed it. So I went back through the bomb bay, not a very nice trip, to the rear compartment where the radio operator's panel also had a compass. But this too had been removed. The radio was sometimes on, sometimes off, but we managed to call back to our takeoff base. They said we could not come back because the weather was worse and the base was closed. We had to keep going. No choice. And no compass to navigate with.

Before leaving, I had followed standard practice and checked with the weather office, which gave me the projected winds for the trip, so I got my courses and distances to India plotted. At this point, I had an idea. I carried a small pocket compass on the dog-tag chain around my neck and once had experimented with it. I had found that by being very careful and holding it in the center of the cabin, I could get fairly good compass readings. Having nothing else to go by, we did this and set the pilot's gyro compass with it. Pilots usually fly by a gyro compass set by the magnetic pole and reset the gyro every few minutes—so were we really going to make it with a pocket compass? (You may think it odd that I carried a compass, but I also wore two wrist watches: one for Greenwich Mean Time, which we used for navigation, and the other for local zone time.)

Running Low on Fuel

Now a new problem: in checking the fuel consumption, I found the airplane was using more than I had ever seen in a B-25, and it was a question whether we could make it into Calcutta. Normally that plane used about 135 gallons per hour, but this one was using about 180. And there were no closer airports. By now we knew this was a very old, very tired airplane. The radio was on and off, and we often could not reach anyone with it. The pilot was doing the best he could with the engines, adjusting prop pitch, mixture, temperature, and anything else he could to improve fuel consumption, and we flew on, resetting the gyro when needed. Eventually, we got to where we should be, beyond the higher mountains, even though still in the clouds, and started to let down. This descent was very gradual to preserve fuel. It was getting later and later.

Finally, we broke out of the clouds and picked out checkpoints on the ground and saw where we were. It was a little off course but still surprisingly good for the kind of navigation we had been doing. However, fuel was still running out.

After a while, we could see signs of Calcutta in the distance—a long, long distance. The pilot tried calling the airbase at Calcutta once more, and this time the radio worked. He explained our fuel problem: that we might not even make it, and certainly could not follow the normal course pattern of circling the field, but requested permission to come in on direct approach. This was unusual, but they agreed and would get other airplanes out of our way.

By now we had used up most of our glide, and it still looked like a long way to go. As we finally approached the runway, the pilot said,

"There's something wrong here! Planes are still taking off and landing. They haven't cleared the runway for us." But by then he had no choice, could not go around, and landed anyway by some sort of squeezing in between those landing and taxiing. They apparently didn't know we were there. The pilot had done a great job, but it was close and scary. What had gone wrong?

Well, what we had done was to talk to the United States base at Barrackpore, whereas we were really landing at the British air base called Dum Dum, also in Calcutta!

We went into the Operations Office and explained our situation. While the pilot took care of the paperwork, I found a crew to fuel the aircraft; there were only a few minutes of fuel left in the tanks. We were tired and it was too late to fly over to Barrackpore, so we went into the city and got a room at the Burdwan Palace, which belonged to the Maharajah of Burdwan, through an arrangement for U.S. Air Corps people to stay there. It was great. We ran into guys we knew from earlier duty in the States and had a great evening enjoying being in a real city again. We even found several U.S. Coke machines that sold ice-cold Coca-Cola—and for five cents a bottle.

The next morning I asked the pilot about our plans for moving the airplane. He said he was too tired from the previous day. OK, this was his responsibility, not mine. So we enjoyed another day in the city.

The next day he agreed to go out to the British field, but it was late in the afternoon, and there was a thunderstorm. Of course the officers wouldn't clear us to fly even that short distance, but they were not happy with us and insisted we be there early the next morning to get that B-25 out of there: they wanted it *gone*!

We got there early the next morning, flew over to Barrackpore in a short time, and went in to Operations to turn in the paperwork. When they heard what airplane it was, everyone stopped work and looked at us. We were in big trouble! No one had thought to report to the United States base that we had landed earlier at the British base: they thought we had run out of fuel on approach and crashed somewhere out there. They had reported to our squadron that we had been missing for three days, and had sent out a search plane to look for us.

We finally got back to our initial destination, the squadron's new base at Hanchung in China, to a mixed reception. I flew some missions there, but most of my time after that was on detached duty at Sian, about 130 miles to the northeast. The squadron's mission there was to extend our range to more targets and to keep the Japanese-controlled railroads and bridges out of commission. We had four B-25s and crews at Sian, the U.S. air base farthest north in China. We were at the end of a very long and dangerous supply line which flew in all our supplies, including fuel and bombs.

North of Sian, China was divided into many territories, some occupied by Japan, some by Nationalist China, and some by Communists. There were also areas controlled by guerillas and warlords. Luckily, none of our people had to make emergency landings in any of these territories.

When the War ended in 1945, I helped move the 490th Squadron's airplanes to an air base in Germany. I was stuck in Europe until the spring of 1946 but found things to do in Paris and Switzerland.

At last, I returned home and was discharged from the service.

On one of Frank's missions from the Sian base both engines over-heated badly and quit. The pilot crash-landed in this turnip field.

After returning to the States, Frank completed college at the University of Connecticut. During his career, he worked on a number of engineering projects. He married JoAnn Kinney. In 1983, both he and JoAnn retired and moved to coastal Maine, where they spent the next 13 years occupied with hiking, skiing, sailing, and gardening. In 1996 they moved to Kendal at Hanover.

MY ACCIDENT-PRONE NAVY

~

Samuel Doak
U.S. Navy

IWAS AWAKENED FROM A DEEP SLEEP by a very loud screaming sound of metal tearing metal, and found that I had been thrown from my army cot onto the deck. The ship had given a tremendous lurch from port to starboard, but there was no sound of an explosion—only the shouts of men out on deck. I had been sleeping in my skivvies, and I quickly pulled on my pants, not bothering with shirt or shoes. I ran out onto the deck looking towards the stern, which, as I gazed, appeared to be moving to my right, detaching itself from the forward part of the ship. The call was shouted out, "Abandon Ship!"

My ship was the *USS Perkins* DD 377, a Mahan class destroyer built in the 1930s. I had come aboard three days before at Milne Bay, a large naval installation at the eastern end of New Guinea—a very green ensign in the Navy Supply Corps. After graduating from Princeton in June 1942, I immediately applied for a commission as a deck officer in the Navy. Much to my disappointment, I was rejected for colorblindness—a condition I had never suspected I had. After being rejected by

Army and Marine Corps officer training programs for the same reason, I had learned how to cheat on the colorblindness test. Thus I passed it successfully on the examination for the Naval Supply Corps, to which I applied when I learned I would be able go to sea.

I was sent to the Harvard Business School for four months of training as a Supply and Disbursing Officer and received a most effective training that proved invaluable later. I had applied for duty on a destroyer and got my wish, being assigned to Destroyers Pacific Fleet in Pearl Harbor, where I waited six weeks before assignment to the USS *Perkins*. At that time, there was no transportation directly to the South Pacific from Pearl Harbor, so I had to hitch rides on a cruiser, two aircraft, and a landing ship dry dock before ending up in Milne Bay, where the *Perkins* was anchored. Milne Bay was a large roadstead filled with what looked like hundreds of ships. I was taken by a small landing craft to the *Perkins*, and as we approached the ship, a slightly pudgy young officer yelled out, "Is that you, Sammy?" He was the Supply Officer and had been waiting anxiously for my arrival, having received a copy of my orders several months earlier.

When reporting to the Captain, I learned that the ship was to sail in three days to perform a shore bombardment at the village of Finchhofen, held by the Japanese on the north coast of New Guinea. Moreover, I was going to have to move fast to transfer all the stores, cash, and accounts, if my predecessor was to be detached and leave the ship before we sailed, which he was most anxious to do. Consequently, the next two days were a whirlwind of activity to effect the transfer. I was able to bid my predecessor goodbye on the second night, and we sailed the next morning.

It was that night that I heard the cry to abandon ship.

The Mae West

My first thought was my life preserver, which I had not had time to try on. It was an Australian "Mae West," inflated by mouth through a rubber hose in the front of the pouch. In my haste, I mistakenly assumed that the ties went under my arms instead of around the neck and waist as they were designed to do. As a result, the "breast" of the life preserver floated up over my face, providing no buoyancy whatsoever.

My second thought was the payroll record book. I had been taught in training that, if your ship sinks, you might as well go down with it if you do not recover the payroll, since it would take months of work to reconstruct it. My office was not far from the compartment where I was sleeping, and I felt my way to it, passing men jumping over the side, and grabbed the payroll, a large book weighted with steel plates so it would sink and not fall into the hands of the enemy. Of course I did not want it to sink, and I was about to jump overboard with the book under my arm when I heard a splash and saw an empty life raft floating in the water directly below me about ten feet from the ship's rail. I immediately threw the book as hard as I could and by some miracle it landed in the middle of the raft. In a flash, a sailor pulled himself onto the raft and, with the most commanding voice I could muster, I shouted, "Sailor, hang on to that book!" He did!

We had collided with the *HMS Duntroon*, an Australian troop transport full of soldiers returning from fighting at Finchhofen, the battle site to which we had been headed. It struck us amidships in our engine room, killing all four men on watch there, and the two hulls of the ship began to bend apart. I climbed over the rail and jumped, with my left arm holding the useless life preserver across my chest, holding my nose with my right hand. The water was warm and calm. I quickly found myself near a life raft, which was surrounded by men holding on to the raft and to each other. There was quite a bit of chatter, mostly about what a great ship the *Perkins* had been. This was in sharp contrast to the talk among the crew I had been hearing the past few days about what a lousy ship it was.

Very soon, the two ends of the ship began to drift apart and almost immediately the bow and the stern rose rapidly in the air, and an eerie, loud noise came across the water. It was the sound of everything loose on board falling, a sort of death rattle. The two ends of the ship stood straight up and quickly slipped into the sea.

At some risk, for there were occasional Japanese planes in the area, the *Duntroon* turned on its lights and put out life boats, which picked us up. They had lowered the gangway, and when I climbed onto it and inquired about the disposition of my payroll, I was sent to the Captain's cabin, where it had been taken. On entering the cabin, I overheard the Captain asking another officer if there had been any damage to the beer stored in the anchor chain locker in the bow of the ship. These were Australians, and Australians loved their beer. With payroll in hand,

I was taken to the ship's galley, where the coal-fired range had been banked for the night, and, one by one, I dried out the pages of the payroll. We lost ten men in the accident.

Back in Milne Bay, we were put aboard the *USS Dobbins*, a destroyer tender. I was quickly able to pay the crew and settle my accounts. About $34,000 went down with the ship, but I was exonerated for its loss after the end of the War by the Secretary of the Navy. A Court of Inquiry held that the *Perkins* was responsible for the collision and recommended that the *Perkins'* Captain, Executive Officer, and the Officer of the Deck be court-martialed.

Survivor's Leave

I received orders to report home to Philadelphia for one month's survivor's leave. The entire ship's complement sailed aboard the *USS United States*, the former flagship of the US Lines, and we sailed full speed back to San Francisco in 21 days. A few days later I arrived home in Philadelphia, only to find that none of my friends were home, and I was relieved when my new commanding officer called me from New York and ordered that I report for duty ASAP. My new station was The Disbursing Office for Destroyer Escorts in Manhattan, where I was assigned to pay the crews of destroyer escorts coming into New York Harbor from convoy duty in the Atlantic.

Although New York was lots of fun, I was most anxious to get back to sea. I managed to arrange a transfer to the position of Supply Officer of a new AKA (Attack Cargo Ship), the *USS Trego*, being outfitted in the Brooklyn Navy Yard. As the Supply Officer, I was responsible for assembling all the equipment for the ship except fuel, water, and ammunition. I commanded the S Division, consisting of one warrant officer, two chiefs, storekeepers, cooks, a baker, laundry men, and black stewards. My division was responsible for procuring, storing, and serving the food, running the two stores and the laundry, keeping the payroll, and paying the crew. As the decoding officer in the radio shack, I also stood watch at sea and at general quarters.

It was obligatory to have a breakdown cruise before commissioning, and the *Trego* cruised up the East River into Long Island Sound, before anchoring for the night. As far as I knew, things had gone well. However, when I woke in the morning, the ship was gently rocking and

I surmised that we had gone out to sea during the night. But when I looked out the porthole, to my astonishment, directly below me, there was a girl riding bareback on a horse at the edge of a long sandbar about ten feet wide. I yelled down, "Where are we?" The reply came back, "This is Oyster Bay." I soon found out that we had dragged anchor during the night and were hard aground. An inexperienced officer of the deck had taken inaccurate bearings on a nearby lighthouse and we had drifted hundreds of yards. It occurred to me that I might be an instrument of bad luck to any ship I served on, but I soon rejected this idea since I am not superstitious. We had to be pulled off the sandbar by a Navy tug and were towed to dry dock at the Bethlehem Steel Shipyard in Hoboken, New Jersey, where we underwent repairs for about six weeks.

Finally, the *Trego* was back in the water and ready to sail through the Panama Canal to duty in the Pacific. Our first cargo, a ship full of beer for the thirsty men at Pearl Harbor, had to be carefully guarded. I stood on the port side of the main deck to get a good view of the New York skyline as we passed down the Hudson River. The ship headed east into the river and should have begun to turn to starboard down the river. But, it did not turn. It continued to head east towards an empty pier in Manhattan at what was probably about 34th Street. Several men who were loitering on the pier watching our progress began pointing toward us, rising to their feet, and I could faintly hear a shout, which I could not understand, but which must have been something like "Run for your life!" because that is just what they did.

At about that point, the Executive Officer came running down the ladder from the bridge and rushed by me toward the stern of the ship. Soon thereafter, the ship very slowly turned to the starboard and at last headed down river. I estimate we came within several hundred feet of the pier, now vacated. It was a close call and had me so shaken that I forgot to watch the New York skyline, so I remember nothing about our exit from New York Harbor. I learned later that the Captain, or one of his officers, had neglected to post a watch in the Steering Engine Room, which should always be done when entering or leaving port. The steering engine malfunctioned and nobody was there to turn the rudder manually. Phew!

From New York, we sailed with a full load of beer destined for the sailors at Pearl Harbor, and then on into the South Pacific. Over a period of two years we dropped anchor at a number of islands, some shortly after they had been captured from the Japanese. I still remember the names of many: Hilo, in Hawaii; Eniwetok; Ulithi; Guam; Guadalcanal; Russell Islands; Samar, Manila, Subic Bay, and Lingayen Gulf, all four in the Philippines; Wakayama and Nagoya in Japan; Milne Bay and Hollandia in New Guinea; and Okinawa at the port city of Naha. It is only there that our ship was in a battle zone. Our fleet was shelling Naha, where, tragically, the inhabitants refused to surrender and were almost all killed. The U.S. fleet there was attacked several times by Japanese kamikazes. A cruiser anchored near us was hit, but our defense on the *Trego* was to hide under smoke produced by generators on our small boats. This was the only action I saw in my entire tour of duty.

The dropping of the atomic bomb brought great relief to our ship, since we had been preparing for the invasion of Japan, and we knew that would be a deadly operation. When Emperor Hirohito ordered the surrender of Japan, he was supported by universal compliance of his people. I did not appreciate that fact until an incident occurred at the harbor of Nagoya, when I was really frightened. Soon after the surrender, we were ordered to unload some cargo at Nagoya, a large manufacturing city, then completely flattened by American bombing. The harbor was protected by mines which had not yet been cleared. A pilot was needed to navigate through the mine field. I was in a genuine panic when I realized that the pilot was Japanese, and that he could be just as suicidal as any kamikaze pilot and deliberately sink our ship. After all, we were the hated enemy! To my great relief, with great dignity he brought the ship into a safe anchorage, and took us out again two days later.

After five more months of island hopping we finally pulled into the Navy yard at Norfolk, Virginia, where the ship was decommissioned. My sister Bea and my fiancée, Kitty Johnson, drove down from Philadelphia to take me home for final discharge in Philadelphia in May 1946.

Sam was born in 1920 in Philadelphia. He attended Quaker schools and entered Princeton in 1938. He was active in sports, majored in economics, and graduated with honors in 1942. In June 1946, he married Katherine (Kitty) Avery Johnson, with whom he had three children. He spent most of his career in the paper business, working for three Massachusetts companies: Crocker Burnham, Weyerhaeuser, and James River. In 1996, he and his wife moved to Kendal at Hanover, where Kitty died in 2005.

RESCUED BY INGRID BERGMAN

~

Robert Encherman
U.S. Army Air Force

Written by his widow, Carolmae Encherman

MY HUSBAND, BOB ENCHERMAN, graduated from Dartmouth on
May 10, 1942. The College had moved the graduation up from
its usual June date so that the whole class could graduate together. He
enlisted, and 10 days after graduation he was inducted into the Army.
After receiving his uniform, he was taken to his assigned barracks.

The first thing he saw there was a man who had committed suicide,
hanging from the rafters. It was a moment he never forgot.

Bob was assigned to the Army Air Corps and sent to Miami Beach
for training. As it was early in the War, the only place the recruits could
be quartered was in a hotel. It didn't last long, but it was pleasant while
it lasted. He was sent to Scott Field, outside of St. Louis, to radio school.
When he graduated, he was assigned to an Army air field near Tampa,
Florida, where he attended Norden Bombsight maintenance school.
What they taught there was so secret, they had to burn their notes.

During the rest of his Army service, he never was to use either his radio skills or the bombsight information.

His next move was to Camp Davis, North Carolina, to Officer Candidate School. He almost graduated, had even been measured for his uniform, but washed out when he marched a whole battery, including the band, into a ditch! It was a bad mistake, but may well have saved his life. Camp Davis was an antiaircraft training camp, but all the men he trained with were eventually sent, as airborne infantry troops, into action during the Battle of the Bulge.

He was then sent to Elmendorf Air Field in Alaska, near Anchorage, where he spent 27 months and had many interesting adventures. One of the most memorable was picking up Ingrid Bergman in his jeep and driving her to the officers club, where they were having a reception for her. She had come to do a USO show, which consisted of the sleeping bag scene from *For Whom the Bell Tolls* with an actor named Neil Hamilton. Bob was very excited to be driving Ingrid Bergman, since she had always been his favorite actress.

While she was at the reception, he remained outside in the jeep. After a few minutes, a lieutenant came out, saying that Miss Bergman, worried that the sergeant would be freezing outside in the jeep, asked that he be invited inside to the reception. He came in, and was the only enlisted man at the party. He would have been all right in the jeep—it had a heater—but he was greatly impressed with the consideration and thoughtfulness of Ingrid Bergman.

Bob stayed in Anchorage for the remainder of the War. During that time he had a six-month assignment, to accompany a captain from the Morale Services Division to investigate the high suicide rate in the Aleutian Islands. The troops there were in a treeless, barren area with nothing to do but wait for an attack that never came.

Just before the end of the War, Bob had an attack of appendicitis and needed an operation. The Army surgeon was angry at being held back from returning home because of having to perform this operation. However, he did his job well and made the next ship home.

Bob was sent home in November of 1945. He was able to get a ride in an Army plane from Seattle to Fort Monmouth in New Jersey, near his parents' home. Nobody was home when he arrived there and the house was locked, so he opened a window and climbed in. A neighbor saw him and called the police. Fortunately, he was able to prove that he belonged there and was not arrested.

Although Bob was accepted by Harvard Law School, and they had kept his place for him while he was in the Army, he chose not to attend. He began work as a columnist for the New York Journal of Commerce *and then became Director of Public Relations for a national trade association. He eventually created catalogs for his own business, which was a buying concern for a group of wholesalers. He and Carolmae were married in 1947 and had three children. They lived on Long Island, New York, until his retirement in 1982, when they moved to Quechee, Vermont. There Bob wrote a weekly column for the* Vermont Standard. *The Enchermans moved to Kendal at Hanover in 1996. Bob died in 2007.*

TIGER, TIGER

George Harris
Air Transport Command

During World War II, tigers still burned bright on the jungle-clad slopes of the Himalayas in Assam in northeastern India. They sometimes came down into the tea fields below, from which the U.S. Air Transport Command flew supplies over the Himalayan massif to China. The tigers were not supposed to be man-eaters, but we who were stationed there could not be sure that one would not change his mind.

One steaming evening in 1942, in the *chota* (short) monsoon, some of us were sitting over drinks of wild lime juice and Indian gin and trying to maintain an illusion of coolness. Fireflies were flashing their lights over the fields—always a spectacle, for in their millions, they flashed, not at random as at home, but simultaneously, forming a brilliant stratum of light that gradually rose above the fields in the gathering darkness.

Suddenly, a young soldier drove up. Leaping from a jeep, he shouted, "Tiger, tiger! He nearly got me in this goddam broken-down jeep!" Still trembling, he said that he had been driving down a long, narrow lane in the tea fields. In the twilight, he saw on the road ahead the glowing eyes of a shadowy figure he took to be a stray calf. As it came closer, he saw that this was no calf but a big Bengal tiger. He stopped, appalled by the thought that there was no room to turn around and that the jeep was prone to stalling and could be started only by hand-cranking.

The tiger continued to saunter down the center of the road toward him. Getting out to crank the jeep was unthinkable. The temperamental engine was still running. Could he put it into reverse without it stalling? With the tiger only yards away, the question might be one of life or death. The great beast might or might not be hungry. Pinning desperate hope on retreat, the terrified young man revved up the idling engine to a high scream and thrust the jeep into reverse. Backing the quarter of a mile to the end of the lane, he must have broken all speed records for driving in reverse. We tried to calm him with lime juice and gin and resolved to insist that the starters on our jeeps be kept in working order.

Stories of man-eating tigers were common but mostly unsubstantiated. When verified, the tiger was elderly and unable to take any prey other than human. Tigers are, of course, dangerous animals to hunt. If cornered or wounded, they can turn the hunter into the hunted. They do not so much seek humans as avoid them, except when yielding to feline curiosity. Some of us were aware of these characteristics, but no one was disposed to test them.

The Yellow Eyes

The living room, bedrooms, and veranda of the junior officers' bungalow were built above the kitchen and storerooms, which were separated by a driveway that passed under the living quarters above. Our mess sergeant preferred setting up his cot in the driveway at night to trying to sleep in his airless room in the storage unit. Late one night, he rushed up the stairs to the veranda, where most of us, unable to sleep in the 95-degree humid heat, were still up. "I'm not sleeping down there anymore," the sergeant announced. "I just woke up. I had the feeling something was watching me. Right there beside my cot was the biggest tiger I ever heard of. His head was big as a basketball. He just stood there looking at me through my mosquito net. Those yellow eyes!

Finally, he walked off. Must not have been hungry!" Needless to say, the sergeant slept on the veranda thereafter. The thought that there was nothing to prevent the tiger from joining us too was not comforting.

Our headquarters was in a long tin-roofed shed from which the tea-drying tables had been removed. The colonel's desk was at the head of the double line of desks of the rest of the staff. Mine happened to be just in front of the colonel's. I was glad to spend most of my time in the field, out from under the colonel's critical eye. One morning, a supply truck drew up. The driver, a corporal, came in and saluted the colonel smartly. Beside him on a leash was a full-grown tiger.

After one startled look, the colonel leapt to his feet and fled through an open door, followed by everyone else.

Everyone but me. As Officer of the Day, I had to remain at my desk and telephone in the event of an emergency.

The tiger, on a leash and undoubtedly tame, was the embodiment of strength and beauty. I was fascinated. The bemused corporal walked over to me with the tiger. "She's really friendly, sir. I've had her since she was a kitten. Somebody shot her mother." Very tentatively, I petted the silken head.

The colonel peered through the door. Glaring at the three of us, he shouted, "Get that goddam cat out of here!"

Outside, the corporal hastily unloaded some office supplies and gave me the manifest. I stood watching as he and the tiger drove off.

George earned a B.A. in anthropology and Chinese studies from the University of Washington and a Ph.D. in anthropology from the Catholic University of America. His military service was in the China-Burma-India theater. From the end of the War until 1954, he held various American government positions in and relating to China. He then became a Research Associate and subsequently Professor of Anthropology and East Asian studies at The American University from 1954 to 1981. In 1981, George and his wife, Elaine, retired to northern Vermont, where they lived until 2003, when they moved to Kendal at Hanover. Elaine died in 2008 and George in 2011.

Ten Days in August

~

John Hennessey
U.S. Army

It all happened in ten dramatic days 66 years ago. On August 6, 1945, the United States dropped an atomic bomb on Hiroshima, Japan. On August 8, the Soviet Union declared war on Japan. On August 9, we dropped a second atomic bomb, on Nagasaki. On August 15, Japan surrendered. World War II was over.

I was an Army officer on Luzon in the Philippine Islands during those ten days in 1945. I remember well the feeling of sensory saturation, even a tinge of disbelief. Was this a dream? The joyful headline was that we had won the War. That was what we had fought for, dedicated our lives to. But, what was this unimaginable technology that had suddenly blasted and radiated whole cities? What is atom splitting? What hath God wrought?

In 1943, at age 18, I had volunteered to be drafted, having been deferred because of my eyesight. I felt fulfilled by the act. Hitler and Tojo were our implacable enemies. War was raging both in Europe and in the Pacific. For me, a bugle had blown, and I rushed into basic training with a youthful sense of chivalry and adventure.

I was impatient with the grinding weeks of depersonalized basic training. Then I was assigned to train basic troops in Mississippi, where my company commander changed my life by telling me he wanted to recommend me for OCS, Officer Candidate School, back in Maryland. I doubted that I would be qualified because I would need an exemption for my eyesight. To my surprise, I was accepted, and I took the train north in high spirits.

Ninety days later I emerged from a tight pressure cooker with 2nd-Lieutenant gold bars and a new persona as "an officer and a gentleman." I studied the Officer's Guide, even the amusingly dated pages about wearing white gloves and leaving calling cards when visiting the home of a base commander! Along the way, I learned about leadership, the uses and limits of war, and the Geneva Convention. I also learned a lot about the enemy. I was enchanted by the idea of Duty, Honor, Country, which I was told many times was the motto of West Point.

The Philippines

A few months after OCS, I embarked from San Francisco on a crowded troopship bound for places unknown. We only knew we were at the Equator when we were put through the traditional dunking ceremony in a pool on deck. Three weeks after leaving the United States, I found myself in the Philippine Islands, where I was promptly assigned to the 580th Ordnance Ammunition Company, ten miles south of Manila in a picturesque Luzon village, on the edge of which the 580th's 10,000 tons of ammunition were stored on a former Japanese airstrip. The 580th had six officers and 250 enlisted men, mostly veterans of the long Pacific campaign. The company employed 100 Filipino civilians in its sprawling depot.

The aversion to all things Japanese fueled our "passionate intensity." The Filipino civilians spoke of a visceral hatred of the "Japs" and of their thirst for revenge. We talked about the imminent invasion of Japan and the predicted 400,000 allied casualties and that made rough sense to us, as long as the result was the epic victory that always glowed at the end of our mission. That would justify the brutal battles since 1942 on one island after another and the persistent conflicts at sea and in the air. The glorious end would justify the inglorious means once more in human history.

The Old Testament image of "an eye for an eye and a tooth for a tooth" was mixed in my brain with notions of civilized rules: sparing innocent civilians, treating prisoners fairly, a sense of "just wars," a concern for proportionality in means toward the ends of war. The reported savagery of the Germans and, especially for us, the Japanese, was toxic to us soldiers in our everyday military lives, of course, and images of retaliation seemed entirely appropriate and motivating. We deeply believed in our "cause" and over time the enemy became diminished in our minds to the status of criminal or worse.

During May, June, and July 1945, we became almost numb from the routine of unloading ammunition crates at the nearby railhead, trucking the matériel to our familiar acres of thatched-roof storage sheds on high bamboo poles arranged symmetrically in an area about the size of six football fields. In the depot we classified and sorted ammunition with an elaborate coding system, stacking the bullet cases, grenades, shells, projectiles, propellants, fuses, and other components. We then doled it out to the combatants who came in their trucks and half-tracks, all for the invasion of the Japanese mainland.

One day blurred into another. We thought the invasion of Japan would surely begin before the end of 1945, but the slow grinding War and the reported suicidal resistance of the Japanese on Okinawa diluted the confidence of our predictions of when the invasion might occur. The continuing War was our obsession, our reason for being. We were totally absorbed in our work and only vaguely aware that we were doing in the Pacific what had been accomplished by the United States and its allies in Europe, ending in V-E Day in May 1945.

Cognitive Dissonance

With the news of the atomic bombs and the sudden announcement of the War's end, my fellow officers and I felt a strange mixture of joy and disorientation, almost confusion or cognitive dissonance. Dominant, of course, was the glowing image of good conquering evil. The powerful idea of making the world safe from tyranny resonated with my understanding of past wars and WW II. But not entirely. The awful power of the new bomb was a radical departure from the past, very different from any concept we understood in our ammunition depot on Manila Bay. The force of an atomic weapon was reported to be more than the power of our entire ammunition inventory. Perhaps much more. I felt a shiver of awe and apprehension.

We were the ammunition experts, after all, and no such weapon existed for us. Surely we would have heard some hint of a super-weapon, one that could do so much. How much? The message implied a whole city had been destroyed. But why would that be so sensational, when we had known of extensive devastation produced by the firebombing of major Japanese cities? An echo of Coventry and Dresden in the fury of the European conflict, controversial acts that were easily spun for us soldiers as the necessary routes to winning a major modern war.

A Loss of Innocence

My fellow officers and I all felt what we called a "loss of innocence." We talked of an entry into a new age of international relations, overshadowed by the atomic bomb, its power and its apocalyptic threats. The evolution of methods of war had suddenly veered off the map. It was as if Henry V had been given a machine gun at the Battle of Agincourt, one of my friends said. The seed of a new term, "weapon of mass destruction," was delivered by the God of Physics. The genie was out of the bottle. A new Faustian bargain had been struck with Mephistopheles. All sorts of images and metaphors (and clichés) brewed in our young brains, as our imaginations worked to fill the void of ignorance. And we experienced the sheer joy that the War was over. We could go home!

We did not debate whether President Truman had made the right decision in ordering the dropping of the A-bombs, of course. Our Commander-in-Chief had pulled off a miracle. In a few short days, our minds shed the expectation of a costly assault on Japanese shores to a vision of a world of peace and the victory of democracy over aggressive totalitarianism. We bathed in the sentiment that we would soon be resuming our civilian lives, turning our swords into plowshares! The letters home were not "what hath God wrought" but "Thank God, the War is over. Thank God for answering our prayers."

At one point our slim line of logic led us to speculate: what if the physicists of Germany and Japan had broken the secret of the atom first? What then? In our exuberance and patriotism, we rejected that as unthinkable. Of course, God was on our side. In my youthful confusion, I remembered Lincoln's wise rephrasing of the question of whether

God is on our side to whether we are on God's side. In that part of my brain I also thought of the *Iliad*, where the playful gods often determined the fortunes of warriors.

Our job at the depot suddenly changed after those ten days in August. Following months of filling orders for ammunition and loading endless convoys of trucks from infantry and artillery companies, we did an about-face. It was like shifting into reverse. Now our task was to take back the ammunition. The troops had been told that there would be no talk of going home until all ammunition had been handed back to the ordnance people (like us) for disposal, demolition, burning, and dumping at sea. We used whatever means of disposal would satisfy military standards and the requirements of the Filipino government. Around the clock, seven days a week, for at least two months, we were once again open for business as a relentless stream of trucks snaked into our sprawling depot and dumped the contents wherever their drivers could find space. We became absorbed in the new and somewhat dangerous routine, and thoughts of going home became indefinitely postponed by the necessities of our professional duties. The concept of atomic bombs, still so unimaginable, seemed totally abstract as we dealt every day with the comprehensible if old-fashioned array of ammunition whose dimensions and power we understood, piece by piece.

A year later, in August 1946, after a series of other adventures, including participating in the celebration of the independence of the Philippines on July 4, 1946, I came home by troopship, passed again under the breathtaking Golden Gate. In the weeks that followed I shed the uniform and daily habits of an Army officer, warmed by public praise for the service we had performed. People had stopped me on the street of my hometown to shake my hand in gratitude and say, "Thanks for a job well done."

Supported by the benevolent GI Bill, I soon became a college student again. But I still felt in the back of my conscience the strange apprehension that the Atomic Age held more threat than promise. Are we going to have future wars in which we drop these A-bombs on cities? I was still working on metaphors such as going "Through the Looking Glass" into a new world. I was now, at 21, a grizzled veteran, ready to go back to college and try both to put my wartime experiences in perspective and to get ready for life on the other side of the Looking Glass.

John grew up in York, Pennsylvania, and entered Princeton in September 1941. After the War, he graduated from Princeton in 1948 and married Jean M. Lande, Vassar '48. With an M.B.A. from Harvard and a Ph.D. from the University of Washington, he joined Dartmouth's Tuck School faculty in 1957 and served as Dean from 1968 to 1976. After he became emeritus in his ethics professorship in 1987, he was named Provost and then Interim President of the University of Vermont. He has served on many governing bodies and chaired the Kendal at Hanover Board from 1998 to 2001, when he and Jean became residents, near their two children and three grandchildren. Jean died in 2004. In 2006, John married Madeleine M. Kunin, former Governor of Vermont.

Journey to Tokyo Bay

~

Alan Horton
U.S. Navy

Prologue

MY FIRST REAL ACQUAINTANCE WITH WORLD WAR II was in 1938–39 when, at age 17 in Strasbourg, France, I was living with a French family. We would occasionally take walks, family style, along the banks of the nearby Rhine. From across the river on the German side there often came the chatter of machine guns. This was said to be target practice. But on the faces of my French family, especially those of two 18-year-olds, a son and nephew, it was not difficult to see an awareness that their pleasant lives were about to be replaced by something else. I left for the United States just before the War broke out.

The Navy Years—First Plunge

On July 20, 1942, I set off for Newport, Rhode Island, to join the Navy. Boot camp seemed routine, somehow expectable. Toward the end I put in for quartermaster school; I explained to civilian friends that, in the Navy, quartermasters were the enlisted persons on the bridges of ships (steering, keeping the log, sometimes signaling), nothing to do with supplies and warehouses.

I had spent a short time working in the Navy library and had been given a "ship's company pass," which permitted an easy exit from and re-entry into the naval base. A bureaucratic mix-up that I never fully understood resulted not only in my keeping the pass but also using it whenever bored by quartermaster training. When the training period was over, one of the sailors mimeographed a "class report" and sought to mention everyone. He carefully described me in less than a sentence as "nocturnal Alan Horton." And after the short graduation ceremony, the Chief Petty Officer who had been in charge of the course drew me aside with a smile and said: "Horton, I'd like to see that ship's company pass you've been using." Astonished, I reached for my wallet and handed it over. "Aha," he said, "thanks and good luck." He continued to smile. I did not push my luck again.

To get to San Francisco, we all inhabited a railroad car for a week or so. Pulled and pushed across the country, we passed the time playing cheap poker and sleeping. From Goat Island in San Francisco Bay two of us were directed to the *USS Nevada*, a tub-like World War I battleship crammed with 2,000 men and bristling with big guns. I was assigned hammock space (nighttime only) on the main deck and put to work as a lookout. Within two days the ship started north, and after several days at sea we were told we were headed toward the Aleutians.

In a few weeks, thanks in part to an assistant navigation officer I had known vaguely at Princeton, I was transferred to the N division, the small group of quartermasters who manned the bridge. Our sleeping quarters were in the bowels of the ship, exclusive and with real bunks, across from the space occupied by the ship's band. My quartermaster colleagues welcomed me and became close friends. I began as a helmsman and in several months became a quartermaster of the watch. I liked the responsibility. Soon I was promoted to QM 3/c, the petty officer status which I had not achieved at quartermaster school because of my nocturnal habits. In retrospect, I think I was growing up.

For several months the *Nevada* and a couple of destroyers patrolled the seas between the outer Aleutians and mainland Japan. Bleak saltwater scenery, back and forth and back again, long hours along designated parallels, occasional savage weather. We feared submarines, but ran across traces of them only a few times. When off duty I occasionally played chess with a bassoon player from the other side of our quarters, but usually it was checkers or rummy or cribbage with other quartermasters. The monotony was broken when, for several days, at battle stations or watch-on-watch-off, we stood off Attu at 5,000 yards, firing 16-inch guns in support of the landing of U.S. ski troops. We could see the shells hit the island's rocky slopes.

Then, after more unexciting patrolling, the *Nevada* headed south. Rumors flew. We stopped in San Francisco, then on to the Canal Zone, where almost everyone was allowed a brief stint ashore. Shortly after entering the Atlantic, our captain came on the ship's loudspeaker and said we were now in "a civilized ocean." He asked all hands to shave the beards so many of us had carefully cultivated in the Aleutians. He told us we were going on convoy duty and that the admiral in charge of the convoy would have his headquarters on our ship. As a fellow quartermaster drily put it, an admiral has to have a comfortable and safe place to sleep. Heading out on our first convoy, we were at the center of perhaps 50 ships, including more than a few destroyers and destroyer escorts equipped with the latest antisubmarine devices. The admiral would sleep safely.

With help from the ship's chaplain, the officer assigned to such matters, I was finally given orders to report for midshipman training at Northwestern University's downtown campus in Chicago. When I left the *Nevada*, more than several quartermasters and two watch officers came to the main deck aft to watch my final salute.

The Navy Years—Amphibious Portion

Abbott Hall, the location of the midshipman school, was on the near north side. And Chicago was the city where I had gone to high school. So it was a busy three months not only of study but also of re-establishing old acquaintanceships—girls I went to school with, families of old friends now in the service. I shared a pleasant room with three others who were younger than I—or so we all felt, because, unlike them, I had been "with the fleet." Soon we were fitted out with new uniforms, and I was appointed a cadet officer. Toward the end of the session a full lieutenant came by and spoke to some of us about volunteering for an outfit called Scouts and Raiders. It sounded good.

So my next stop was the amphibious base in Fort Pierce, Florida, where Scouts and Raiders had its special training area at the seaward tip of the base. Along with about 20 young ensigns and 100 enlisted men, I was put through a rigorous three-month training program that left me in the best physical shape I've ever been in. We became familiar with every aspect of swimming with fins and face masks, of maneuvering with rubber boats, of handling 30-foot landing craft. Our principal conditioners were large logs, each lifted by six men in long exercise sessions.

Scouts and Raiders had made a name for itself off the shores of North Africa in 1943 and at the Normandy landings, but apparently their abilities were deemed less useful for Pacific warfare. The officers were shipped out of Fort Pierce and for some reason assigned first to a short course in naval intelligence in New York near Times Square. After some five weeks of uninspiring lectures (combined, of course, with urban entertainment), we reported to the Hawaiian island of Maui, where some of us were immediately thrown into the ranks of already experienced UDTs (Underwater Demolition Teams). My assignment was UDT#7, which had already done its considerable bit at the landings on Saipan, Tinian, and Peleliu.

It was February 1945 when Team 7 tucked me into its routines. I became the second officer of one of its four platoons. The team had two jobs. The first was reconnaissance, reporting on conditions for bringing landing craft onto the beach. The second was blowing up the obstacles—both man-made and coral. On the way to Okinawa, the team's next assignment, we had a major practice session at Leyte Gulf, in the lovely warm water of the Philippines. Then it was on to the real thing, the chilly water off Okinawa's Yellow Beach, where we did the crucial reconnaissance on March 29, 1945. The swimmers had only mask and flippers, a sheath knife at the belt, a waterproof wristwatch, and a special Plexiglass slate and "pen" for taking notes.

We were dropped from rubber boats attached to the seaward side of landing craft driven by very savvy coxswains. Most of the swimmers went straight in from 500 yards out at intervals of 50 yards. I was one of four "cross-swimmers," who swam along the length of the beach at a distance of 100 yards from shore. All of us were covered by battleships firing at 5,000 yards and destroyers at 2,000 yards. Fire from shore was only sporadic. When the swimmers had finished their reconnaissance, they swam out and waited in the water until they were flipped back into the same fast-moving rubber boats 90 minutes later by equally savvy sailors squatting in the rubber boats holding out looped ropes for the swimmers to grab.

The following day, the rest of the team did the demolition of wooden posts and coral barriers, but I was transferred by a tricky over-the-water conveyance to a destroyer and then to the headquarters ship of the oncoming task force. Along with two others from other demolition teams, we sat down with our reconnaissance information in a roomful of admirals and generals and told them about the beaches. The generals expressed their gratitude for the information we provided but were astonished that we had swum in with no weapon but a sheath knife. When I got back to our destroyer escort, the demolition work had been completed—without casualties. On D-Day (April 1) a few members of the team were assigned to guide the landing craft onto the beach, and as we watched the Marines stream off the landing craft I thought about the casualties they were about to incur.

Kamikaze Attacks

Other events that followed included a sudden attack from a small nearby island. When doing a routine reconnaissance, our ship was hit by shore batteries resulting in ten wounded and one killed. And of course this was the time when the Japanese were launching kamikaze suicide attacks on Navy ships. One such kamikaze was brought down three yards from where I stood on deck.

Along with several other demolition teams, we were put ashore on the atoll of Ulithi in the central Pacific. Both officers and men had pleasant cabins to relax in for six weeks. The mail finally arrived in large sacks with many letters for each. A letter from my father, written in longhand, sought to tell me important news in a code we had worked out long ago but I had completely forgotten about. My father's scrawl, the part anyone could read, said simply: "MHM and I are to be married." Nothing more. Who the hell was MHM? On the floor by my cot was a copy of the wartime *Time* magazine with a cover picture of a certain Mildred H. McAfee, head of the Waves.

My reaction was immediate: "No, it couldn't be." But putting scattered bits of information together, I eventually realized that not only could it be but in fact it was. Given Mildred's position, the need for keeping the engagement confidential was obvious. I got a special leave and was best man at their wedding in Connecticut on August 10, just four days after Hiroshima. The Japanese surrendered on August 15 and the surrender was signed on September 2. All leaves were cancelled, including mine—and all those of Team 7, who (it turned out) had been given 30-day leaves after I left for the wedding.

I made it back to California just in time. I arrived to find that several of our officers had been transferred to other teams or jobs. A different destroyer escort was ready and waiting for us at Oceanside, and we went straight to Tokyo Bay, which was packed with U.S. ships. While waiting around for orders, we went ashore several times and had some fascinating and revealing conversations with Japanese we met in the streets. On one occasion we were invited into the home of a delightful man who spoke passable English. With the War over, I think all of us felt somehow liberated. Certainly a heavy burden had been lifted away. Had it been necessary to do the reconnaissance and demolition work for an attack on the Japanese homeland's fabulous defenses, we all knew we would be dead.

At one point we were sent up to reconnoiter a beach near Sendai on the east coast, and two platoons went ashore in rubber boats. I was in charge of a group and carried a Colt .45 at the waist. When our rubber boats first landed, we were surrounded by rural poor, smiling and friendly, from a village of fisher folk nearby. Suddenly one of them saw my revolver, and they began to drift away quickly. But one young woman had left her baby lying on the beach and was both terrified and determined. She stood uncertainly about 50 yards away. A sailor in his thirties knew immediately what to do. He went over to where the baby lay and sat down making cooing noises and other parental sounds and gestures. The mother edged back, and little by little so did all the fisher folk. They ended up carrying our rubber boats along the dune line and back to the surf.

The following morning we returned to Tokyo Bay, where we encountered a severe typhoon, and we then took off, by way of Guam and Pearl Harbor, for San Diego and the neighboring amphibious base of Coronado, where post-war demolition was to make its headquarters. Our destroyer escort was loaded with unused demolition materials, and our team members were loaded with rumors about the future. Coronado, it turned out, had our future very much in mind: a series of unexpectedly quick decisions and re-assignments. Team 7 began to disintegrate. Quite a few men and most officers were eligible for immediate discharge, most by virtue of medals such as Bronze Stars and Silver Stars. Our commanding officer, who had just been promoted to the position, asked me to serve as the team's Executive Officer (the team's #2). A week later, on October 27, 1945, he asked me to march the team's enlisted personnel to a certain office on the base in a final gesture of the team's dissolution. He said he did not wish to accompany me. Sentimental fellow.

The Navy Years—Final Page

The team officers, the few that remained, were given several innocuous choices for their few months left in the Navy. I chose the Shore Patrol, the Navy version of the Army's Military Police. Along with others anxious for an easy transition to civilian life, I reported for two weeks' training in San Diego on how to be a Shore Patrol officer. There was little they could teach me, but I enjoyed the streets of San Diego, a true Navy town where every main street was a sea of undulating white sailor hats.

To my delight, I was assigned to duty in Manhattan. Conveniently, my father and stepmother had a nice apartment on Riverside Drive near Columbia University, an area of New York I knew well and where I had a smattering of friends. The Shore Patrol office to which I reported was on 52nd street just off Fifth Avenue, next door to a New York Police precinct office. Every third day—all 24 hours of each one—I was the officer in charge of Navy Shore Patrolmen for all of Manhattan from the Bowery to 125th Street. I was answerable to an over-age commander of whom I saw very little. I cannot remember the number of patrolmen who were theoretically under my control (perhaps 250); what is important is that I was assisted by a chief petty officer who was almost old enough to be my father, who in pre-War days had had two decades of experience as a Manhattan cop. When he suggested a course of action, I agreed immediately. Together we patrolled all of Manhattan's areas south of Harlem—ethnic, racial, rich, poor—and often sampled restaurants where the headwaiters knew him and refused to charge us for our food, as if my friend the Chief were still on the force.

As we checked on our wandering patrols, he filled me with information and gossip about every corner of Manhattan—his experiences of people, institutions, stores, the staff and residents of particular apartment buildings, academic campuses. My usefulness to him came only on the more than several occasions that commissioned officers were involved, such as the time a major hotel phoned in and asked us to squash an unruly drinking party made up of full lieutenants and lieutenant commanders; on the Chief's advice I simply stood at the door, arms folded, until the officers took their women and left. On another occasion a lieutenant commander in the French navy got into a brawl with an American chief petty officer; an awkward incident was averted when my fortuitous knowledge of French allowed the Frenchman to let off the steam of his indignation.

This fascinating and very short tour of duty had to stop. The Princeton spring term was about to start. I put in for a discharge earlier than the so-called points allowed, mentioning also that I was expecting a Silver Star for action off Okinawa. When an affirmative answer came back with approval for immediate discharge, I went to 90 Church Street and left the Navy—in March of 1946.

Epilogue

A week or two later I received a letter calling me back to 90 Church Street to pick up a Silver Star. Directed to an office with a petty officer at the desk, I handed over the letter. He asked me to wait a moment, went to the inner office, then came back with the suggestion of an embarrassed smile. The commander would like to see you, he said. Inside sat a commander, probably retired, who asked me to sit down. Clearly he was anxious to put a bit of ceremony into the occasion of handing over my medal but did not quite know how to proceed. Finally, after a few awkward phrases, he stood up from behind his desk, simply held out the medal, and shook hands. I felt that the sooner I left, the easier it would be for him.

The Underwater Demolition Teams (UDT) of World War II evolved into Navy SEALS some time before the Vietnam War. The veterans of both groups have formed what might be called an alumni association and apparently have annual get-togethers. Having lived abroad for many years and not being much of a joiner, I missed almost all of this, though Team 7 kept in touch by mail by way of a few faithful volunteers. I was brought back into the fold when one day, about a decade ago, the phone rang in my family summer house in Randolph, New Hampshire, and a voice asked if this was the Alan Horton who had been on UDT 7. It was the current volunteer-in-charge, who happened (astonishingly) to live in the town next door. Thus I became re-involved. Now there are only two officers and six men left. The man in the next town has gone and our commanding officer is age 93—and he has asked me to take some responsibility. The extraordinary widow of the man in the next town has agreed to do all the paperwork and keep the records.

The War is almost over.

Alan went to Cairo in 1947 to study Arabic on the GI Bill and stayed on in the Arab world. He taught at the American University in Cairo (AUC), served with the American Friends Service Committee in Gaza, where he met his wife, Joan, and worked for the United Nations in Beirut. He did his doctoral work in anthropology at Harvard and North Syria in the early 1950s. He returned to Cairo in 1955 and became academic dean at AUC. Later he was Middle East correspondent for the American Universities Field Staff, then its Director in New York and Hanover, New Hampshire, and finally in Rome in semi-retirement. He and Joan entered Kendal at Hanover in 1999. Joan died in 2010.

PRISONER

~

James Keeley
U.S. Army Medical Corps

Based on records provided by his widow, Mary Keeley

JAMES KEELEY WAS A MEDICAL CORPS RESERVE OFFICER with a graduate fellowship at the Mayo Clinic when he was summoned to active duty in August 1941. Less than two months later, he was aboard ship, heading to the Philippines. At that time, the United States and Japan were officially at peace; however, for over a year the United States had banned shipment of gasoline to Japan and had pretty much stopped the shipment of scrap iron, steel, and other material as well. Although the European theater had first call on supplies and other assistance, the Americans were doing what little they could to improve the defenses of the Philippines. Keeley was one of those posted there as part of that effort.

Rapid conquest of the Philippines was a crucial element in the Japanese plans. Officially, the islands held a Commonwealth status, with the United States the sovereign power. Thus, the American military was responsible for their defense. But the Japanese could not tolerate a situation where American power lay athwart the sea lanes that the Japanese thought essential to tie their empire together. Therefore, immediately after Pearl Harbor, December 8, 1941, they launched an offensive against the Philippines. Despite the valiant efforts of American and Filipino troops, by May 1942, after the fall of Bataan and Corregidor, General Wainwright ordered all American forces in the islands to surrender. Keeley and his men became prisoners of war.

Until the end of 1942, Keeley and a thousand other soldiers were held in Malaybalay, in northern Mindinao. They were then transferred to Dapecol, the Davao Penal Colony located about 20 miles inland from the port of Davao on the southern coast of the island. A bit later, an additional thousand prisoners came to the camp from Luzon. There they remained until May 1944.

Dapecol

Carl S. Nordin, in his book *We Were Next to Nothing: An American POW's Account of Japanese Prison Camps*, describes Dapecol's layout, organization, facilities, and personnel as they existed during Keeley's stay. The camp comprised thousands of acres set in a thick jungle, a harsh, remote environment providing its own deterrent to escape. The camp was self-sustaining and also produced agricultural products for use elsewhere.

In the center of this vast complex lay the main compound, fenced with many layers of barbed wire. The compound was guarded at all times, from guard towers and perimeter patrols, and was brightly illuminated all night. Armed guards accompanied all work details outside of the main compound.

The varied foodstuffs grown in camp were not for the prisoners' table. The normal prisoner diet for breakfast, lunch, and dinner was rice, a soup made of a tubular plant boiled in water, and tea. This diet inevitably resulted in malnutrition and disease. Everyone lost weight; the normal average weight of the soldiers dropped to about 105 pounds. Malaria was endemic. The Japanese put Keeley in charge of the malaria patients who were not hospitalized, which involved over 90% of the 2,000 prisoners in camp, but they gave him few medicines or other supplies. Beriberi and other diseases became common. Prisoners nonetheless had to work in the rice paddies and other fields. Keeley, however, evidently was able to keep some very sick men out of the fields, although it is not clear how he accomplished that.

The Japanese guards were often brutal. Prisoners were subjected to slaps, beatings, or much worse, often for no apparent reason. The Japanese took away mess knives and forks because they might be used as weapons, leaving prisoners with only a spoon, mess kit, canteen, and cup. Bibles were also forbidden, and violators were harshly punished. At night, when the Japanese guards were not harassing the prisoners, hordes of lice, bedbugs, and rats took over.

By 1944, the tide of war was changing. Allied troops were moving northward from the South Pacific and the Japanese had to move the prisoners. In the middle of May, all the prisoners were marched 20 miles from Dapecol to Davao harbor. The weak, malnourished men suffered terribly during such marches. Some passed out, some reeled drunkenly trying to stay upright. At the harbor, the prisoners were herded into the hold of a freighter that had recently carried horses. Crowded into inadequate space, provided with reduced rice and water, without furniture or bedding, they made their way to Manila.

The Trip to Japan

After a couple of weeks in Manila, Keeley and 1100 other prisoners were again loaded into a freighter's hold, in this case a dilapidated vessel that had evidently been sold to Japan for scrap. Again horse manure testified to its previous occupants and again the prisoners were allotted so little space that one could not stretch at full length to rest or sleep. A five-gallon can was provided for urine and stool. Food and water were limited. Veterans who were familiar with this and similar vessels understandably called them Hell Ships. The July heat, the stench, the seasickness, the ill and undernourished men with no chance to wash or change: it was a voyage from hell. Six men died on the journey. And it was a very long voyage: this time the destination was Japan. The ship broke down several times and had to stop in available harbors for repair; on one occasion, the ship's power failed and it drifted for two days in the China Sea.

Once in Japan, prisoners were divided into smaller groups. One hundred and fifty Americans joined two hundred British prisoners who were taken to Funatsu, a newly built camp located in an isolated wooded area in central Honshu, the main Japanese island. Rations were reduced, malnutrition worsened, there was more beriberi. Keeley noted that 90% of the prisoners showed gross dependent edema, swelling of the lower extremities due to fluid accumulation. Their daily ration consisted of radish soup and rice.

After almost a year in Funatsu, Keeley alone was brought to another camp near Toyoma, where the prisoners included enlisted military men and civilians; there were no officers and no doctors. The Japanese appointed Keeley camp Commander and Doctor, and he was told that he would be shot if anyone escaped. Nobody tried.

It was at the Toyoma camp, on September 2, 1945, that a couple of American pilots suddenly walked in and announced that the War was over. The surviving prisoners were swiftly transported to San Francisco, where they received medical examinations and, when their conditions permitted, were sent home.

Despite his long travail, the doctors in San Francisco pronounced Keeley to be without disability and, all things considered, in satisfactory physical condition; he could resume his life. But the War was still not quite over for Keeley. About four years later, the Army informed him that a number of men who had been incarcerated as he had been now had schistosomiasis, an ugly disease they probably contracted in the Philippines from water in which certain species of snails live. Tests showed that Keeley indeed did have the disease. He was cured after undergoing an arduous regimen.

Forty-four months separated the attack on Pearl Harbor and the Japanese surrender; that was the length of America's war with Japan. For most of that time—39 months, to be precise—James Keeley survived the daily horror of being a prisoner of war. In the scraps of existing material relating to his long imprisonment, only a few provide hints of his work to protect his fellow prisoners throughout their long incarceration.

After the War, however, when the Army learned of his work in the camps, Keeley was awarded the Bronze Star. The citation accompanying that award provides some idea of his accomplishments under the most severe conditions imaginable:

Major James K. Keeley, while a prisoner of war in Mindinao, Philippines and Yokaichii and Funatsu, Japan from May, 1942, to September, 1945, performed merito-rious service to his co-prisoners of war. With very poor medical facilities and scant supplies of medicine, he was very patient in treating the sick. Through his ingenuity and at the risk of his life, he was able to keep the sick men from working as required by the Japanese. Major Keeley's bravery, self-sacrifice, loyalty and devotion to his medical profession were an inspiration to his co-prisoners and a positive contribution to their morale.

Jim was born in 1912 in Ridgewood, New Jersey. He graduated from Dartmouth College in 1934. After completing Dartmouth's two-year medical school, he graduated from Harvard Medical School in 1937. After the War, he returned to the Mayo Clinic to finish his three-year fellowship in surgery. He then set up a practice in General Surgery in Poughkeepsie, New York. He and his wife Mary entered Kendal at Hanover in 1991. Jim died in 2007, leaving Mary and four children.

PROBLEM OF THE BAMBOO POLES

~

Robert Stanton
U.S. Army

A STAPLE CHARACTER IN HOLLYWOOD WAR MOVIES is the officer who is so committed to strictly obeying formal regulations that he ignores common sense. That officer was alive and well in the Philippines immediately following World War II.

In November 1945, I arrived at the American Army base in Batangas, at the southwest end of Luzon. The region had been liberated from Japanese control only a few months earlier, and American forces were just getting settled into a post-war routine: mopping up remnants of enemy troops, concluding unfinished business, and preparing for peace. I had been assigned to the post of Purchasing and Contracting Officer. When I reported to Headquarters, I found it located in a huge, ostentatious, castle-like building. I entered and went to one end of the long hall to check in. While I was on the way in, and still a bit awestruck by the unexpected surroundings, my attention was drawn to a noisy commotion at the other end of the hall. It turned out to be a group of Filipino natives, ordinary workers, clamoring to be paid by a flustered American officer who was trying to explain that there was no way he could pay them. That was my introduction to the problem of the bamboo poles.

The campaign to liberate the area had produced a good deal of destruction. When American forces took over, they wanted to prepare for peacetime use. Among other things, that called for building many new structures for storage, PX, barracks, and so forth. For such construction, the Army needed wooden poles, and in the Philippines that meant bamboo poles. So the military agreed to pay native workers 50 centavos per pole. The area was still not completely pacified, and conditions precluded a cash-and-carry operation, so the Army developed an ad hoc payment system. When a worker brought some poles, he would receive a chit indicating the number of poles he had delivered; the next time he brought poles, he would get another chit; and so on. Each chit had to be signed by the enlisted man immediately running the operation, who attested that the number was correct, and then it had to be countersigned by the officer in charge. The workers were promised that, when the work was finished, they could turn in their chits to Army headquarters, where they would receive the cash they were owed.

That was a common-sense, workable system, but it had one flaw. The officers who were supposed to countersign the chits were frequently not available: many were still in the jungle rounding up Japanese or were otherwise occupied. Therefore, they left the supervision of pole collecting to perfectly competent and reliable sergeants or corporals. The result was that most workers accumulated a batch of chits that, while accurately showing the number of poles they had delivered, did not accord with the rules set out by the American Army: they were not countersigned by an officer. Therefore, when workers sought to get paid, and discovered their chits were worthless, they became very agitated, to say the least.

The decision not to pay for un-countersigned chits was made by the colonel commanding the base. He was a crusty regular Army officer with many years of service. He believed that Army rules were created for very good reasons and should be followed to the letter. Departure from the rules was bad for discipline, ultimately undermined morale, and simply created chaos. He would certainly not violate the rules because of a bunch of clamoring Filipinos whom he didn't like very much anyway. His chief subordinates tried diplomatically to change his mind, but he would have none of it. Chits not countersigned were not to be paid.

A New Agreement

I was very disturbed by these events. I empathized completely with the workers and felt their sense of outrage at being so shabbily treated. Moreover, I felt ashamed that my country should be represented—or, rather, misrepresented—by an officer who was so petty, inflexible, and devoid of compassion; that was not the America I wanted foreigners to see.

One of my chief tasks in earlier postings and, in fact, as a civilian before joining the Army, had been to negotiate supplemental agreements to contracts between the military and civilian companies. When, for example, specifications agreed upon in a contract had to be changed because of unforeseen circumstances, I would draw up a supplemental agreement modifying the contract to take cognizance of all the financial and other effects of the new arrangements. It seemed to me that the problem of the bamboo poles needed a supplemental agreement.

Therefore, without consulting anyone, I wrote such an agreement between the U.S. Army and the Filipino workers. In it, I incorporated the idea that the unavoidable absence of officers fighting in the field necessitated changing the rule so that certification by an American non-commissioned officer was sufficient to justify payment. I sent this to the Commanding Officer, which was like dropping it into a black hole. I was not surprised to get no response. All my dealings with the CO had shown me a man who would never depart from the letter of regulations, so I sadly assumed that nothing would come of it.

A few months later, however, I received a letter from the mayor of Taal, a town in Batangas Province near a celebrated volcano, thanking me for arranging for the payments to his constituents. That is how I discovered that the supplemental agreement I had fashioned out of whole cloth had in fact been accepted by the Army, and the workers had received their pay.

I later concluded that my suggestion had somehow found its way to Washington and had been approved, so our CO had to implement it.

The regulations had changed. However it came about, it was one of the most satisfying experiences I had in the Army.

Bob was born in 1920. He grew up in New York, attended North Carolina State College, and worked in the textile industry before entering the Army as a private in 1942. In the Army, he quickly advanced through noncommissioned ranks and in 1945 graduated from Officer Candidate School as 2nd Lieutenant. After a stint in Batangas as Purchasing and Contracting Officer, he was sent to Manila as member of the Liquidation Commission, disposing of American wartime matériel. Following the War, he went into manufacturing and was Vice President and Treasurer of the Standard Equipment Company when he retired in 1985. In 2002 he and his wife, Ruth, moved into Kendal at Hanover. He died in 2010.

FROM NASHVILLE TO NAGASAKI

~

William K. Tate, Jr.
U.S. Navy

ON DECEMBER 7, 1941, I WAS SEVENTEEN and a senior in a college preparatory school in Nashville, Tennessee. Several of us boys in an automobile were trying to decide which of our girl friends we were going to visit that Sunday afternoon. When we heard the news about Pearl Harbor, we did not fully comprehend what it meant until getting home and listening to our parents.

At the time nothing changed much for me. I graduated from high school, enrolled in Vanderbilt University, and did not turn 18 until November 1942. My dad had been in WW I and knew what war was all about; he convinced me to get into V12, an intensive program designed to transform college students into commissioned Navy officers. I am sure he was trying to protect his only son, rationalizing that I would spend the next three years getting an education and perhaps by then it would all be over.

In May 1943 I entered Georgia Tech in the V12 program but soon became concerned that the War was going to pass me by and my only contribution to it would be getting an education. I asked my dad how I could hold my head high when in later years my future son would ask me what I did in the Great War and all I could tell him was that I went to school. This problem was soon resolved: I flunked out of Georgia Tech. I was transferred to boot camp in Bainbridge, Maryland, after which I was sent across the country on a troop train to San Francisco and put on a troop ship with 5,000 others. I wound up in a Navy staging area in Milne Bay, New Guinea, getting yellow from Atabrine tablets, meeting the natives, and finding out how indescribable a tropical rain forest really is.

A month later I was assigned to the *USS Regal* in Hollandia, New Guinea, as a seaman deck hand but also as a crew member on the Captain's Gig (small boat). The ship's function was to repair troop landing craft damaged in the island invasions. My introduction to the devastation of war came when I first saw landing craft that had been in battle: I learned how damaged a ship could get and still float, and what a bomb can do in distributing body residue throughout a ship's interior.

After a few months the *Regal* sailed for Sydney, Australia, where we spent a month getting overhauled. After this we were ordered to the Philippines and I was assigned as a helmsman. We were in the middle of a large convoy protected by destroyers and destroyer escorts, and I was at the helm. One moment everything was OK and the next all hell broke loose when we lost the ability to steer the ship: apparently the hydraulic system failed and we were unable to get the auxiliary steering to operate. The *Regal* was a very large and slow ship. Before we recovered we had made a 360-degree turn, barely missing a dozen ships, and wound up out of and well behind the convoy. It took a day and a half to catch up, and during this time we were on our own.

The USS *Flusser*

As we approached Leyte Gulf in the Philippines, I requested and was granted permission to transfer to a destroyer, the *USS Flusser* DD368, part of the Seventh Fleet. When the United States entered the War this was the latest design. It had two smokestacks, four five-inch guns, an arsenal of 20 mm and 40 mm antiaircraft hardware, and a top speed of 35 knots. The ship had on board a full Captain Squadron Commander who had seven destroyers under his command.

During my time aboard the *Flusser*, our area of operations was throughout the Philippines and Borneo. The ship was awarded eight battle stars in the Pacific and I was on board for the last two. It was known as the luckiest ship in the Navy because it survived the War without much damage. That was not the case for several of our sister ships. My duties included being the Captain's talker, a function I will describe below and, at battle station, a team member of a 20 mm antiaircraft gun. In port, I was the coxswain of our 20-foot motor whale boat and I also drove a landing craft when we needed to transport stores and ammunition.

The battles we were involved in were similar to most of the island landings. There was the initial bombardment, then deployment of the troops followed by support bombardment. There was counter bombardment from the shore but no suicide planes.

On the way to Borneo I learned about one person's perceptions. We had a contingent of troops on board, and in a conversation with one of them I allowed as how I would not want to trade places with him. To my surprise, he did not want to trade with me either because, as he put it, "you can't dig a foxhole on a ship." I'll still take the ship.

I spoke of my duty as the Captain's talker. This can best be described in terms of an action we had chasing a Japanese sub in the Philippines. My station was on the bridge, and I followed the Captain wherever he went. I had a head phone set that was connected to the radar, radio, and sonar rooms. Any information for the Captain that came from these three places came through me, and I reported every detail to him. During this attack, sonar bearings were changing rapidly, and radar tracking of our proximity to other ships kept coming in, as did a few radio messages. The Captain made decisions based on what I relayed to him. It was amazing to me how quickly I learned to listen and talk at the same time. But more amazing was the Navy's use of this method of communicating, and the possible consequences of an error. Fortunately, I did not make any (at least any that counted), and I often laughed when I told my shipmates that I, a first class seaman, was the one who told the Captain what to do.

Manila

After Borneo, we sailed to Manila and had our first real R & R (Rest and Recuperation) in over nine months. Manila had been bombed; it was a mud hole, and it rained. Typically Navy, we were required to wear white uniforms. I drank too much and bought a phony Japanese flag, which I stuck in my white jacket, where it proceeded to turn everything red. Somehow I ended up at the ship where the Officer of the Deck thought I was wounded and called the medic to shuffle me off to the sick bay.

In Manila the ship was overhauled. Later we moved to Lingayen Gulf, northwest of Manila. This is a large body of water and was one of the staging areas for the invasion of Japan. We were there when the atomic bombs were dropped and the Japanese surrendered. I was and still am very supportive of the decision to use the bombs.

For me there were several significant events that occurred during my four remaining months in the Navy.

The first was the most life-threatening event I ever experienced. While in the Lingayen Gulf, a typhoon came through. It devastated Okinawa and the Philippines. To ride it out we put to sea and, at its height, I was on the bridge. Mounted on the back wall was an Inclinator, which showed how many degrees the ship rolled to either port or starboard. Every Navy ship has a critical point and, if exceeded, it will roll over. Ours was 44 degrees. Many times we rolled over 40 degrees and at one point reached 42. This got our attention; we all put on life jackets, ready to jump. Several ships in the area sank. I believe Herman Wouk's novel *The Caine Mutiny* was based on this storm.

After the War ended, our Squadron Commander was selected to accept the surrender of the large Japanese naval base at Sasebo, Japan. This was our first face-to-face encounter with the Japanese. The population was mostly old people, and we were probably the first Americans they had ever seen. It is difficult to describe their reaction, but, in simple terms, it was weary but curious.

Nagasaki

We had only been in Sasebo for two days when the next typhoon warning was posted. To ride it out, we sailed to Nagasaki for protection. The Nagasaki bay is actually a bowl. When the atomic bomb hit, the upper rim was completely leveled but the bay was protected. It was here that I had my next close call. As the whale-boat coxswain I was sent out to pick up one of our officers. Before we could get back, the storm had intensified to the point that our boat was taking on water faster than we could bail. We made it to the ship, but the boat was half under water. All jumped out and about a minute later it sank. It was that close.

While in Nagasaki I took several officers to the shore and I walked up to the rim and saw the area where the bomb hit. It was off limits but this made little difference because, for miles, there was nothing to see but rubble. Seeing the real thing is much different from seeing a picture, and one's imagination runs rampant. Later, in reflecting on the experience, I felt very sad, but that feeling diminished when I thought of the carnage that would have occurred with an invasion of the Japanese Islands.

We returned to Sasebo for a period of time and then left for home around November 1, 1945. About halfway between Hawaii and San Diego, on November 13, I had my 21st birthday and was now old enough to have a legal drink. About that same time, I was on the bridge and spotted an object on the horizon. It turned out to be a beautiful three-masted clipper ship under full sail. We changed course to get a close view. It was an Australian ship that had been stranded in England at the beginning of the War and was on its way home. Sometime later I saw a documentary about this ship.

The realization of missed opportunities came later in life when I looked back on my experiences in the Navy. As mentioned above, I was attached to the small transport boats on both ships I served on. This provided the opportunity to leave the ships frequently whenever we were in a port. Most sailors, particularly on a destroyer, hardly ever got off. But wherever we were anchored, I continually carried officers, personnel, and supplies to and from the ship; this put me in close contact with the native people. We operated over a large geographical area: Milne Bay and Hollandia in New Guinea; Sydney, Australia; Leyte Gulf; Zamboanga, Mindanao (where the monkeys have no tails); Davao Gulf; Balikpapan, Borneo; Manila; Sasebo and Nagasaki, Japan; and many places in between. At best I had only a detached curiosity about those areas and their inhabitants. At no time did I attempt to really know the people or learn anything about their culture. How unfortunate: a 20-year-old not having the imagination to see the opportunities in front of him.

World War II was responsible for one of the most significant changes in my life. Before the War, I had lived in Nashville, Tennessee, and thought the sun rose on the east side of Belle Meade, a residential area of Nashville, and set on the west side. My exposure to life was that narrow. My world was populated mainly by WASPs, and African-Americans were only welcomed as long as they had on their servants' uniforms. During the War I discovered the diversity of the human race and learned to like and depend on most of those I met. When I got home, the social attitudes had not changed, so I decided to finish school at Vanderbilt University and then leave. Fortunately I married a woman who had the same feeling about the South, and both of us knew we would never fit in. A week after graduation we moved north and never looked back. We are two of the most liberal-thinking people where our fellow man is concerned.

It is sad to think it took a war, with all of its destruction, for me to mature socially.

Bill was born in Tullahoma, Tennessee, in 1924, but grew up in Nashville. After the War he returned to Vanderbilt University and earned a degree in Mechanical Engineering. He started work for General Electric Company in January 1949 and remained there for the next 36 years, progressing through middle management positions to Department General Manager. He retired in 1985 and moved to Hanover, New Hampshire. In retirement, he was particularly active in SCORE, the Service Corps of Retired Executives, counseling individuals in small businesses. He also apprenticed as a cabinetmaker with his son in Dorset, Vermont, and now has his own woodshop in Lyme Center, New Hampshire, where he pursues this activity. Bill and his wife Barbara moved to Kendal at Hanover in 2001. Barbara died in 2011.

An Avenger Pilot

Arthur N. Turner
U.S. Navy

Arthur Turner, left, and crewmate

"MR. TURNER, YOUR ALTITUDE IS LESS THAN 200 FEET!" My radioman's shout snapped me out of my "vertigo" and saved our lives. I was flying in circles above the shore of Guadalcanal in order to rendezvous with two other Avengers (who never appeared). We had been told to torpedo two Japanese destroyers headed for Guadalcanal. It was a very black night with no visible horizon. Having little instrument flying experience, I had become confused until my radioman reminded me to get out of the turn and climb to a more sensible altitude.

I still couldn't see anything, but proceeded cautiously northwest up "the slot" between the Solomon Islands which I sensed on either side of me.

Finally I saw flashes of gunfire in the distance, probably destroyers firing at one another. But if I went over there, how would I know which destroyer to hit? Again my radioman solved the problem. "There's a Jap destroyer under your left wing!" There she was, faintly visible, definitely a Japanese DD, and she wasn't firing at me! I dove down and dropped my torpedo, proud of myself for the first time that night. I landed triumphantly at Henderson Field, only to be told on debriefing that my Jap destroyer had been abandoned on that reef two weeks ago.

Why and how did I get to Guadalcanal anyway?

Becoming an Avenger Pilot

In the fall of 1941 I was enjoying my junior year at Yale, especially because Nancy, a student at Yale Music School, was also in New Haven, and I was stroking the lightweight varsity crew. But I was increasingly wondering why America was not at war with Nazi Germany and why I was not in that fight. So on December 7 it was easy to decide to quit Yale and become a naval aviator; I liked the ocean and thought I was physically qualified to be a good pilot.

During most of 1942 I was learning to fly, at Floyd Bennett Field, New York, and Jacksonville, Florida. Nancy was able to visit her stepmother in Jacksonville and we became engaged in October. After I got my wings and commission, the Navy reluctantly allowed us to marry on the Naval Air Station, Jacksonville, with only 24 hours "liberty." The NAS Chaplain agreed to marry us after we told him, truthfully but incompletely, that the reason we wanted to marry was that we enjoyed talking with each other so much.

Soon after our December 30 marriage we drove our 1937 Chevrolet coupe down to Fort Lauderdale for torpedo bomber training. Getting to know the new "Avenger" model TBF or TBM was daunting at first, but it turned out to be a reliable, friendly airplane, not very fast or maneuverable but hard to shoot down and easy to land on runway or flight deck—also on water, as I discovered on two occasions, although it didn't stay afloat long.

But for the wife of a new torpedo bomber pilot life was tough: horrid places to live, very little time together, no nearby family or friends. And one afternoon when Nancy came to pick me up, the Marine at the gate told her not to worry—her husband had been rescued and was OK. On a low-level practice bombing run I had misjudged the distance to the water and my propeller had hit a wave, knocking out the engine. I landed nicely on the water and was picked up by a helicopter.

As a result of this misadventure, I would have to face a panel of senior officers. I would probably be grounded and have to become a supply officer! How terrible, I wailed to Nancy, who thought that sounded pretty good, but somehow I persuaded them not to take away my wings.

Soon after my accident I got orders to go to San Diego for further assignment. So we raced across the country in a nice Plymouth convertible which my parents "lent" us for some reason. We arrived in San Diego with worn-out tires and nothing to do except worry about my next assignment: to proceed by ship to Noumea.

Noumea, New Caledonia, was the main U.S. base for operations in Southwest Pacific. Soon I was on the *Lurline*, a former Matson liner converted to a troop ship, together with other "replacement" pilots and a large number of marines. Nancy somehow sold the car (useless tires and all), visited relatives in Los Angeles, and returned to Connecticut.

The *Lurline* zigzagged unescorted across the Pacific to Fiji, where the marines disembarked. I clearly remember them gathering on the wharf in a torrential rain, with all their gear, and thinking how bad their next landing would probably be.

After a couple of lazy weeks in Noumea, and a couple of flights around beautiful New Caledonia, seven of us replacement Avenger pilots were ordered to join VT 21, a squadron which had been based on Henderson Field, Guadalcanal, for several difficult months.

Guadalcanal

It was as a brand-new member of VT 21 that I was awakened in the middle of the night and assigned to the lonely and pointless mission that I described above. As a consequence of the American advances, there were no Japanese troops left on Guadalcanal, but some remained on the other Solomon Islands. We dropped many 2,000-pound, 500-pound, and 100-pound bombs on Japanese airstrips and bases. Back home, Nancy saved local newspaper accounts of two of those strikes. One of them—greatly exaggerated—had me earning a Distinguished Flying Cross by dropping a bomb on one of the Solomon Islands. I don't even remember that raid at all.

There was one major Japanese air raid on Guadalcanal and its harbor while I was there. Most of the Japanese aircraft were shot down by American and Australian fighters. It was a spectacular air show which we bomber pilots enjoyed watching from the ground.

In return, the Navy launched a large air raid against Japanese shipping in Rabaul Harbor, a well-defended Japanese base several hundred miles northwest of Guadalcanal. I dove from over 12,000 feet with a Zero on my tail, which my gunner hit or chased away. I released three 500-pound bombs on the side of a Japanese freighter. One bomb had failed to release, so as I left the harbor I tried to hit a lighthouse with it. I probably missed, though when Nancy and I visited Rabaul on a cruise in 2008, the beautiful harbor looked familiar, except there was no lighthouse—so who knows?

Anyway, I do remember that raid and felt I had earned that DFC.

When VT 21 was finally ordered home, the replacement pilots were taken to Espiritu Santos to wait for another squadron which needed replacements. While there, in October 1943, I recall two important events. I learned that our son Nick had been born, and I came down with a nasty case of dengue fever.

The *Princeton*

Eventually orders came to join Air Group 23 on the *USS Princeton*, a "light" carrier (CVL), with a short and narrow flight deck on a hull originally designed for a light cruiser. Relearning how to land on such a small flight deck was difficult when we had been land-based for so long. One of us, a Texan named Eubank and a good friend, was killed in the attempt to land, but the rest of us somehow managed to do it safely.

VT 21 was a small and friendly squadron with lots of combat experience. According to another local newspaper account which Nancy kept, in eight months on the *Princeton* I "participated in forty strikes against the Solomon Islands, Rabaul, Nauru, Gilbert Islands, Marshall Islands, Palau, Hollandia, and Truk." Many of these strikes were supporting Marine landings; some were against Japanese shipping and bases.

At some point, the *Princeton* had to go back to Oakland for repairs, but sadly the Air Group had to wait behind on Maui. We did have a good short Christmas holiday on a sugar-and-cattle plantation on the Big Island.

In May or June 1944, Air Group 23 was relieved from the *Princeton* and sent home. Some months later, with her new air group, the *Princeton* was sunk during the Battle of Leyte Gulf, with major loss of life.

When I finally got home, Nick was eight months old, and the three of us had a good vacation in Maine before a short assignment to a new squadron that was training on Martha's Vineyard.

The *Bennington*

Unfortunately for Nancy and me, the influential skipper of VT 82 was in Newport News training to board the *Bennington*, a new fleet carrier. The skipper had mostly new pilots or older flight instructors and he wanted more pilots with combat experience. So, I was ordered to Newport News. And before long, I was on the *Bennington* for its shakedown cruise, to the Caribbean, then through the Canal and back across the Pacific.

By this time, January 1945, so many Japanese ships had been sunk, so many Japanese pilots killed, and so many American ships built and pilots trained, that Japan had no chance of winning the War. But many bloody battles remained—and the *Bennington*'s Air Group 82 would be in most of them.

After a brief stop in Honolulu, where VT 82's skipper was killed in a jeep accident, we teamed up with a large task force for a series of bombing attacks on airfields and bases on Hachijo Jima, the Japanese homeland Kyushu, and Chichi Jima, during which two Avengers were shot down.

Then the *Bennington* joined a large fleet to support the landing of 75,000 Marines on Iwo Jima on February 20-22, 1945. Flying over the Marines on that deadly black beach was frustrating because we could not really help them very much.

Next, we steamed north to drop incendiary bombs on Tokyo. I was glad not to be assigned to that strike. Probably I was on antisubmarine patrol that day, flying a long, narrow, low-level triangle ahead of the fleet: boring, because you never saw a submarine. Sometimes, when returning in bad weather, it was hard to find the carrier. And it was not enjoyable landing on a pitching flight deck with unused depth charges aboard.

After Iwo Jima and Tokyo, the *Bennington* joined an enormous fleet being assembled in Eniwetok lagoon for the invasion of Okinawa: over 20 American and British aircraft carriers, many battleships, and hundreds of cruisers, destroyers, transports, etc. We were at Eniwetok for nine days, with nothing to do but drink beer on a barren little island called "Mog Mog."

Before the main Okinawa landing on April 1, 1945, U.S. carrier aircraft, including VT 82, raided bases in Kyushu, Japan, during which the *Bennington*'s sister ship USS *Franklin* was bombed and severely damaged, with the loss of over 800 lives. The first landings on Okinawa were relatively unopposed, but ferocious fighting continued for two months.

During most of that time we flew low-level support flights over Okinawa, dropping bombs and firing rockets at what we hoped were Japanese troops, or parachuting supplies to American soldiers and Marines. Our skipper since Honolulu was shot down on one of those dangerous flights.

The fleet off Okinawa suffered many kamikaze attacks, but with luck and good antiaircraft gunnery, the *Bennington* narrowly escaped several of them.

On April 7, hundreds of Allied carrier aircraft were launched to attack the Japanese super-battleship *Yamato* and nine escorts which were on a suicide mission against the Allied fleet. But VT 82 was late for the party, and we saw only one little Japanese support ship. We dropped nine torpedoes on her and felt we had sunk the last Japanese ship still afloat.

The *Bennington* was finally disabled, not by kamikazes, but by a huge typhoon. I still dream about those tremendous waves. As the ship slowly steamed into them, each wave lifted her bow high and then crashed it down into the crest of the next wave until the front of the flight deck crumpled down on either side of the bow—bad for the *Bennington* but good for the Air Group, because we were soon on a slow freighter back to California.

I got home soon after our daughter Anne was born in June 1945.

It's Over!

After a short vacation Nancy and I set off for Pensacola, where I was to be a flight instructor. On the drive south suddenly all the horns were blaring to celebrate the dropping of the Hiroshima atom bomb. Japan would not have to be invaded after all! Okinawa had shown how dreadful that would have been.

I got out of the Navy as soon as I could and enrolled again at Yale in September 1945. I was tired and in a sort of daze, dreaming of battles and suffering recurring bouts of dengue fever. I was hardly any help to

Nancy and the two babies in a little house in Madison, Connecticut, with a coal furnace and no washing machine or dryer for the diapers. All I accomplished was to get very good grades for my senior year at Yale.

The following fall, all four of us were on another Matson liner, in a very fancy cabin, sailing to Honolulu, where I taught ninth-grade English at Punahou School for two years. Not a fun job, and low pay, but we all enjoyed the climate, the flowers, the scenery, the beaches, the fruit, and some good friends. A lot better than my previous Pacific adventures.

Arthur and Nancy Turner entered Kendal at Hanover in 2007, after three winters and 50 summers in Small Point, Maine. While Arthur was a professor at Harvard Business School (1958-1985), they lived in Belmont, Cambridge, and Concord, Massachusetts; New Haven, Connecticut; and Ithaca, New York. They also traveled on teaching and consulting assignments to Canada, United Kingdom, India, Pakistan, Indonesia, New Zealand, Nigeria, Japan, and Kenya. As a professor at Harvard Business School, and after retirement, Arthur, with Nancy's help, undertook many teaching and consulting assignments to corporations, government agencies, and management education institutions overseas. They have three daughters (their son died in 2007), nine grandchildren, and, so far, four great-grandchildren.

GUINEA PIGS IN NEW GUINEA

~

John Weeks
U.S. Army

THIS IS THE SHORT HISTORY of the Special Company, General Service, Separate, at Gamadodo Mission on the shores of Milne Bay,
Papua, New Guinea, U.S. Southwest Pacific Area (SWPA), in the early
summer of 1943. I was a second lieutenant with the so-called Airborne
Engineer group, whose specialty was building airports on terrain that
was accessible only by air—but that's another story.

Having arrived in Brisbane, Australia, shortly before this story
starts, the GIs in the Replacement Depot at the Ascot-Doomben racetrack just outside of town were on edge as to what was to come next.
Since it was certainly to be in New Guinea, the prospects were probably
going to be interesting. And interesting it proved to be.

A group of us, officers and men, were selected out, declared to be
engineers in a general service company, and set to work loading ourselves and equipment onto a small old P & O freighter. My job developed into being Motor Officer, observing the dockers as they loaded a
dump truck or two and various earth-moving equipment aboard the

143

ship. When everything was properly loaded and ready, we were mustered on board and assigned living spaces, then settled in as we steamed north out of Brisbane harbor.

During the voyage we occupied ourselves in getting acquainted and planning our mission. This was revealed to the officers first and later, only in part, to the enlisted men: we would carry out an experiment to test the efficacy of a new type of malaria drug under field conditions. The GIs were to be divided into three platoons. One was to receive the standard Atabrine preventive (effective, but it colored the complexion a distasteful yellow); the next platoon was to receive the new stuff, effects unknown; and the third platoon, the control, was to get a placebo ("to calm you"), guaranteed to have no medicinal effect whatsoever. Officers were all in the Atabrine group and so were not part of the experiment. So to the armed forces, the enlisted man was a useful guinea pig as well as a soldier.

We would be encamped on the southwest side of the bay opposite the docks and main settlement, several hundred yards from a native settlement known to be fully infected with our target disease, malaria, endemic in that time and place. The presence of malaria was said to be proved when an "80% palpable spleen" was found on periodic physical examination of each of us.

A Torpedo across the Bow

Once we absorbed this information, we started to approach the bay. We had been accompanied by a little sub-chaser for the latter part of the voyage, and we were at morning "stand to" in formation on deck with life jackets on (part of every morning and evening routine at sea when the sun can silhouette the target for an enemy submarine) when we found that we really were under attack. A torpedo crossed our bow: so close was it that the first sergeant, on the forepeak of our ship, said later, "If I'd had a broom, I could have swept it away!" (When this is pronounced by a man with a harelip, as indeed he had, the effect is unforgettable.)

The sub-chaser immediately went into action and, after some extended maneuvering and an explosion or two, passed us, displaying a broom at the masthead—the traditional "mission accomplished" signal. We all cheered, having come to realize what a close call we had just experienced.

Anticlimactically, we docked and unloaded and, there being an extensive road network around the bay, trundled our equipment and selves to our new station. It was a coconut plantation, still owned by Palmolive-Peet; we were warned that the Army was accountable for any damage or despoliation. The area was named Gamadodo Mission, I believe by a pioneer group of religious recruiters many years before, although we saw no evidence of that sort of activity while we were there.

We settled ourselves into as much of a military space organization as we could, considering the abundant (and immovable) palm trees. Our attendant medicos set up a small clinic down by the beach. We found, soon after we set up, that the beach was a well-used route to one of the fishing grounds used by our neighborly natives. Of course there was an immediate assessment of the figurative charms of the grass-skirted female populace, with cataloging of all types of mammary development, but because Micronesians are quite small and have unfamiliar Negroid features, there was little temptation to exploit their charms—but then we hadn't been in New Guinea very long.

To keep us all busy and out of mischief, we were set to building a road toward the local village. Decisions had to be made on the best way to get a bulldozer onto the beach; low tide was the obvious choice, and we were able to pull that activity off. We were kept as busy as was practical; among the projects was the construction of a few living areas and/or bed-spaces. We had to learn, among other things, the best ways to fasten together pieces of wood that were harder than oak; nails and spikes required pre-drilling the wood before they could be hammered home.

After we landed, word soon got around among the natives that there were doctors nearby, and the medical clinic established to support our experiment was able to provide many services to these islanders, keeping the medics busy. Once, a trading lugger—a schooner-rigged sailing ship—came in and took the officers for a short sail. But for entertainment, that was about it.

Another of my duties—since the motor pool no longer existed—was to censor outgoing mail written by the enlisted types. This was V-Mail, remember, which involved photographing each letter and sending the film roll containing hundreds letters back to the States, to be printed out and sent by the U.S. Postal Service. Well, I remember especially one gent who wrote the same impassioned letter to three women. This guy made two carbons—and sent one of them to his wife!

The Harvard Unit

After a month or so of all this feverish activity, and amid the usual small bothers that go with closed groups, we eventually were ordered to pack up just our personal stuff and company records and proceed to our next assignment, which was a military general hospital outside of Brisbane, Australia. It was manned by medics and nurses from the Massachusetts General Hospital (dubbed "The Harvard Unit") and was located in what had been an agricultural college in Toowoomba, a town an hour or two inland from Brisbane. We were there, of course, for close observation on the effects, if any, of the new drug.

The end result of the malaria project, as far as I could see, was "negative." Since I never heard another word about it, I assumed that the results weren't good enough for the Army to change to the experimental drug. The experiment did result in several deaths (from malaria, I presume), a few Section Eights (insanity discharges), and some disability discharges.

In retrospect, an experiment such as this would now be considered unethical in a civilian population without individual assent. Whether it could be considered ethical in a military population without participants' assent, under circumstances similar to those in our experiment, is an interesting question.

John enlisted in the Army Corps of Engineers in 1941 while a student at Dartmouth College and was commissioned 2nd Lieutenant in 1942. He served three years in the Southwest Pacific area, and after the War used the GI Bill of Rights to return to college and pursue post-graduate education. His career thereafter was with a computer manufacturing company, writing bids and manuals. After he and his wife raised six children and retired, they were drawn again to their early haunts. They entered Kendal at Hanover in 1991. His wife Jeanne died in 1996.

Stateside Service

THE FLIGHT OF THE WASP

Louise Bowden Brown
Women Airforce Service Pilots

I WAS HOOKED ON FLYING BACK IN 1941 when I was 25 years old. I was living on a farm in Elmer, New Jersey, with my parents and had a good job as an X-ray technician at the local hospital. A co-worker, a nurse, invited me to Bucks Airport, which was owned and operated by her brother and his family. I responded, "Sure, I would like to visit the airport!" Before I knew it, I had joined the flying club, was elected secretary, and was taking flying lessons. I soloed in under eight hours and earned my pilot's license in about 29 hours. The cost of the lessons was only three cents a minute, or $1.80 an hour. So, for less than $55.00 I received my pilot's license.

It turned out to be a very good thing, because the government did not want to teach women to fly.

I don't remember how I first heard about the WASPs, the Women Airforce Service Pilots. They were a group of just over 1,000 young women between 19 and 34 years old who were selected from among 35,000 volunteers to enter a very special training program for flying military airplanes within the United States. New airplanes, sometimes untested after they came off the assembly lines, needed to be flown from the factories where they were made to military bases all over the country and to ports of embarkation, where male pilots took them overseas.

Back in the 1940s, there was a lot of opposition within the military establishment to women in the armed forces—and certainly to women flying combat missions. But the male pilots were needed overseas, and there were not enough men to do the job in the States. Over powerful opposition by political and military leaders, in 1943 Congress succeeded in creating the WASP experiment, with the dual purpose of freeing up men for combat duty and finding out whether women could effectively and safely fly military aircraft. Congress did not, however, provide for WASPs to be part of the U.S. Military Service: WASPs were to be civilian employees.

I found out later what that meant.

Stringent Requirements

When I first learned about the WASPs, I became very excited. A stint in the military would give me a chance to serve my country, get out of Elmer, New Jersey, and have the glamorous life I had always dreamed about, all at the same time. The qualifications even to apply were very stringent and similar to those for men who applied to become pilots. Women applicants had to be between 18½ and 34 years of age, have completed high school, be 64 to 72 inches in height, have 20/20 vision (uncorrected) in each eye, *and* hold a valid CAA (Civil Aeronautics Administration) student pilot certificate with a minimum of 35 hours of certified flying time. The applicant also had to pass the Aviation Cadet Qualifying Examination and an Army physical for flying. Besides all this, she needed to submit character references and pass a personal interview.

Feeling sure I could meet all those qualifications, I sent in the application and started rushing to the mail box every morning. The notice that I had been accepted into the training program came quickly, because there was now a war on and a frantic demand by the Air Force for pilots.

I quit my job immediately and was soon on my way to Texas to my glamorous new career as a woman wartime aviator. As ordered, I reported for duty to Avenger Field in Sweetwater, Texas.

Basic Training

Avenger Field, located in central Texas, was one of many training fields around the United States that were built to train the thousands of men required for the rapidly expanding Air Force. Avenger Field was similar to all the others, with two important exceptions. First, it was the only U.S. Air Force training site where all the trainees were women; second, the benefits and compensation were very different. The risks and training were almost the same as for the thousands of male trainees, but we were civilian employees: we had only the benefits and the obligations that go with civilian service. WASP trainees were paid $150 a month and had to pay their lodging, food, clothing, and personal transportation expenses. Male trainees received only $75 but were provided with lodging, food, clothing, life insurance, and complete medical and dental care. On the other hand, though, we had the nonmilitary rights of optional resignation and rejection of assignments.

Soon after we arrived at Avenger Field, Jacqueline Cochran, Director of the WASPs, gave a short speech about the training program, and we were on our way to earn our wings. Miss Cochran was already a famous woman aviator with a commercial pilot's license. Back in 1939, she had written to Eleanor Roosevelt, wife of the President, strongly recommending a women's branch of the Air Force, with full privileges and responsibilities. Throughout the approximately four-year lifetime of the WASP program and its predecessors, she always fought hard for militarization—and she always lost.

A large group of women from all parts of the country gathered on the parade ground at Avenger Field for the start of our basic training program. We learned that a new class would be starting every month and that our class would be known as 43-W-4, which meant that we were the fourth class of women trainees in 1943. Only three classes had gone before us, and there would be 15 more before the WASP program was suddenly terminated at the end of 1944.

We were issued ill-fitting training uniforms designed for men. Our living quarters were military barracks, also designed for men, and were divided into areas for six beds with a shared toilet room and shower.

We stuffed the urinals with socks and used them to wash our under-wear. There were plenty of other disadvantages. Sweetwater, Texas, was a small town on the prairie, with only 6,000 people and with abso-lutely nothing to do. There were no men except our instructors, and they were in big trouble if they socialized with us. Even with all the shortcomings and indignities, the girls got along just fine and had great times together. The idea of being independent and the prospect of fly-ing airplanes were all we needed.

The tough 30-week training program for Class 43-W-4 began on February 4, 1943, and ended on August 9, 1943. When it was sum-mertime in Texas, the temperatures were in the 90s most of the time, including nights. We would often take cold showers after classes with our clothes still on. Some girls dragged their cots outside the barracks to catch a little breeze.

Basic training taught the military way to do everything, including how to fly an airplane. The broad objective was to demonstrate the ca-pability of females in the military through the observed performance of a select group of candidates. The specific objective was for each can-didate to demonstrate proficiency in the flying of small aircraft and to learn how to maneuver safely under any hazardous contingency.

I'll tell you, the first time I flew an AT-6 Valiant, an advanced train-ing plane, tears rolled down my cheeks. I just thought, "I'll never mas-ter this. Take me back to the farm." But you get over it. It's a funny thing, but you do.

Basic training finally ended, and we had a traditional graduation ceremony. Lined up on the drill field, we were presented with our silver wings, a Class 1 flying rating, and a pay increase to $250 a month. Even though we had the same status and the same skills as the new lieuten-ants who had just graduated from flight school, we remained civilian employees and still had no military benefits. But we traded in our over-sized khaki uniforms and received a clothing allowance of $600 for an official blue WASP wardrobe. We all felt and looked very good.

Active Duty

The members of Class 43-W-4 then went their separate ways, glad to get out of Sweetwater. Military service is a procession of on-the-job training and going to school, even after the early training is over. In my own case,

I was eager to get as far as possible up the training ladder. It was obviously desirable to become qualified in many different kinds of airplanes in order to receive frequent assignments. By 1944, there were 635 WASPs in flying operations. Separate licenses had to be earned for increasingly more demanding groups of planes. There were six different groups:

	Type of aircraft	WASPs qualified
Group I	Trainers: C-64 Norseman, AT-6 Valiant,	121
Group II	Cessna: AT-17, two-engine advanced trainer	158
Group III	Douglas: DC-3, C-47 Sky Train	216
Group IV	Medium bombers: B-25, P-38	59
Group V	Heavy bombers: B-17 Flying Fortress, B-24, B- 29	14
Group VI	Fighter planes: P-47, P-63, P-51 Mustang	66

Most of us went to one of four regional bases in Michigan, Delaware, Texas, or California that had been designated for advanced WASP training and active duty. We could request service at any of these air bases and also request the type of service we wanted to pursue. Most of us chose either the Air Transport Command (ATC), which meant continued active flying, or the administrative command. The latter included things like towing targets for antiaircraft practice, flight testing new planes and materials, and becoming flight instructors. I chose the base at Romulus, Michigan, and the ATC option: I wanted to learn to fly bigger and more powerful planes, and I did not like the idea of being target practice for some yahoo.

The promotion to active duty was a great step upward. We were now at the junior officer level and got a lot more respect, although we still had to pay for our room and board. Another WASP and I shared a room in the Bachelor Officer Quarters on the air base. I really felt I had become a big shot.

We reported to a branch of the Air Transport Command, which had units at most air bases. As requests were received for ferrying missions, pilots who were qualified for that type of aircraft were selected from the roster, and flight orders would be written. It wasn't easy, but I finally made it through Pursuit School and was one of 66 out of 635 women qualified to fly Category VI fighter planes. The travel orders included the details of the mission and all the clearances for travel and return to base. We often flew in formations of three but sometimes had solo assignments.

Flying high-powered military airplanes is a dangerous business. Almost everyone had close calls, sometimes ending in tragedy. In 1944, two of my good friends were among the 38 killed in action in 1943 and 1944. We had all been together in basic training classes at Avenger Field in Texas.

Alice Lovejoy, my roommate, went to Pursuit School in Browns-ville, Texas, to learn how to fly powerful fighter planes like the P-47, the P-51, and the P-63. That was when the worst thing in my entire time as a WASP happened. On September 13, 1944, Alice was on a training exercise with three AT-6 advanced training planes, flying in close formation. She was flying the lead plane and was in the rear seat. Her instructor was in the front seat. The other two planes were flying close behind on either side. One of the other pilots made a miscalculation, and his wing came into contact with Alice's plane, causing a major midair collision. Alice's instructor wasn't seriously hurt, but Alice was unconscious. Unable to get to her, he bailed out and survived. Alice went down with the plane and was killed.

Another WASP and I traveled from the base at Romulus, Michigan, to Brownsville, Texas, to claim her body. We then accompanied her casket on the train to her home in Scarsdale, New York. We had to tell her parents that she had been killed. I didn't like that job. There were no military honors and no government official at the funeral to recognize her service to her country. The costs of taking her home were covered not by the government but by contributions from our fellow WASPs.

Hazel Ying Lee, another of my good friends and the only Chinese-American in our class, was also killed in a tragic accident. Hazel was an experienced flyer: in her own words, "I'll take and deliver anything." Described by her friends as calm and fearless, Hazel, on an earlier occasion, had made a forced landing in a Kansas field. The irate farmer who owned the field confronted her with a shotgun, set on capturing the "Japanese" invader. Hazel managed to talk him out of it.

Growing up in Portland, Oregon, Hazel had always had a passion for flying. Like Alice Lovejoy and me, she had gone to Pursuit School and so was qualified to fly fighter planes. In November 1944, she received orders to go to Bell Aircraft in Niagara Falls, New York, to pick up a P-63 Kingcobra fresh off the assembly line for delivery to the air base at Great Falls, Montana. Great Falls was the busy transfer point where other pilots ferried aircraft to Alaska to be picked up by our Russian allies. Her plane and others were grounded by bad weather in Fargo, North Dakota, for several days.

On Thanksgiving Day, November 23, the sky above Great Falls was crowded with airplanes trying to land, including many P-63s. One of them had lost its radio contact with the control tower and was making an emergency landing. At that same time, Hazel had received clearance to land and was in her final approach. When the tower realized that a collision was imminent, the controller shouted, "Pull up!" The upper pilot could not get the message on his dead radio, but Hazel followed the order. Her plane collided with the underside of the other. There was a loud explosion and a ball of fire as the two planes crashed to the ground. The upper pilot survived with minor injuries, but Hazel suffered serious burns. She was pulled out of her smoldering flight suit and taken to the base hospital. There she endured for 48 hours before she died. Although she was fully conscious the entire time, she never complained.

Again, another WASP and I went to Montana and accompanied her casket back to home base in Romulus, Michigan. And, once again, WASP contributions covered the expenses.

The Vertical Propeller

My own closest brush with disaster occurred while I was flying a P-51 Mustang. I'm very lucky to be here to tell about it. The P-51 Mustang is a very fast and very powerful airplane propelled by a single huge 1500-horsepower engine. Its wings don't look large enough to keep it in the air, but it handles very well. I was on a solo ferrying mission to deliver the Mustang from a factory in the midwest to an air base on the east coast. Everything was perfectly normal. I was cruising along at about 6500 feet—when suddenly the engine quit. It just stopped running. I looked at the propeller and saw that it was standing still—straight up and down. I pushed all the proper switches, but nothing happened. Nothing.

There were only two possibilities and not much time to decide. I could try for a dead-stick landing, hoping the plane would stay airworthy

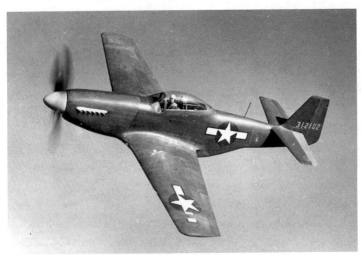

(Courtesy of National Museum of the U.S. Air Force)

Louise's plane, the P-51 Mustang

long enough to find a soft field. Or I could try to bail out. You don't practice either of these things in training. I quickly ruled out the first option as a sure loser.

Next, I tried to remember how to bail out of that type of airplane. My parachute was in its harness and I was sitting on it, so that part was OK. I might get the hatch open, but I could never climb up high enough to jump out. Even if I could, the tail section would come by in a fraction of a second and wipe me out.

Then I remembered the lesson from all that training: unbuckle your seat belt, open the hatch, and lower a wing until you fall out of the plane.

It worked! I was free of the plane and drifting down to earth at a quiet eight miles per hour. What a wonderful feeling!

My fall into a field was partly broken by a tree, and I was completely unharmed. A naval plane was circling overhead, and I knew the pilot had spotted me. I waved my arms and then kicked each leg, so he would know that I hadn't broken any bones. He dipped his wings to show he'd seen me.

A soldier and his wife who were driving down a nearby road had seen it all happen and rushed to help me. They insisted on taking me to the local hospital to get checked out. Then they got me to an airport so I could get back to Romulus and report the loss of a valuable airplane. Nancy Love, the most prominent female aviator in the United States after Jacqueline Cochran, actually helped show me how to report the disaster. She suggested that the base hospital staff send in a report, which they did.

Many years later at a P-51 Mustang reunion, one of the men explained that you would never be able to bail out of a Mustang. I straightened him out by remarking, "Look, sonny, I'm here to tell you that you *can* bail out of a P-51 successfully, because I did it."

The Caterpillar Club

That is not quite the end of my story.

A few weeks after my big adventure, I received a letter and a small package from the "Caterpillar Club." The letter said I had just become a Life Member of the Club with no dues or obligations, and I was invited to attend its annual reunion. The small package contained a beautiful little gold-plated pin in the form of a caterpillar. It seems the English company that created the original parachute—made of silk—carried on a tradition of registering as lifetime members every person anywhere in the world whose life had been saved by the lowly silkworm. I still wear my pin when I get dressed up, and I get a lot of questions about it.

The basic training of new WASP classes at Avenger Field in Texas and the active service of WASPs around the country continued through 1944. However in June 1944, the battle of militarization of the WASPs heated up again in Congress. Returning military pilots were being rotated back to the States looking for jobs. On June 21 the bill in the House to give WASPs military status was narrowly defeated. General Hap Arnold, who had been a proponent of militarization, said in a speech he delivered at Avenger Field in Sweetwater, Texas. on December 7, 1944:

> The WASPs have completed their mission. Their job has been successful. But, as usual, the cost has been heavy. Thirty-eight WASPs have died while helping their country move toward victory. The Air Force will long remember their service and their final sacrifice.

We had the best airplanes in the world and the best instructors. We had it made. And then all of a sudden, the Army said, "We don't need you any more." The Women Airforce Service Pilots was discontinued on December 20, 1944.

Those of us on active duty at air bases around the country went on with the next phase of our lives. Some were able to enlist in parts of the armed services that now admitted women. Some found a place in the civilian aviation industry. And some bought their own tickets back home and started a new life.

Epilogue

Between September 1942 and December 1944, the WASPs had flown an estimated 60 million air miles. They had delivered 12,650 aircraft of 78 different types from factories to airfields and ports of embarkation in the continental United States. Exactly 1074 women had earned their wings from WASP training schools, and 38 had lost their lives in service to their country—11 in training and 27 in active duty.

All records of the WASP were classified and sealed for 35 years. The contributions of the WASPs to the war effort were little known and inaccessible to historians. In 1975, under the leadership of Colonel Bruce Arnold, son of General Hap Arnold, the new "Battle of Congress" was fought—and won. Finally, in 1977, the records were unsealed, with the essential support of Senator Barry Goldwater, who had himself been a World War II ferry pilot. President Jimmy Carter signed the legislation giving the WASPs full military status with benefits. In 1984, each WASP was awarded the World War II Victory Medal. Those who served for more than a year were also awarded the American Theater Ribbon/American Campaign Ribbon for their service during the War.

Final recognition came on July 1, 2009, when President Barack Obama and the United States Congress awarded to each WASP the Congressional Gold Medal. This medal, along with the Freedom Medal, is our country's highest civilian honor. Three of the surviving WASPs were on hand when Speaker Nancy Pelosi presented the bill for the President's signature. On March 10, 2010, 200 of the 300 known surviving WASPs gathered in the rotunda of the Capitol to receive their medals.

Louise Bowden Brown was not able to attend the Washington affair, but her medal was presented in a ceremony at Kendal at Hanover by two representatives of the United States government: Leigh Marthe, from the office of Congressman Paul Hodes of New Hampshire, and a delegate from Senator Jeanne Shaheen. Arrangements were made to send the medal for safekeeping to her home-town bank in Elmer, New Jersey. It was put on display in the bank's front window until a brick was tossed through the window in an unsuccessful robbery attempt. Louise Brown's Congressional Gold Medal is now safely in the bank's vault.

After leaving the WASPs, Louise gave flying lessons at various aviation schools and worked as a medical technician in Alaska and other places, including San Diego. She became a missionary with the Presbyterian Church and spent many years in India and Nepal. Married at age 78, she was widowed three years later and in 2001 came to Kendal at Hanover, where her sister, Emily Connolly, was a resident.

This memoir was written as a collaboration with Louise and Kendal resident Bob Stambaugh, assisted by Jane Barlow, another resident. Now a lively 95 years old, Louise lives in a pleasant private room in the skilled nursing wing of the Kendal Health Center. She generously gave many interviews as the memories came surging back. We also received help from Joel Godston of Haverhill, New Hampshire—who interviewed her in 2007—and from her sister, Edith Eldridge, of Indialantic, Florida. Additional anecdotes came from an interview with several WASPs, including Louise, broadcast on December 18, 2002, on National Public Radio's program All Things Considered. *We are especially grateful for the records in the WASP archives at Texas Woman's University in Denton, Texas.*

EARNING MY CRAMPONS

Ann Brooks Carter

Ann with husband Ad in 1942

THIS IS THE STORY OF HOW I BECAME INVOLVED in testing new mountain-troop equipment in winter.

In the early 1940s the U.S. Army was finally persuaded by some of the country's outstanding mountaineers, of which my husband Adams Carter was one, that mountain troops would be necessary if the United States entered the War. Those soldiers became the famous 10th Mountain Division. Adams, known as Ad, was one of the knowledgeable mountain men to be attached to the Army's Office of the Quartermaster General (OQMG) in Washington, D.C., to help develop the equipment needed for mountain warfare, including that needed in cold winter conditions.

Ad and I were married in June 1942. Our first week of married life included living on nothing but the Army's developing K rations for testing purposes. No cheating! Dehydrated everything from egg powder to ice-cream powder, all of which, of course, had to be rehydrated. Far more interesting was the testing of cold-weather equipment for the mountain troops. A location which provided cold, snow, ice, and wind was needed. In winter, Mt. Washington in New Hampshire would provide all this in abundance. As it was Ad's home territory, he was chosen to do some of the preliminary testing in January 1943. I was to be his assistant.

Ad's family house in Jefferson, New Hampshire, was our headquarters. On a frosty clear morning with the temperature in the single digits, we readied the equipment to be tested in Pinkham Notch at the base of Mt. Washington: nylon mountain tent, down sleeping bags, different kinds of boots, clothing from wool underwear to parkas, packboard, nylon climbing rope, crampons, ice axes, plush sealskins for skis, primus stove, and cooking kit. To transport it, we each had an Army backpack, heavy even before it was loaded. What did not go into our packs was to be loaded onto another test item, a long, convertible toboggan-to-sled, which Ad was to pull. It was started in sled mode, as the trail up Mt. Washington was fairly well packed.

We attached the plush sealskins to our ski bottoms, to keep the skis from slipping backwards, and started the hike up the Fire Trail toward Tuckerman Ravine. The sled was unwieldy and uncooperative, so Ad decided to try it as a toboggan. It was supposed to transfer easily. It did convert, but easy it was not. Ad suggested that I keep going as he wrestled with the contraption.

It was beautiful! Brilliant blue sky, sparkling snow festooning the trees—and so still. No wind—yet. I was climbing slowly, steadily, easily. My 30-pound pack was riding well. Suddenly the stillness was broken by a shout from Ad, now unencumbered by the sled. In total frustration, he had finally unloaded it and thrown it into the woods. He had piled what he could into his already heavy pack and left the rest for subsequent trips. He continued on up the trail at a faster pace than I was capable of, to leave the first load at the Harvard Cabin just off the trail not far below where we planned to camp. We had expected to make this picturesque ascent together.

Toward the end of the morning, as my pack was beginning to feel intolerably heavy, I was startled to have it silently lifted off my back by a stranger who continued without a word.

"Hey, wait a minute! What's the idea? Who are you?"

"Your husband sent me," was the reply. He turned out to be Bill

Putnam, an old friend of Ad's, whom I had never met. Finally, toward the end of the afternoon, thanks to Bill's help, camp was set up at the base of the Little Headwall below Tuckerman Ravine and all loads were accounted for.

Not only Bill, but another friend, Andy Kauffman, added greatly to our pleasure and productivity. That evening we supped with them in the Harvard Cabin, complete with wine. We brought along the Army K rations which supplied most of our food.

But the warm coziness of the cabin had to come to an end. So, out into the frigid night, illuminated by a full moon. Gorgeous! However, the wind was beginning to blow as we skied our way up to camp.

During the night the experimental wool underwear and our heavy down sleeping bags kept us comfortably warm as the temperature dipped into the minus numbers. The wind was anything but comforting. But it was just what we wanted in order to test the strength and stability of the tent. The constant loud flapping and snapping in the little two-man tent made sleep next to impossible for me. I couldn't help wondering whether the tent might collapse on top of us. Not so for Ad, who slept peacefully through the night. With dawn the wind started to let up, and I slept until Ad shook me awake to be greeted by bright sunshine. We breakfasted on ample portions of K Ration instant oatmeal and tea. Melting the snow, a slow process, provided the water. The new design of stove worked in the cold. The cook-set and utensils were quite adequate.

Tuckerman Ravine

The real work of the day was about to begin. Ad slung the experimental nylon climbing rope around his shoulder. We loaded two different kinds of crampons and boots into our packs, attached an ice axe apiece to the outside, donned our skis still with skins, and headed up above the tree line into the great bowl of Tuckerman Ravine, with its precipitous headwall and cliffs. I felt very small in the stretching expanse of white as Ad and I stood in the flat bottom of the bowl, taking in the beauty and considering where best to try out the crampons.

An ice-covered cliff was to the left of the headwall. As the snow was wind-blown and solid, we swapped skis and poles for crampons and ice axes. This was my first experience with crampons, but not the last, and

I was a little apprehensive about this ice climbing, though I knew Ad would be in the lead and belaying me with the rope. A shout of greeting interrupted my reverie and, to my huge relief, Bill and Andy appeared from below, with their crampons and ice axes. Enthusiastically Bill swapped his old crampons for an experimental pair.

At the ice cliff Bill roped up with Ad while Andy and I watched. That was quite all right with me. It was a short climb. At a possible stopping place, Ad suggested to Bill that he would like to jump free with Bill belaying him, to see if the unacceptable stretch in the nylon rope had been corrected. Ad jumped and I held my breath as the rope stretched instead of going taut. Luckily he stopped before hitting anything. Bill and Andy had brought the standard manila climbing rope, which then took the place of the faulty nylon one. Andy had his turn on the cliff. Then Ad looked at me and said, "Next." After all, that's what I was here for. So I roped up, with Ad belaying me, and quickly lost my anxiety. It was an ideal place to have my first lesson in ice climbing. The day was perfect. The bright winter sun warmed things up a bit.

We continued testing, trying different boots and crampon combinations on the ice. For lunch we consumed granola bars and dried fruit, sitting on a big rock in the sun. I longed for a cup of tea instead of the very cold water in canteens which had been wrapped in wool within the packs, supposedly to keep the water from freezing.

I finally got my tea when we returned to camp. Bill and Andy joined us for a tea party, complete with cookies which I had tucked into my pack at the last minute. Supper again with our friends in the Harvard Cabin and then a sound sleep with only a gentle flapping of the tent.

Next day was moving-down day, easier said than done for me. The beautiful weather had ended; it was snowing and blowing, fortunately not too hard. The skins were off the skis, our packs were loaded. We waved goodbye to our successful camp-site and pushed off down the Sherburne Trail, with Bill and Andy again helping. They and Ad went ahead of me, as their descent would be more rapid than mine, and they would have to return for another load that they had left behind in the Harvard Cabin because it was snowing.

My pack was heavy and unwieldy and didn't help my skiing. The Sherburne Trail is not difficult, but it is fairly narrow. It wasn't long before I took a spill. I couldn't get up, try as I would. Solution: take the pack off, stand up, then heave it back on. The rest of the descent was punctuated by more falls. About three-quarters of the way down, Ad turned up and took my pack. I felt as if I could fly and whisked to the bottom in style. We gave each other a big hug. Thumbs up! Mission accomplished! Then off to Jefferson, a warm house, delicious dinner, and a comfortable bed. Bliss!

Back in Washington, Ad turned in the equipment, except for the sled, and a detailed report. The nylon rope was all that needed major change. The plans for a toboggan-sled were abandoned. For me it had been a wonderful indoctrination in the ways of winter camping and climbing. And I got huge satisfaction from being able to share this experience with Ad as well as to contribute something to the war effort. Ad commented that I had "earned my spurs"—or, rather, my crampons.

After the War, and a nine-month stint teaching in Chile, Ann and Ad returned to Massachusetts, where they were involved in the preparatory school world for 35 years. They hosted many foreign students and took students on mountaineering expeditions in this country, Alaska, and Peru. Their three sons grew up skiing and mountaineering. The mountaineering world brought them in touch with interesting places and people around the globe and brought many foreign guests to their ample house in northern New Hampshire. Ad died unexpectedly in 1995, and Ann came to Kendal at Hanover in 2005.

WHOSE WAR *IS* THIS?

Elinor Clark Horne

Elinor Clark discusses a point of Japanese grammar with Toshio Kono

Ohayo gozaimasu. Konnichi wa. Ikaga desu ka?
Arigato gozaimasu. Sayonara.

THESE JAPANESE EXPRESSIONS—most of them widely familiar to Americans nowadays—are a few of the conventional phrases you need to know when you speak with Japanese people in their language. Straight out of Lesson One, they were among the first words learned by many a U.S. soldier who participated in Army Specialized Training Program (ASTP), which the Army had established in December 1942 with the purpose of training academically talented enlisted men at major colleges and universities across the country. One of its branches was the Intensive Language Program.

I spent my war years teaching in the ASTP Japanese language program at Yale University. Yale was one of the several colleges breaking new ground with an innovative method—pretty much being developed as it went along—for teaching foreign languages in a hurry. The immediate goal was to prepare selected soldiers for interacting with Japanese people by speaking with them in *their* language on *their* soil when the War was over and the anticipated occupation had begun.

Soldiers selected for the ASTP Program were a bright bunch. Taken from various Army training camps around the country on the basis of their IQs and educational background, they suddenly became college students at universities here and there in the United States. Quite a switch from their day-to-day lives in the Army!

I, too, had been recruited for the Program—plucked from my job in Washington, D.C., where I was working at the U.S. State Department in the Office of Foreign Relief and Rehabilitation (OFRRO, the forerunner of UNRRA), a great place to feel right in the thick of things. I would occasionally pass Secretary Cordell Hull in a hallway, sagging wearily at the end of his long day but still carrying home a bulging briefcase. The State Department was at that time right next door to the White House, and from our windows we could look down on the back lawn. Franklin D. Roosevelt sunned himself in plain view every so often and sometimes received exciting visitors there. The word would go round our office: "Look who's talking with the President!" and we'd all rush to the windows. Once it was Winston Churchill: there he was, stomping around a seated FDR and puffing on a cigar.

This was the milieu I left when, on the basis of a college language major and a bit of demonstrated aptitude for language, I was recruited by the Intensive Language Program and sent to Yale University, to study Linguistics (which I had never heard of) and join the linguistics staff of the Japanese program (a language I knew not a word of).

The program, I found, was conducted as a close collaborative relationship among three teams: a small staff of linguists, who organized and devised teaching materials and observed the results in the classroom; a staff of several dozen tutors, men and women whose first language was Japanese; and the students, young enlisted men whose task was, essentially, to immerse themselves in Japanese-ness—especially the language.

Students? Soldiers?

These ASTPers were playing a dual role: "Soldiers first, students second" was the dictum from above. As students, they were housed in

Yale College dormitories and took their meals in Yale College dining halls; as soldiers, they were under strict military discipline at all times. They wore regulation uniforms, obeyed reveille, were subjected to Saturday morning inspections, put their lights out at 10:30 p.m., marched to classes and meals—counting aloud or singing as they went:

> A friend on the left and a friend on the right, Viva la
>   Compagnie!
> In one and good fellowship let us unite, Viva la Com-
>   pagnie!
> Viva la, viva la, viva l'amour! Viva la, viva la, viva
>   l'amour!
> Viva l'amour, viva l'amour, Viva la Compagnie!

In their pockets they carried their copies of *Beginning Japanese*, the manual being developed lesson by lesson by the linguistics staff (a few giant steps ahead of classroom needs) and printed by the Government in a horizontal format designed to fit in the pocket of an Army uniform.

Elinor poses for a photo with her students

Our soldier-students worked hard. Along with a weekly hour-long lecture by the linguist who directed the program, and the evenings devoted to study, they spent hours each day closeted in small "drill groups" under the charge of a Japanese tutor, whose task was to speak Japanese to them and require them to do the same, sentence by sentence, in direct imitation of the Japanese tutor. Gradually the students began conversing in Japanese on their own, always under the tutor's guidance and supervision.

One of my jobs was to visit these drill groups in action—to go around from one to another observing the students' progress and making sure the program was being conducted properly. This latter meant, most particularly, enforcing Rule #1, the most important one and the hardest to obey: *Nihongo daké!* "Japanese only!" Not a word of English was to be spoken in the classrooms.

I enjoyed these visits—only partly because I learned a good deal of Japanese while making them—though I found later that those I was viewing regarded my visits more as a police action.

The academics were intense and the standards rigorous. Not everyone made it. If you just couldn't get the hang of speaking Japanese, you had to leave the program and be assigned elsewhere, mostly to an infantry, airborne, or armored division still in stateside training. One of these less linguistically gifted ones, returning to Yale some time later to visit, dropped by my office. At his new training camp, it seemed, he was *teaching Japanese* to his fellow trainees! He showed me some of the lessons he had drawn up—the way they *ought* to be done, he implied.

Of course it's entirely possible that time has added a rose-colored tinge to my spectacles, but as I look back on the teamwork we all engaged in to accomplish this highly important wartime work, my top recollection is that it was *fun*. Stimulating, productive, demanding, eminently worthwhile, arduous, collegial—and fun. Serious, yes; solemn, no.

In relief from the academic intensity of their task, the ASTPers devoted most of their meager free hours to good times and social activities, especially those involving girls. The occasional dances they put on were big, joyous affairs: they dressed up in their best uniforms and escorted pretty girls wearing long dresses, upswept hairdos, and corsages. Everybody was invited to these affairs, faculty and tutors included—one more example of the comradely spirit that pervaded the program.

Talk about fun! A particularly memorable event was the elaborate stage show the ASTPers put on, giving full vent to their creativity, for the entertainment of everyone connected with the language program.

A series of skits, all in Japanese, revealed a whole new take on their day-to-day labors, aimed in large part at *us*, their slave-drivers. They parodied our gestures and eccentricities so aptly as to be unmistakably identifiable. One skit depicted a typical drill-group scene with students making wildly hilarious mistakes in Japanese and being guided by the tutor into more acceptable directions, when the door opened and in walked a "visitor" (I recognized myself) who, though welcomed with smiles, was uneasily aware of whisperings that sounded very much like a Japanified version of *Cheese it—the cops!*

And then there was the Little Red Riding Hood skit (still all in Japanese): A student in a red cape and carrying a little basket was saun-tering through the forest when (s)he was accosted by a wolf—a human one. Hard-pressed by the increasingly aggressive wolf and on the verge of being overcome, LRRH finally panicked and cried out, "Help! Help!" Instantly a policeman rushed in, shook a stern finger at her, thundered *Nihongo daké!* ("No English!")—and rushed out again.

All of this was so plainly delivered in a good-natured, comradely spirit of fun that it could only be taken in the same spirit

Some things, of course, are inevitable among any population of healthy, normal young folks, regardless of status or rank. Occasion-al hints would circulate of romances between an ASTP soldier and a young Japanese tutor. A marriage took place between a faculty member and a student. And we learned of at least one broken heart.

The spirit of fellowship that prevailed among our student-soldiers at Yale was shared in ASTP programs elsewhere and long outlasted their training time. We soon began hearing the universal theme song (to the tune of "My Bonnie Lies Over the Ocean"):

> Some mothers have sons in the Army,
> Some mothers have sons on the sea;
> But take down that service flag, Mother:
> Your son's in the ASTP.

Along with typically wry ASTP self-perception, might this song have reflected a touch of guilt felt by soldiers lucky enough to be living the life of a more-or-less college student?

The ASTP endured for only a few years. The trainees were to have served as Army officers both during the War and in the restoration of civilian governments afterwards; but as the invasion of Normandy neared, and the need arose for additional manpower in the ground forces in Europe, the Army disbanded the ASTP in early 1944 and assigned the trainees to the infantry, where they fought in both the European and Pacific theaters.

Their caliber is suggested by a short list of those who later became illustrious in widely dispersed fields: diplomat Henry Kissinger; New York Mayor Ed Koch; sports commentator Heywood Hale Broun; Senator Frank Church; newscaster Roger Mudd; author Gore Vidal; actor Mel Brooks.

Friends? Enemies?

What about those tutors—the team of Japanese speakers who constituted the backbone of the ASTP language program?

They were among the first people I met at Yale. Recently out of college, and a victim of the prevailing wartime propaganda, I of course knew exactly what to expect from these slant-eyed people: they were devious, secretive, full of mystery ("you never know what they're thinking"); they were all alike and altogether different from "us."

Miyo Okada and Senzo Usui helping Elinor speak and understand their language

Who were they? As required by the new teaching method, the primary qualification was that they speak Japanese as their first language. Most of those born in Japan spoke heavily accented English, while the second-generationers were fully bilingual. Recruited from many areas, they ranged from a young recent Pomona College graduate to an elderly widow who had spent many years as a conscientious schoolteacher. One was a young man in his middle twenties who had just begun to prosper in his cleaning and dyeing business on the west coast when he and his family were abruptly ordered into an internment camp. There were shy young girls and less shy young girls. One tutor was a middle-aged businessman who, along with his American wife, was now coping with two fully Americanized teen-aged children. Another was an older Korean man who had assumed a Japanese name and identity after the Japanese had invaded his country and renamed it *Chosen*. There were a dignified, cultured middle-aged couple who instantly commanded everyone's respect; a young Japanese wife who was waiting at home while her young Japanese husband fought in the U.S. Army in Europe; a Buddhist priest who was something of a hypochondriac.

We all worked closely together with the collaborative goal of teaching American soldiers to speak good Japanese. As I learned it myself, I found that the more you know of someone else's language, the more you come to understand the cultural values and world view of its speakers. I also found—to my growing amazement—that the Japanese weren't so different from us after all. What a surprise! They had senses of humor, tempers and temperaments, hangups and idiosyncrasies. Some were easy to get along with and some were a pain. They all seemed to share, with "us," the apparently universal human appetite for gossip. In short, they were ordinary human beings! To be sure, some of their cultural attitudes differed to some extent from ours, and they spoke Japanese a whole lot better than any of us ever managed to, and there wasn't a blue-eyed blond among them, but still...

I wished that more people could share the opportunity I had of getting to really know some of "the enemy." It became increasingly mortifying to observe the treatment they underwent in our society—these people who had been leading dignified, productive lives among us before the War. Many had been torn from their homes and humiliatingly interned as suspicious enemy aliens, in utter disregard for everything except their ethnic origins. Never mind that they had all been thoroughly checked out by the FBI: it was constantly made clear to them that they were *other* and *undesirable*. New Haven landlords shared the

Bob Midzuno, Fred Okada, Ken Yamamoto, and Jimmy Shiozaki being "Japs"— having fun with the wartime propaganda stereotype

prejudice: Japanese people who had traveled from elsewhere to join our staff had trouble finding apartments. Once at a social event when I told a new acquaintance that I was teaching Americans to speak Japanese, she sniffed and said, "I wouldn't even want to talk to them."

Close friendships developed within our group of Japanese and Americans. I spent much time with their families and entertained them in my home. We worked together, laughed together over *New Yorker* cartoons, got mad at each other, played charades at parties (complicated by the fact that the Japanese concept of a syllable differs substantially from ours), shared movies and meals (in my kitchen, they taught me to cook rice in the Japanese style so that each grain remained separate: you start by measuring water up to the first joint of your index finger). We played bridge together sometimes and poker often. *Side benefit*: I eventually scraped together my winnings and spent them on a very-much-used car.

During a visit to New York, several of my young Japanese friends took me to their favorite Japanese restaurant, where I said a few friendly things in Japanese to the young waiter. Apparently this pleased him, because when he brought the check, he slipped me a note reading *Ai shite orimasu, watakushi wa anata ni*—which, after the word order is sorted out and the honorifics overlooked, means "I love you." The note has long since vanished; the cherished memory remains.

And then...

On Monday, August 6, 1945, the news crashed down around us.

The United States had dropped an atomic bomb on the city of
    Hiroshima.

The reports from Ground Zero were unbearably horrifying.

A profound hush pervaded our restrained talk.

Here in New Haven, thousands of miles away, business had to
    go on as usual in our offices and classrooms. But nothing
    was the same. It was hard to look directly at one another.

Then three days later...Nagasaki.

We "others" were no less appalled than our Japanese friends.
    But the ultimate impact was available only to them.

For quite some time nobody said much of anything about it at all.

What was there to say?

What about all these months we've been working together so
    harmoniously and constructively—we and our Japanese
    colleagues?

What about our mutual friendships and affections, our shared
    enjoyments, our intermingling in each other's lives?

Was the dropping of the atom bomb *our* fault?

Had the attack on Pearl Harbor been *their* fault?

Whose war *is* this?

*In 1948, Elinor Clark married David Horne—a World War II veteran
who had been wounded not long after participating in the D-Day invasion at Normandy Beach. Over the years they raised three daughters
and, in the course of David's career in Shakespeare scholarship and
University Press publishing, they moved from Yale to Harvard to Dartmouth. David died in 1999. Elinor has continued to work and teach in
Linguistics and in her secondary field, Traditional Oral Folktales. She
has published several books on languages of the Far East. She moved
into Kendal at Hanover in July of 2007.*

THE BIRTH OF THE UNITED NATIONS

Elizabeth Morrison Hunter

IN 1941 I WAS LIVING IN BATON ROUGE, Louisiana, where my husband was on the faculty of Louisiana State University—a happy, stay-at-home young faculty wife. But the Japanese bombed Pearl Harbor that December, and we immediately knew, as did many other young people, that we had to go to Washington to help our government in any way we could.

My husband had professional skills, but I only knew how to type and take Gregg shorthand. Soon after we reached Washington I joined a typing pool in the Lend-Lease Administration, and he found a job with the Bureau of the Budget using his special skills in budgetary matters. The Lend-Lease bill had been stalled in the Senate because many people felt that we should not get involved with a European war.

Early in 1941, President Roosevelt sent Wendell Willkie—a staunch Republican—to London with a handwritten introduction to Churchill, so that Willkie could learn firsthand about England's wartime problems. On his return, he reported to Congress that Britain was running out of military supplies and warned that if we continued to be isolationists, there was no telling where "the madmen loose in the world" might strike next.

Shortly thereafter, Congress passed a bill, signed into law on March 11, 1942, authorizing the President to "transfer munitions and supplies to the government of any country whose defense the President deems vital to the defense of the United States." Roosevelt pulled another political coup by bringing into Washington leaders of industry who were reputedly lukewarm about his war policies. In 1941 he chose Edward R. Stettinius, Chairman of U.S. Steel, to head up the new Lend-Lease organization, with offices in the old Federal Reserve Building. On the first floor were young people hoping to be given a job. It was a very noisy scene —I know, because I was there as part of the typing pool.

One day a man from Mr. Stettinius's office asked me if I ever made a mistake in my work. I replied, "No." I then passed a test by typing a memo dictated to me and, to my astonishment, learned that I was to listen to all of Stettinius's telephone conversations, record them in shorthand, and type them. Later I also became responsible for his appointments, arranging his conferences and meetings and locating interpreters when needed. A white telephone on my desk was used only to receive calls from the White House.

In 1943 Stettinius was moved to the Department of State, first as Under Secretary and then, a year later, as Secretary of State to replace the ailing Cordell Hull. I was asked to go with him—and thus became part of the drama within the State Department, particularly in its planning of a San Francisco conference where 50 nations would be joining together to create an organization dedicated to maintaining international peace in the post-War world.

Then Roosevelt died, in April 1945. The Department, though stunned, realized that it must go ahead with its plans for the Conference: the date had been set and the names of the delegates had been announced. The U.S. delegates included Edward Stettinius as chairman, Cordell Hull as the senior advisor (though he was too ill to attend), and Democratic and Republican members of the House and Senate. Among the public representatives, Virginia Gildersleeve, a Barnard College Dean, was the only woman delegate.

Late at night on April 23, 1945, at Washington Airport, we boarded the Secretary's C-54, a four-engine propeller plane, for a nonstop flight—all the way to San Francisco in thirteen hours! Aboard that plane were all the delegates, plus some State Department people.

Our flight was not without incident. As we flew into an ice storm over the Rockies, the plane had to climb to 14,500 feet, and four of us shared an oxygen mask. I think we all survived because my Catholic friend was frantically fingering her rosary.

The morning we landed in San Francisco was sunny and beautiful. Welcoming officials were standing at attention, civic ladies presented us with large bunches of flowers, a brass band played, and the press hovered with poised pencils. We found fleets of cars at our disposal and learned that the Opera House and Veterans Building had been turned into offices and conference centers, while hotels and apartment buildings had been requisitioned to house the hundreds of men and women from fifty nations. Another secretary and I shared a small, dark room overlooking the fire escape in the Plaza Hotel. We either walked up Nob Hill to the Fairmont Hotel or paid seven cents for a cable car.

We were immediately put to work. Members of the American delegation were waiting to be greeted by Stettinius. An off-the-record news conference had been scheduled. Vyacheslav Molotov, Foreign Minister of the USSR, with his U.S. interpreter, Chip Bohlen, and Averill Harriman, U.S. Ambassador to the USSR, had appointments with Stettinius. And that evening he was to give a radio address.

My office was in a suite on the fifth floor of the Fairmont Hotel in what I think had been the dining room. Just outside my office there was a private elevator, run by the FBI, that went up to the penthouse, where Stettinius lived and held private meetings. Large and ornately furnished, this suite looked out over beautiful San Francisco. Standing at the window you could see our warships in the harbor; often you would also see the sharp point of a rifle carried by one of the several members of the armed forces who paced back and forth along the parapets, day and night.

In the largely male world of the 1940s I was delighted to learn that many women's organizations from all over the world, both public and private, had sent representatives to the Conference. Four residents of Hanover, New Hampshire, were directly involved: John Masland, Assistant Secretary in Committee Two of the First Commission, who later became provost of Dartmouth and the husband of Kendal's Mary

Masland; Waldo Chamberlain, Documents Officer, later Dean of Dartmouth's Summer School (and the husband of Kay Chamberlain, a former Kendal resident); John Sloan Dickey, Public Liaison Officer of the U.S. Delegation and later president of Dartmouth; and Dickey's deputy, Richard Morin, who was to become Librarian of Dartmouth.

All through the years I've kept my notes and letters to my devoted husband, Donald Morrison, describing those fascinating days in San Francisco:

May 4, 1945—What a day! Chip Bohlen dictated a top-secret memo about a conversation he had had with Molotov. News came over the telephone from the press section that Eisenhower was accepting the surrender of German forces in Denmark and Holland. I telephoned the news up to the penthouse. Stet (Stettinius) came downstairs immediately and announced the news to an in-progress subcommittee meeting about war criminals, which was attended by Molotov (who had said "Good morning" to me in English) and members of the U.S., British, and Chinese delegations. Through the open door I could hear their laughter and conviviality. Then Stet asked John McCloy, Assistant Secretary of War, to call Chief of Staff George Marshall to make sure the news was true. A formal ticker tape arrived confirming the surrender. I held it in my hand for a minute or two. When Stet took it he shook my hand and said, "Congratulations." Wow!

At that point photographers arrived, along with the rest of the U.S. delegation, who then had their pictures taken right in front of my desk before going up to the penthouse for lunch. The hall filled with reporters, but only a few were allowed in.

In the afternoon Stet and Anthony Eden, British Foreign Secretary, went out to Berkeley, where Stet received an honorary degree. On his return, with the hood he had just received, Stet dictated a letter to his wife: "Dear Ginia, Here is the hood just received from the University of California. You can add it to the others. Devotedly..."

All the amendments to the Charter document must be in by midnight. More meetings. By mistake I stopped at the office of Alger Hiss, Secretary General of the Conference, as I was taking a memo to James Dunn, Under Secretary of State. There were lots of people opening bottles in celebration. Alger asked me if I wanted a drink. I refused, saying

I would fall flat on my face if I did, I was so weary. He said he would fall flat on his face if he didn't have a drink, after this wild day.

May 5—Molotov asked for a sudden appointment with Stet this evening, said he had something important to take up with him. No one could find Bohlen, so I asked the FBI to get one of their men to act as interpreter. Molotov agreed to two issues that had been unresolved. Everyone was very pleased.

May 12—Today heard that the first few feelers of surrender from Japan had come in from the same source that had announced Germany's early feelers. This afternoon Anthony Eden winked at me as we passed in the hall.

All of us at the Fairmont office felt that under the surface of gaiety and excitement, we had a grave responsibility to the United States and to the world. We were well aware of the complicated work being done at the Civic Center—by the Secretariat and staffs, who were doing the substantive work of drawing up the complicated terms of the United Nations Charter; by the corps of telephone operators who spoke foreign languages; by the hundreds of delegates with their supporting technical committees that met every day and often at night—all working to determine the extent of the Big Powers' duties, the responsibilities of the permanent members of the Security Council, the terms for handling breaches of the peace, the procedure needed for admitting a new member; and all the other complicated issues that the Charter had to address.

The Russians had come to the Conference with suspicion. They felt there was a solid front against them in the United States and that the Latin American countries were over-represented. Molotov didn't want Argentina to be admitted and this became a *big* issue because the United States felt it important to include them for Latin-American unity. After the vote, and the admittance of Argentina, Molotov walked out of the Conference and many people were concerned that he wouldn't return. That night, however, he asked for a meeting with Stet. They had a long talk in the penthouse. And the next morning, Molotov called a press conference to announce his agreement.

Another *big* issue was Poland. Russia wanted them admitted, but they had a puppet government under the control of the Soviets. Russia also wanted three seats on the Security Council—Byelorussia and the Ukraine as well as its own. The tug of war between the countries challenged the whole structure of the Conference. But Stet was marvelous. He had come to this world scene without great knowledge of international affairs, but he had dynamic energy, a lot of patience, and the determination to make the Conference a success. At times the stalemates seemed impossible to resolve, but with renegotiations again and again, the Russians began to lose their initial suspicions, and differences were resolved.

June 6—Today at noon we learned that there was a break in the Russian deadlock. Stet was as elated as I have ever seen him. He called Andrei Gromyko, Russian Ambassador to the United States and a participant in the writing of the Charter, with the news. Another Big Five meeting was called this afternoon at the request of the Soviets. Tonight Charles Spyros of 20th Century Fox gave a dinner party honoring the American delegation. There were about 150 people there, including me, and it was indeed a very special occasion. We women were each presented with three orchids at the door, cocktails before dinner, soup and fish and filet mignon—and I'd come from wartime Washington where food was rationed: we were grinding nuts flavored with Bovril, pretending it was hamburger, and were lucky if we had enough coupons to buy a chicken for Sunday dinner. After our grand dinner, a sleight-of-hand specialist, Dr. Giovanni, persuaded Vandenberg, California Governor Warren, Stassen, Stet, and a few others to join him on stage. He then proceeded to lift their wallets and other valuables without their knowledge—to the delight of the audience. A truly gala evening.

June 7—A day of celebration. Few meetings. Late in the day Stet asked me to get the President on the phone and then to "listen to every word" as they discussed the President's upcoming trip to California. The United Nations Charter was completed and signed by all fifty sovereign nations. The document, under the protection of Secretary General Alger Hiss, was then sealed in a padlocked steel case, had a parachute strapped to the top of the case, and was flown to New York.

June 26—President Truman addressed the last meeting of the Conference, held in the old Opera House. He said, "The Constitution of my own country came from a Convention which, like this one, was made up of delegates with many different views. Like this Charter, our Constitution came from a free and sometimes bitter exchange of conflicting opinions. When it was adopted...it grew and developed and expanded. And upon it was built a bigger, a better, a more perfect union...Let us not fail to grasp this supreme chance to establish a worldwide rule of reason—to create an enduring peace under the guidance of God."

The United Nations Conference was over, and everyone headed home with confidence and hope. James Byrnes was named Secretary of State and Edward Stettinius was named the United States' first Ambassador to the United Nations. I went back to Washington and moved from the State Department to a small office in the East Wing of the White House as Stet's secretary, but he shortly left for London and I came to Hanover with my husband to once again become a faculty wife.

Over the sixty-plus years since San Francisco, our nation's confidence has sometimes been threatened, but we have never lost hope. The United Nations must endure. The UN Charter cannot prevent war, nor check aggression with military force, but it can be invaluable as its international agencies strive to reach compromises and settle disputes and work to alleviate the poverty and hopelessness that sow the seeds of anarchy and terrorism.

Elizabeth grew up in Grand Rapids, Michigan, and graduated from Oberlin College. While working in Princeton, New Jersey, she met and married Donald Morrison. The War brought them to Washington, where she worked as Edward Stettinius' secretary during the creation of the United Nations. After the war Elizabeth moved to Hanover; Donald became Dartmouth's first provost. He died suddenly in 1959. A year later Elizabeth married Ralph Hunter, a neurologist, thus adding five children to her own three. Ralph died in 2000. Elizabeth enjoys her seventeen grandchildren, recorder playing, and her house on the coast of Maine. She came to Kendal at Hanover in 2002.

Secret Weapon?

John M. Jenkins
U.S. Army Air Force

IT WAS SUNDAY AFTERNOON, DECEMBER 7, 1941, and I, a student at Dartmouth College, was studying in Baker Library. The quietude was suddenly interrupted by staccato voices and a low rumbling. Disconcerted, I went to the desk and found students clustered around a small blackboard. In large letters it said, "JAPS BOMB PEARL HARBOR." I ran to my room and turned on the radio.

Like most of my classmates, I attended college the following summer so I could graduate from Dartmouth before entering the service. On December 20, 1942, three days after receiving my degree, I became a private in the U.S. Army Air Force—colorblindness having ruled out my becoming a pilot—and was sent to Camp Upton on Long Island, New York, for basic training.

As I attempted my first "hup, two, three, four" through Grand Central Station on my way to Upton, I looked at the commuters dashing for trains and wondered if I'd make it through the War to become one of them in later years.

After a brief time at Camp Upton, I was sent to Basic Training Center #10 near Greensboro, North Carolina. Friends of my parents, Harry and Mary Alice Carter, lived in Greensboro and they entertained me in my free moments. Mary Alice also sewed new stripes on my uniform each time I was promoted. By the following December she was beginning to complain about the constant sewing and was delighted to learn that I was going to Officers Candidate School, where I would trade my sergeant's stripes for a gold bar.

In late February 1944, I became an intelligence officer in the Army Air Force and married my college love, Mary Mecklin. Together we headed for my first assignment as an officer: Victoria Army Air Force Base just outside Hays, Kansas. Victoria was training crews for the brand-new B-29s, long-range bombers designed for use in the Pacific Theater—the planes later used to drop the atomic bombs on Japan. The crews at Victoria, along with similar bases scattered through the midwest and south, would be the first to take the new planes overseas and into action.

The B-29 was huge. At nearly 30 feet tall, it was far larger than all previous planes. Designed for long missions, its range was 5600 miles.

(Courtesy of National Museum of the U.S. Air Force)

To pilot this new plane, the military brought veteran pilots back from the European theater, so the base was overrun with rank. As a second lieutenant I spent all my time saluting captains, majors, and colonels. Worse yet, I wasn't a pilot: I was just part of the support group the pilots delighted in deriding as "gravel agitators" or "desk grippers." Still, I had something of an upper hand: I was one of those who briefed the crews before their practice missions and debriefed them on their return.

The Victoria Base

Maybe the spirit on the base was a natural offspring of the War, but there was an unusual closeness among the men at Victoria. The old hands, back from the European theater, felt a special camaraderie that spilled over to everyone. Receptions of various kinds were fairly common, particularly because there was a constant stream of visiting generals anxious to see how the training of the new B-29 crews was progressing. Since Kansas was a dry state, liquor had to be found elsewhere and there was no hesitation about sending planes to Chicago to load up.

At one of those receptions I asked the sergeant-bartender for a bottle of liquor. I was wearing an Army overcoat with double pockets—accessible from the inside as well as the outside. I carefully put the bottle in my pocket, stepped away from the bar, and—CRASH—the bottle fell to the floor with a noise that stopped all the action in the room for a second or two. I had missed the pocket altogether. A few minutes later, when life around me had resumed, I tried again. The sergeant was still agreeable and all went well for a moment and then—another crash. I hurried toward the door and was intercepted by an annoyed general: "Where's that man who was just at the bar?" "I don't know, Sir. I think he went that way." I pointed out the door. The general left in hot pursuit. I tried to make myself invisible.

But the tension on the base was palpable. The veteran pilots distrusted and feared the B-29s. With good reason. The planes had several engine problems that could lead to sudden fires and, all too often, to the crash of the planes. A few times I arrived at the airfield to find a huge crashed plane on fire at the end of the runway. Sometimes the crews escaped. Sometimes they did not. The problems were not entirely resolved before the planes departed for Asia in the spring of 1944.

The pilots' concerns about the B-29s were apparent in the way they swarmed around Sergeant Ashe, who had been a trans-Atlantic Pan Am pilot. When he tried to enlist in the Air Force, Ashe was told he was over age and couldn't be a pilot, so he found himself on an Air Base but never in the air. He was, however, an incredible source of knowledge and information for all the flying officers. Walking by his desk, looking at the rank always crowded around him, you couldn't miss the most frequent question: "What would you do if...?"

At the Oil Well

As the time of departure neared— and no one knew exactly when that would be—the crews became more and more anxious. In dry Kansas, the only bar away from the airfield was in the basement of the local Hays Hotel. Called the "Oil Well," the bar only admitted commissioned officers and their wives. One evening in March, when tension was at its peak, Mary and I were in the bar with a group of pilots and their wives. The small room was crowded and by mid-evening was hazy with cigarette smoke. The men were drinking heavily and, with increasing concern, talking of how they'd never make it to Asia, let alone return from their assigned missions. They spoke longingly of the B-17s and B-24s they had flown in Europe—great planes in which they had total confidence, planes they knew could take a beating from flak and other enemy fire. The B-29, they scoffed, couldn't even manage the enemy-free skies over Kansas. Late in the evening a small group gathered and, with arms around each other, sang "Mairzy doats and dozy doats..." Watching them, you could feel the nostalgic tears just below the surface and sense their fears of what lay ahead.

Departure came soon after that evening in the Oil Well. The secrecy surrounding the take-off of the B-29s vanished the moment the planes were in the air. Our Victoria group joined other groups, some from nearby airfields, creating a pre-dawn roar that woke everyone living within a wide swath of central Kansas. A great air armada on its way to Asia. They flew east and across the Atlantic, a ruse that was supposed to confuse the enemy. Two of our Victoria contingent, caught in the B-29's ever-recurring problems, didn't make it to the east coast. All who did not encounter problems ended up on air bases in India and China, and eventually the Mariana Islands, from which they bombed Japan.

Later, as the War was ending, it became apparent that I was the government's secret weapon.

Why?

No sooner had my orders been cut for a transfer to the European theater than V-E Day was announced.

After another few months I was sent to Utah in preparation for assignment to the Pacific theater. Just as my departure date was set, Japan surrendered.

The cutting of my orders seemed to precipitate surrender.

A war hero? No. But don't tell me I wasn't a secret weapon!

Born in Bronxville, New York, John was educated at Culver Military Academy and Dartmouth College. After the War he worked for three different companies in sales and marketing. Starting as a salesman, he eventually became Vice President of Sales and a member of the board of directors of Imperial Schrade International, manufacturers and importers of cutlery and hunting, fishing, and pocket knives. John and Mary retired to Kendal at Hanover in 1999 without a moment's regret at leaving New York City commuting and the hectic life of southern Connecticut.

ENCRYPTED MESSAGES

~

Charles Latham
U.S. Army

WORLD WAR II BEGAN FOR ME, in more ways than one, on Pearl Harbor Day, December 7, 1941. I was 23 and was doing my first year of teaching history and Latin at Salisbury, a small boarding school for boys, in the northwest corner of Connecticut. I was pretty thoroughly convinced, by what I had heard around home in Indiana and by what I learned in an American Foreign Policy course I had taken at Princeton, that Hitler was not a real danger to the United States, and that Americans should avoid European entanglements. I wasn't militant about it, but in my one year of graduate study at Harvard I thought that President Conant might spend more time speaking to students and less in running down to Washington to urge more aid to the British.

But that Sunday afternoon in 1941 changed the world. Like thousands of other Americans on that day, I realized—just like that—that I had been dead wrong about American foreign policy.

I didn't run down the next morning and enlist, like some of my friends, but taught till June. I did my warlike duty by standing once a week in a high field to watch for the highly unlikely possibility that an enemy plane might fly by on its way to a secret rendezvous. At the instruction of my draft board, I underwent a physical exam in Hartford, where a technician drawing blood broke the needle off in my arm and where the psychological exam consisted entirely of a man who leered at me and asked, "Do you like to go out with girls?" ("Yes" equals "normal.")

Drafted in Indiana in July, I was assigned to the Signal Corps and shipped off to Camp Crowder in the Ozarks of southwestern Missouri, where I got toughened up and learned to like and respect the decent, clean-cut farm boys from nearby states. Then there was a six-day train ride, via Texas, Chicago, and several points between, to Fort Monmouth in New Jersey.

For those six days I shared an upper berth (a tight fit) with a young man named Myrl Leedom from Anderson, Indiana, the only person I ever knew who belonged to the Epworth League. One of the two denizens of the lower berth was a proficient gambler, whose mother ran a pool hall in Richmond, Indiana. He wore octagonal rimless green glasses which made him look as though he knew something you didn't. He chose me as his stakeholder: he never took more than a hundred dollars into a game. I held his surplus winnings, and by the end of the trip I was holding more than two thousand dollars for him in cash—a healthy sum for 1942, and almost twice what I had earned by teaching in the previous year. When we reached New Jersey, he went right to a post office, bought a money order for the whole amount, and mailed it to his mother. The last I heard of him he was serving as an assistant chaplain.

Under Bill Bundy

During my short stay at Fort Monmouth, the Army tried unsuccessfully to make me a typist. Then one day a group of us were shipped to a station in the Virginia countryside near Warrenton. There, life was part rustic and part technical. The barracks were in the woods, a mile or so from the mess hall. Our company commander was Bill Bundy, whom I had known pretty well in graduate school at Harvard—a product of Groton and Yale who did everything by the book. We got up good and early—say 4:30—and he marched us to the mess hall for breakfast. "We'll fall in again at 5:13. Let's synchronize our watches." We operated on Bundy War Time. (After the War was over, Bill served in the CIA and then in the Kennedy and Johnson administrations as Assistant Secretary, first of Defense and then of State.)

After a couple of months at Warrenton, where we divided our time between studying cryptography (secret writing) and cryptanalysis (finding ways to read secret messages) and various kinds of hard physical labor, we shipped to Arlington, outside of Washington, D.C. It was there that I spent most of my Army service. The Arlington base had been a girls' school, but was now a center for signal intelligence—in other words, obtaining information about enemy forces by electronic means like radio and telegraph.

My first job there was as an instructor in the Army correspondence courses in cryptography and cryptanalysis. We were a small group: three enlisted men, two of us lowly privates, and one sergeant; a captain who was active in the work; a couple of civilian secretaries; and a West Point colonel who didn't know the business and spent his days going down to the branch bank to get rolls of coins that he went through looking for rarities. He was head of the board that selected candidates for Officer Candidate School (OCS). On the day before I went before this board, I traded him an 1879 San Francisco silver dollar for a 1900 New Orleans silver dollar. I passed.

As instructors, we corrected students' lesson papers, which came in from all over the country, made up some new lessons, and worked on our own advanced courses. There were two courses in cryptography and four in cryptanalysis, each with ten lessons. In the highest two courses, a lesson could take a couple of months. Solving was a process of trial and error, and when a message finally began to "break" it gave you a real sense of accomplishment. By the time I moved on, I had finished the fifth lesson of the fourth course. The group had a generous table of organization, and when I left I had five stripes (technical sergeant).

All of this was good mental training, but what we were teaching dated back to the First World War. After a year or so, our superiors decided we should be doing something connected to the current War, and we were moved down the hall to where the work was called Radio Traffic Analysis.

Monitoring the Japanese Network

By the time of Pearl Harbor, the Japanese had conquered basically the whole western half of the Pacific Ocean north of Australia and west of

Hawaii. To bring home the products of this vast empire, which they called the Greater East Asia Co-Prosperity Sphere, they created a system of ship convoys which sailed directly from the conquered territories to Japan.

To communicate over the thousands of miles of island-dotted sea, the Japanese set up a radio network that had two characteristics. First, wanting clear transmission over great distances, they made no effort to use low frequencies, which would have made it more difficult for us to intercept. Second, they gave a great deal of information on the outside of their messages—time filed, addressee, source and destination, type of encrypting.

As traffic analysts, our job was to get as much intelligence as possible from these outside features, while other sections worked on the actual "breaking" of the messages. We also tried to identify each circuit, by frequency and call signs and location and army unit, and to make sure that all circuits were assigned for interception. There were intercept stations all around the Pacific, from Australia to Alaska, and the traffic they intercepted was sent to Arlington by radio and teletype and occasionally mail. We had machines, sort of early computers, which sorted these messages in different ways.

My work in this department was to supervise about twenty young women, of varying abilities and amounts of training. Each kept track of certain assigned circuits on which she made a weekly report. All of this I edited and pulled together into a published report.

Pinned to the wall above my desk was a huge Dutch map of the East Indies. From this I learned something of the strategy our troops were carrying out, attacking from east to west, skipping and isolating Japanese posts, and slowly cutting off convoy routes until, with the capture of the Philippines, there was none left except along the coast of China. And you could see another characteristic of the Japanese: their stubbornness in holding onto places that were virtually lost but from which they filed daily reports from dwindling garrisons.

After several months in this new area of work, I went to Fort Monmouth for OCS. I think it was a three-month course. First we had classes as dull, but as necessary, as Mess Management: (True or False: "Pork must be cooked to an even pink throughout" or "Meals should present a pleasing variety in color, texture, and taste"), or as challenging to me as firing a machine gun.

Our last month of training was spent in the scrubby flatlands of eastern New Jersey, acting as the signal company of a division that, with its three regiments, was constantly on the move, and maintaining telephone and radio contact among its four headquarters. The aim was to exhaust us physically and mentally and see how we reacted to the strain. I think most of us came out of it pretty well, with a lot of mutual help and cooperation. My feet simply gave out, and my colleagues arranged for me to be the frequent driver of a two-and-a-half-ton truck with a motorized reel in back, which distributed and picked up endless miles of telephone wire along the roadside ditches. Coordinating the speeds of the truck, the reel, and the man walking along behind with a pulley to guide the wire into the ditch or back onto the reel, was a bit tricky. I have two photographs of our OCS class: at the beginning, cold and thin and not very happy; at the end, in spring sunshine and new uniforms, confident and smiling.

Back in Arlington, it was more of the same work, except that all messages solved elsewhere that dealt with frequencies and call signs were sent to me, and I had a translator to put them into English. With that and other material I put together a short daily report of "net intelligence" that was forwarded to Military Intelligence Headquarters. In late July 1945 I got a bunch of messages setting up new circuits in the northern Ryukyu Islands, between Okinawa, their capital, and Kyushu, the southernmost island of Japan. This seemed to indicate that new garrisons were moving into those islands and that southern Japan would be defended just as stubbornly as other territory had been. This possibility may have been one factor in our decision to attack Hiroshima and Nagasaki a week later.

With the collapse of Japan, we wrote histories of the work we had done, and after a few months of waiting I was free to pursue my chosen profession of "training steel-trap minds" in American youth.

Charles taught in independent schools, mainly at Episcopal Academy in Philadelphia. Retiring in 1982, he worked part-time as an archivist at Indiana Historical Society. He also wrote three books and edited several others. He traveled quite a bit, alone and on fifteen Elderhostels, in southern Europe and the Mideast. After coming to Kendal at Hanover in 1997, he kept busy as president and librarian of the historical society in Thetford. He died in 2010.

A Quaker's War

~

Frank Miles

Frank, second from left, in China, 1948

WORLD WAR II WAS COMING ON IN 1941 when I graduated from high school and entered Oregon State College. My family was Quaker: I did not take ROTC. My father had been in France as a Conscientious Objector during World War I, and we shared the sense that a stand against violence was the way it should be. Taking the pacifist position was not all. I registered for the draft as a Conscientious Objector (CO) and wanted to serve overseas. The draft board suggested I take a training course for overseas service, saying they would delay my induction until the course was completed. I entered such a training course at Guilford College in Greensboro, North Carolina. To get there, I took a train from Portland, Maine, where we lived at that time.

When I was about halfway through the course at Guilford, Congress passed a new law denying any financial support for Conscientious Objectors outside the country. The government also refused to issue passports to COs, fearing they would be bad for troop morale. I was very disappointed, and told my draft board so. Since they had suggested the Guilford training, I was permitted to complete the course. Then I revisited the draft board and was drafted into the United States Army as a Conscientious Objector.

My first assignment was to Smoky Mountain National Park at Gatlinburg, Tennessee, where alternative service was managed by the American Friends Service Committee (AFSC). I cleared trails and did maintenance work in the Park, a lovely place. On the weekends, we were free to hike the Appalachian Trail. It was a beautiful time of the year, with the rhododendron and mountain laurel in full bloom. But there were times when I thought of my friends in the South Pacific, or facing danger somewhere else during the War, while I was here not doing much for the world. After a few more months of this, I'd had enough of trimming trails and scything grass along the roads and asked for a different assignment.

When I was offered a chance to be a medical guinea pig in Philadelphia, I jumped at the opportunity. At that time, the doctors didn't know how infectious hepatitis was acquired and transmitted. The Hospital of the University of Pennsylvania was running experiments to discover how people became infected. Along with 30 other young volunteers, I lived for six months in isolation in a house at the University. We could walk the streets to our hearts' desire, but we were isolated from any contact with other people indoors. Every three months, we were involved in other experiments. For one of these, I was part of a group which used mouthwash that had been previously used by infected patients. None of our group contracted the disease: infection was not passed along orally. Eventually, they discovered that it was spread by contact with fecal material.

My next year of alternative service was spent at a state hospital in Trenton, New Jersey, looking after what they called "the violent wards." Many on the regular staff didn't want to have us COs— "yellow-bellied sons of bitches"—around, and they encouraged the patients to feel the same way. As we walked the corridors, we were sworn at frequently for the first month. When spring came, though, we played softball with the patients and staff, and soon we were just people like everybody else.

For my third and final year of alternate service, I was assigned to the psychiatric wards at Duke University Medical School at Durham,

North Carolina. The Conscientious Objectors there were accepted as part of the staff, and each of us worked with 10 to 15 patients. It was a great place to complete our service. As a bonus, we had regular access to the beautiful music at Duke's famous chapel.

On to China

The War was over for us, and we were relieved from alternative service in mid-1946. Most of us felt we had done our bit for the war effort, but some were still finding it difficult to re-enter normal society. I was one of those. Fortunately, I had maintained contact with my friends at Guilford College. The business manager there had gone to China for the Friends Ambulance Unit of the AFSC and had written suggesting he could line up a job for me in China. This was very satisfying to me: I continued to feel I had done nothing that involved real risk or was comparable to what my friends did in the military service.

Three weeks later, I was on my way to China, traveling by boat for 21 days. I arrived in Shanghai and was assigned to a post up on the Yellow River, a three-day trip by train. This was an area where, during the Chinese-Japanese war, the dikes of the river had been destroyed to stop the Japanese. It didn't stop them, but it did displace about 10 million people from their homes. When I arrived, the United Nations was just finishing rebuilding the dikes: there were about 100,000 men carrying baskets of soil to build them up again, a very optimistic scene.

The AFSC was operating three hospitals in the area, and my first job was as a truck driver. Another fellow and I made many trips up to the coal mines in the north to bring down supplies for heating the hospitals in the winter. On one trip, we became impossibly mired in mud, but we had to stay with the trucks; otherwise, both they and the coal would disappear. Since the only communication was by mail, it was many days before we were rescued. The local peasants from the village took us in, though, and it worked out very well.

I worked for the Friends Ambulance Service in China for four years and then came home ready to get on with my life.

Frank finished his B.A. degree at Haverford, where he met Pat Beatty. They were married in 1951 and had four children. After spending 14 years in the Philadelphia area and earning a Mechanical Engineering Degree from Villanova University, he worked at Firestone Tire for 20 years, 12 of them overseas and the last years in Canada. After retirement, he became a staff member for the Canadian Quakers. Later, he and Pat spent 10 years at Kasco, British Columbia, and then joined their daughter's family in Piermont, New Hampshire. They came to Kendal at Hanover in 2002, where Pat died in 2003.

Matters of Destiny

~

Avery D. Post
U.S. Navy

M Y REFLECTIONS ON WORLD WAR II take me back to the 1920s. Like others born in the twenties, I was a post-World War I child. My father had been a First Lieutenant in the Army and had served in France. I was very proud of him. His Army trunk had been stored in the attic and I loved going up there to open it, to admire his uniforms and try on his helmet. When he marched on Armistice Days on Chelsea Parade in Norwich, Connecticut, I was moved to see how erect and serious he was as he marched, his eyes front and his chin trembling.

In Post family lore there were stories of family members in the Revolutionary War, the War of 1812, the Civil War, and the Spanish-American War. I had a boyhood pride in those stories. As a child in New England, I was bred to loyalty to what had happened in our country's history and to the expectation that someday it might be my turn to go loyally to war.

Happy childhood years during the 1920s came to an end with the great economic depression, and—for our family, an experience to me as harsh as war—a break in the family that resulted in divorce. My two brothers and I experienced severe dislocation and emotional distress, yet were lovingly supported by each of our parents, who fortunately remained in good communication.

From the early to mid-1930s, with a boy's awareness, I watched a war—a second war—begin to develop in Europe. My orientation to war continued to carry images of my father's dedicated service, and I remember how I loyally joined my father in Armistice Day parades—he with a veteran's cap, I in a Boy Scout uniform.

The changes of those years took us to new homes, new neighborhoods, and new friendships, as well as a new church. The members of that church, and particularly two of its pastors, made a major impact on my life. It was there that a vocational commitment began to take shape.

From 1938 to 1942 I was a student at the Norwich Free Academy. War awareness grew year by year. Like almost everyone, I remember exactly where I was sitting when I heard about the bombing of Pearl Harbor on December 7, 1941. Seniors began to enlist, deferring their college education.

I registered for the draft and left for Middlebury College in September 1942. It was clearly a wartime campus, with students and faculty members leaving regularly for military service. Life sobered in the college community that year as the news of the deaths of recent graduates reached the campus. My draft board in Norwich kept pressing me. Ultimately I received a deferment until May 1943.

October 6, 1942, was the most signal of days in my young life. On that day I met Margaret (Peg) Rowland, a freshman from Teaneck, New Jersey. First a delightful date, then a serious date, and then falling in love, the relationship had meanings for both of us far beyond our imaginings. So it was for many couples in those wartime years.

Peg, too, was a post-World War I child. Her father, a Presbyterian minister, had been a chaplain during the first war. As with my father, Chaplain Rowland regarded his commitment to the war effort as a service to the nation. In fact, at the age of 49, he enlisted again in World War II and had a long and distinguished service as a chaplain in this country and abroad. Peg's father, a thoughtful, scholarly minister, became, during the War and over time, the major and supportive guide in my choice of vocation.

The completion of my freshman year at Middlebury College was followed by a memorable interview in the recruiting center in Hartford, Connecticut, where the Army representative handed my papers to the Navy representative and I found myself in the U.S. Navy, soon bound for basic training at Camp Sampson and later to the Signalman School at the University of Chicago. Then, proud of my new rank as Signalman, Third Class, I was assigned—in fact by counting off one-two, one-two—to the Atlantic theater rather than the Pacific, for armed guard services on merchant ships bound for Russia with military matériel. Ready to sail, Peg and I had a tearful goodbye at the Middlebury, Vermont, railroad station. We were part of those anxious years for lovers, mothers and fathers, brothers (my older brother was in the Army), and sisters. Moreover, many of us as young people were carrying the grief of losing friends in the War.

Orders for V-12

I was sitting on a sea bag in the Brooklyn Navy Yard, waiting to board a ship leaving the next day, when I was startled to hear the following announcement over the loud public address system: "Will Third Class Signalman Post report to the Education Officer?" I went off to find the Education Office, where the officer handed me orders to report in six weeks to the V-12 unit at Ohio Wesleyan University for officer training and a recently announced pre-chaplaincy program.

I recall experiencing in that moment a storm of emotion, even breathlessness, as I made my way back to my sea bag. First, there was gratitude for good news, at so many levels. Second, release from tension, for I had been more apprehensive than I openly admitted about the journey into the north Atlantic, where, at that time, scores of merchant ships were being sunk. Then, suddenly, there was the unexpected loss of an assignment, a duty, work for which I had trained, and about which I felt confident. After six weeks of guard duty and liberty, I went off to the V-12 unit at Ohio Wesleyan University in Delaware, Ohio, a long way from the sea.

V-12 was, of course, very much part of the Navy, with Naval Education, "falling out" for drills and exercise, saluting petty and commissioned officers, laundering uniforms, and standing inspection. But available also was a full campus life, the declaration of a major (mine combined literature and religion), participation in sports (shot put and discus) and organizations, life along Main Street and in the neighborhoods of an attractive town, and the freedom to welcome Peg for occasional visits. For several months I even became the pastor of a congregation in the Ohio countryside.

So this is my story of an incredibly privileged time during World War II, for which I will always be grateful. If there is any unease as I recall my story alongside others, I am nonetheless grateful for a whole world of experiences and friendships. But above all, there were the unexpected wartime gifts: time and occasions for nurturing a lifetime partnership with Peg, a first-rate liberal arts education, and the experience of testing and living into a vocation as a Christian minister.

The V-12 pre-chaplaincy program at first included extended education and a degree at a theological seminary, leading to a commission as a naval officer. Following V-E Day and V-J Day, the program was terminated and I was formally separated from the Navy at Lido Beach on Long Island in November 1945. In the meantime Peg had graduated from Middlebury College and begun work in Boston.

On January 1, 1946, deferring the award of a B.A. degree until June, I entered Yale University Divinity School with benefits from the GI Bill of Rights, another incredible privilege. On June 8, 1946, Peg and I were married in the Village Congregational Church in Wellesley, Massachusetts. After a couple of weeks along Lake Champlain in her family's cottage in Keeseville, New York, we moved to Eden, Vermont, where we served in a summer pastorate in Eden Mills and Eden Corners before returning to Yale for further study.

Peg and Avery moved to Kendal at Hanover from Norwich, Vermont, in May 2002. They have four daughters and eleven grandchildren. Over the years they worked side by side in pastorates in Woodmont and Clinton, Connecticut; in Columbus, Ohio; and in Norwich, Garden City, and Scarsdale, New York. From 1969 to 1977, Avery was Minister and President of the Massachusetts Conference of the United Church of Christ and Peg taught at the Kingsley School in Boston. From 1977 to 1989, Avery served as National President of the United Church of Christ. Peg died in 2010.

Our Floating Runway

Benjamin Sanderson
U.S. Navy

I HAD ALWAYS DREAMED of one day piloting an airplane. I grew up hearing heroic stories of my uncle Corry, a decorated WW I Navy flyer, who, after being thrown from his biplane in a crash, was killed trying to rescue his co-pilot from the burning wreckage. While still in high school, during the first days of WW II, I saved enough money for 20 hours of flight training and took my first lessons at a municipal airport near Buffalo, New York. I sat behind an instructor in a Piper Cub two-seater. I managed to take additional flying lessons while I was at Hobart College.

Because I had acquired enough credits to graduate halfway through my senior year (December 1942), the U.S. government decided my chemical engineering skills were essential to the war effort and I found myself involved in the manufacture of powerful explosives. After a brief and unsatisfying stint starting up a new plant for Holston Ordnance, I requested a change to a 1A rating from the draft board and enlisted in Navy flight school.

In February 1944 I reported for duty in New York City and was promptly put on a train with six other inductees. We had no idea where we were going. One of us was given an envelope, to open on the train, containing our orders and our destination: Philadelphia. We completed several months of aeronautical studies in Philly and flight prep in Chapel Hill, as well as physical conditioning meant to whip our bodies into shape; we were then designated as AFT (Approved for Flight Training). This was followed by six months of primary training at Bunker Hill, Indiana, to prepare us for actual flight training in a Stearman biplane. Among our training group was a rather well-known recruit: baseball star Ted Williams, who later became a Marine pilot.

I began the long journey toward becoming a fighter pilot in a most forgiving aircraft, the Stearman biplane. After learning basic maneuvers, I gradually progressed to more complex maneuvers in increasingly powerful and less forgiving aircraft such as the F6F Hellcat and the F8F Bearcat. Along the way, up to one-third of the aviation cadets washed out of the program or were sent back for additional training. After making the cut at each step, I opted to become a fighter pilot and trained at various airfields across the country, eventually earning my wings and my commission in 1944.

A Dangerous Endeavor

Learning to pilot a Navy fighter plane off an aircraft carrier is a dangerous endeavor—almost as dangerous as the combat missions themselves. Things could, and sometimes did, go wrong in a hurry. Part of the challenge was to keep from killing yourself long enough to acquire the very skills necessary to keep from getting killed. Even experienced pilots lost their lives on routine training missions. One week before I joined my squadron, the skipper and the exec (both expert flyers) were killed instantly in a midair collision while practicing gunnery runs over the end of Long Island.

As most people appreciate, taking off from an aircraft carrier is not at all like taking off from a runway. You are flung off the deck by twin steam-driven catapults designed to launch multiple aircraft in quick succession. I once had the misfortune to be assigned a bunk directly under one of these catapults, which announced every launch with a tremendous roar.

Navigation was one of the essential flying skills you had to master in the days before GPS. A typical carrier mission required flying over a featureless ocean searching for enemy aircraft, while at the same time charting compass heading, time, and wind drift on a small pull-out navigation table in the cockpit. Most importantly, you had to keep track of a floating runway that was sailing away from your starting location at 15-20 knots the whole time you were aloft. Wind drift had to be estimated by looking at ocean whitecaps and waves. So it was with some relief that you came back into visual contact with the carrier when returning from a mission, knowing that you had done your navigation calculation correctly. That relief was followed, however, by a white-knuckle landing on a runway heaving in the ocean swells. Carrier landings necessitated dragging a hook from your plane's tail over a cable that brought your aircraft to a rather abrupt but most welcome stop. If the landing wasn't perfect, you could overshoot or bounce over the cable, so several backup cables were positioned across the carrier deck to decrease the chances that you'd miss the cables completely and end up in the drink.

Landing was a critical maneuver that we practiced often. On a carrier there was little margin for error, and it was essential to approach at the proper altitude. Flying past the carrier in preparation for landing, you watched an LSO (flagman), who would signal if you were too high or too low. If you were extremely low, he signaled to pull up and abort the landing. The engines on our fighter planes toward the end of the War were so powerful that the torque on the propeller generated by accelerating too fast could literally flip the plane over. In horror, I once witnessed such a scenario at Guantanamo Bay, when seven of us were being qualified for carrier landings in the F8F. The test required a pilot to execute five simulated landings. I had completed my qualification and was standing on the ground with the LSO who was signaling the passing aircraft. As I watched, he signaled to a pilot in our squadron to abort his landing. The pilot gassed the engine too quickly, flipped upside down, and crashed directly into the ground 50 yards from us. I ran to the flaming crash site, but there was no way the pilot could survive.

The crash was a stark reminder of the slim tolerances of our planes when flying at low altitude.

A Missing Wing Tip

Our fighter planes represented the cutting edge of technology from the U.S. aerospace industry—and we found ourselves testing the limits of that technology.

The closest I ever came to crashing was while practicing high-speed rolling maneuvers. Following a high-speed dive bomb maneuver, I heard a loud bang and suddenly found myself in a steep dive. The force of pulling out at that speed would likely have ripped off the wings, so I used the "dive recovery flap," which was designed to increase drag, reduce speed, and allow the pilot to pull up in one piece. As I pulled out of the dive, my gauge was still showing a dangerous number of Gs and I was alarmed to see that one of my wing tips was missing. This was an extremely dangerous situation—worse, in fact, than if both wing tips had been ripped off, because the wings were now unbalanced, making the plane difficult to control. I had known of other pilots in the same situation who had crashed, unable to fly the plane with a missing wing tip.

My first reaction was to reach up to feel for the rip-cord on my parachute as I contemplated bailing out. In the F8F there was no ejector seat; bailing out required a pilot to release his canopy, climb out of his seat, and jump from the plane. This was not a maneuver I was anxious to try, and I was relieved to find that I was able to control the plane even if just barely. I radioed the base about my predicament and, after making several test passes at altitude, determined that I had enough control to land.

This event, combined with some fatal crashes, prompted Grumman to modify its design to include explosive charges in the wing tips, so that if one tip was lost a charge would automatically blow off the other, eliminating the deadly wing imbalance and improving the pilot's chance of recovery.

My only other close call, though somewhat less dramatic, was an example of how important it was to stay calm and make good decisions in tense situations. We were practicing bombing runs off Cape Cod, dropping "dummy" bombs on a little island appropriately called No Man's Land. While looking for the puff of the dummy bombs to see how close I had come to the target, I was alarmed to check my instrument panel and see that my oil pressure had dropped to zero. I climbed to altitude, but the oil gauge still read zero. This could be either an instrument failure or a prelude to an imminent engine failure. I radioed the base and quickly set course for the municipal airport on Martha's Vineyard 10 miles away: better to be embarrassed by a false alarm than have my engine seize up. My worst fears were confirmed as I landed and discovered the brakes on my landing gear were covered with oil streaming from a blown gasket. Had I tried to make it back to the original landing spot, I most likely would have had to ditch the plane.

After V-E Day, I was assigned to a carrier in the Mediterranean. After all my training, I never had to apply these skills in active combat.

I stayed in the Navy reserves after my tour was completed, and, while studying for a Ph.D. at Ohio State, I continued flying in a reserve squadron on weekends. I was able to combine delivering planes to the east coast with visits to a Yale nursing instructor, Betsy Barber, whom I was then courting. As it turns out, my most successful missions were flown during this time; we were married in 1952.

After completing his Ph.D., Sandy worked as a research chemist and in management at NL Industries. He was also an adjunct professor at Rutgers, specializing in spectroscopy, statistics, computer science, and x-ray diffraction. After retirement, he taught computer science and coached the chess and tennis teams at Christian Brothers Academy. The family spent their summers hiking and camping. In 1996 they moved to Kendal at Hanover, where Sandy served on many committees, including Residents Council. Diagnosed with Parkinson's in 1993, Sandy now lives in the Health Center, but he still participates in many Kendal activities. He and Betsy have four children and seven grandchildren.

A CONSCIENTIOUS OBJECTOR'S TALE

~

Robert Sokol

Robert as a "lightkeeper" in 1946

IT WAS A DECEMBER SUNDAY. I was attending a reunion of kids from a summer camp, where I was trying to show off my skill at bowling. The target of my blowhards was a tall, almost skinny 12-year-old girl who—unbeknownst to both of us—would be my wife 10 years later.

In the midst of my song and dance, somebody shouted, *The Japanese attacked Pearl Harbor!*

Everything in the bowling alley stopped. After moments of staring at each other, we asked, almost as an ensemble: *Where's Pearl Harbor?*

Probably because most of the adults there were cosmopolitan New Yorkers, nobody could answer the question until one faint voice timidly ventured, *Hawaii.*

Later that afternoon, we understood that this meant the United States was going to declare war on Japan—as President Roosevelt did, the next day.

At 14, and freshly pleased with myself that I had been admitted to what I considered to be the best high school in the world—Stuyvesant, in New York city—a comma was inserted into my life. From that day on there was constant discussion at home, in school, on the radio, and in the cover pages over the sports section of *The New York Times*. Yes, I had heard something about a conscription law, but that I would be drafted never dawned on me. I stayed busy and, with a modicum of success, tried school politicking, since Stuyvesant's preëminent chess and fencing teams begged me not to join.

Our family essentially escaped the travails of the Great Depression, but as a longtime syndicalist/socialist and opponent of capitalist and imperialist wars, my father was in constant dialogue with people of diverse political persuasions. On every May 1st during the 1930s we marched down Sixth and Seventh Avenues to Union Square in Manhattan, waving placards denouncing Hitler, Mussolini, Emperor Hirohito, and then Stalin and the Communist Party.

Concomitant to these activities, and because of my father's *Weltanschauung*, my brother and I attended a unit of the The Modern Sunday School on Sunday mornings. It is difficult to recall the specific information we were exposed to and the projects we worked on, but one in particular made an impression on me: that murder, killing, and wars were all—and equally—bad.

The Draft

During my senior year in high school I registered with Selective Service, as all 18-year-old men were required to do. This turned out to be a conflictful year for me.

Very prominent in my thinking was the political and moral argument that the Nazis had to be defeated to stop the horrid elimination of Jews, socialists, homosexuals, Romanies, and political dissenters in Europe. It held moral force for me.

At the same time, my earlier training in The Modern Sunday School and the teachings at home convinced me that all wars had to be abolished and mass killing stopped. Toward that end, bearing personal witness against wars was imperative.

With considerable ambivalence, I chose the latter path.

When initially registering with a local Selective Service Board, it was necessary to complete a questionnaire that included a place to sign the following statement:

> By reason of religious training and belief I am con-
> scientiously opposed to war in any form and for this
> reason request that the local board furnish me a spe-
> cial form for Conscientious Objectors, which I am to
> complete and return to the local board.

Also required were the reasons for the registrant's objections, organizational memberships, references, and an affidavit supporting his
claim. One could also ask for exemption from combatant training and
service, or for complete exemption from all military activities and assignment to *work of national importance under civilian direction.*

The local board declined my request for a Conscientious Objector
classification, forwarding instead the one for I-A: ready for induction. I
appealed the decision to the New York Appeal Board, requesting a IV-E
classification that would lead to my assignment to a Civilian Public Service camp to do work of national importance under civilian direction.
This second appeal also failed, leaving one last appeal. From that time
on, the Department of Justice assumed jurisdiction of my case, with
the FBI doing a widespread investigation of my background, family,
friends, and their politics and organizational memberships. I appeared
before a federal judge who, as the Hearing Officer, would make a recommendation to the Presidential Appeal Board that finally granted my
request for IV-E classification. I later heard that this Board was composed entirely of military officers, leading to the conjecture that they
believed the Army and Navy would do better without Conscientious
Objectors of my sort. However, the armed forces did welcome—and
have good evaluations of—approximately 25,000 COs who served in
noncombatant roles, usually medical units, during the War years.

In comparison, from 1941 to 1947, somewhat over 12,000 COs
served in about 150 Civilian Public Service (CPS) work camps across
the country. The large majority of camps were administered by the
Mennonites, Brethren, and Friends, and the remainder by the government under civilian control. Records show there were about 4,700
Mennonites, 1,400 Brethren, and 1,000 Friends in those camps, together with COs from many other denominations.

On to Civilian Public Service

I had never crossed the Hudson River alone, but on August 3, 1945, there I was, wet behind the ears, riding on a stump-nose ferry, leaving Manhattan, my only home ever. At the Hoboken Lackawanna Railroad Terminal, I took a steam-locomotive train to Elmira, New York, on my way to the CPS camp in nearby Big Flats.

After being instructed on rules and procedures at the camp, I was soon out in acres of beds planted with millions of conifer seedlings that required careful plucking of invasive weeds.

A few days later came the announcement that an atomic bomb had been dropped on Hiroshima, Japan. Weeding stopped. We listened to two fellow COs explain the physics and chemistry of an atomic explosion and what an atomic bomb mostly likely did to the fabric and people of that city. This was an intellectual response to a human catastrophe. My dorm-mates included a man who ran for Vice President of the United States; a boogie-woogie-piano-playing Jehovah's Witness from Maine; the Jewish son of a college chaplain; and a Japanese-American Friend. Being the only atheist in the place, I sometimes had to mediate between men with different visions of God and Grace.

As COs in CPS, we received no pay for the work we did, except for $2.50 provided each month by the American Friends Service Committee. In our off-duty time we volunteered in Elmira, where I worked as a hospital orderly.

"Yellow Bellies"

When winter arrived, we stopped weeding and shifted to forestry work in the hills around the city of Corning, New York. It was during these trips that I had my first encounter with hostility from local residents, who shouted "Yellow bellies!" "Cowards!" "Draft dodgers!" and at times threw things like eggs and fruit at us. This experience, together with the dull and wearying daily work, prompted me to seek transfer to another camp.

I tried to volunteer for the yellow-jaundice and lifeboat-starvation experiments, but my father refused to sign the release papers for me (I was 19 and still under age). Instead, I was accepted by the U.S. Coast & Geodetic Survey and assigned to its traveling camp #98, then located in the small ranch town of Wilcox, Arizona.

Reporting to Wilcox, my Jehovah's Witness friend and I were assigned our tent and instructed in how things were done with the triangulation survey equipment, trucks, and jeeps. Along with the other 30 members stationed with the unit, we had to organize our own mess tent and elect a rotating cook and a treasurer who coordinated our monthly government $60, per diem payments, and insurance.

The men were organized into three groups. As a "builder" of the "benchmarked" sites for surveying I slept under the stars a few nights in the legendary Boothill Graveyard in Tombstone amidst the ghosts of the Clanton brothers and Wyatt Earp. However, most of my time was spent on the observation party that aimed a theodolite at a series of lights positioned strategically at high and low points in the valleys, desert, rangeland, and mountains. Most viewings started at dusk. The observations ranged from the 4,000-foot valley flats to almost 11,000 feet for Mt. Graham and the dramatic range topped by Superstition Mountain. Government and private sources still depend on our data for mapping and boundary determination.

"NO COLORED"

Later, while billeted in Mesa, a group of us had an opportunity to participate in a sit-in demonstration in Phoenix. On our own time, we accompanied a group of local black men to a Walgreen drugstore that had a NO COLORED lunch counter. A week earlier, this group had been refused service and sternly warned not to ever come back. With some trepidation they tried another technique that was eventually to become the basic passive-resistance tool used by CORE (Committee on Racial Equality): we organized ourselves into a line consisting alternately of white, black, white, black, etc., and sought to be served at the counter. When the lead white was served, the pattern was established; it was reinforced when the first and subsequent blacks were refused service. Except for the first white, no white accepted service, claiming there were other people ahead of them. Eventually all counter seats were occupied by our group, essentially ending counter business.

In a few hours, the store manager came over and instructed the counter staff to start service for everyone. In later weeks, lunch-counter integration was in full operation. Not long afterward, the lunch counter at the Newberry 5-and-10-cent store was similarly integrated.

In retrospect, it was one of the first—if not *the* first—sit-in "direct-action" demonstrations in the south, even though it had taken place in the southwest. The outcome was particularly gratifying because direct action and passive resistance echoed the mantra invoked by Mahatma Gandhi.

In August 1946, a year after the end of the War, many COs across the country who had been drafted in 1942–44 were still in camps, not having been discharged in line with the pace of discharge officially decreed by the President. This precipitated work stoppages at CPS camps around the country. Soon afterward, old-timer COs started to be discharged and the work stoppages were discontinued, but some so-called "ringleaders" were arrested by the FBI and convicted or dishonorably discharged. The two-day work stoppage at my camp had ended when release papers arrived for two of the long-termers in the unit.

When our Arizona USC&G Survey unit was closed down, I was reassigned to the CPS camp at Gatlinburg, Tennessee, to help in the maintenance of Smoky Mountain National Park. I was not allowed to take my accumulated furlough time but was told to report immediately; nevertheless, rather than disembarking from the train at Knoxville, I continued on to New York City for home cooking and visiting with family and friends. This behavior was chancy: technically I was Absent Without Leave—AWOL—and that was punishable with jail time. After a week's furlough, I reported to the Gatlinburg camp; my legitimate leave time was honored and I was not punished.

In addition to fighting forest fires and bumping into some colorful bourbon whiskey stills, our jobs were generally to help in servicing paths and roads throughout the National Park. I became the "weather man," driving every day to sites all over this beautiful park collecting meteorological data: cloud formations and temperature, rain, wind, and barometric measurements. Thinking back to those months, I recall that Gatlinburg was an unfriendly place for COs. Upon arriving by train or bus we had to take a taxi to camp, bypassing the danger of hitchhiking. We rarely ventured into town: several COs had been assaulted there. When the camp arranged for some local men to play basketball with us, the game had to be cancelled midway because we were literally manhandled. Despite our repeated attempts, none of them would speak to us, probably because some of them were veterans with understandable animosities toward Conscientious Objectors. Apart from those occasions, the dazzling fall foliage of the Smoky Mountains tempered my mood.

On December 10, 1946, I was discharged and given a train ticket to New York City. Shortly thereafter I was a college freshman—and a Conscientious Objector veteran, but of course ineligible for the GI Bill of Rights!

Postscript

In 1950 I was recalled for induction during the Korean War. My beliefs about war had not changed, but the Selective Service Law had. To gain the IV-E classification, a CO had to demonstrate his convictions by virtue of *religious training and belief* and *with a belief in a Supreme Being.* This was the phrasing used in the law for World War II with the significant addition of a belief in a Supreme Being. Since my convictions were not based on a belief in a Supreme Being, I lost all my appeals. Ordered for induction, I refused to step across the white line that signified the end of one's civilian life and the beginning of life as a member of the armed forces. The Army officer in charge of the induction sympathetically urged me to reconsider my refusal, saying my case would be reported to the Justice Department. I wasn't happy about this, having recently married and started graduate school, but hopeful that the American Civil Liberties Union and the War Resisters League would be successful in arguing in the courts that the addition of the phrase *a belief in a Supreme Being* constituted a definition of religion that they deemed unconstitutional.

With the possibility of a jail term looming, two years later I received notification that since I was now 26 years old I had been reclassified as too old for induction.

Manhattan born and bred, starting on May 26, 1925, when the War came Robert enrolled as a Conscientious Objector in 1945. His career path after his discharge from CO service included Long Island University, Princeton, and a Ph.D. degree from Columbia in 1961. He was appointed a research assistant at Harvard 1953 to 1956, taught at Boston and Tufts Universities from 1955 to 1961, and then was appointed Assistant Professor of Psychiatry and Sociology at Dartmouth. He acquired emeritus status as professor upon his 1996 retirement. He and his wife Hilda moved from their Hanover home of 49 years to Kendal at Hanover in 2009.

SECURITY: NAVY STYLE

Robert Stragnell
U.S. Navy

Y EXPERIENCES AS A MEMBER OF THE MILITARY SERVICE during World War II were very brief and somewhat unusual. I was raised in a family of many doctors. Both of my grandfathers, my father and his sister, and my mother's brother were all physicians. As a consequence, I was driven to this profession and in my senior speech at the conclusion of high school I told of my expectation of pursuing a medical career.

I entered the freshman class of the University of Virginia in September of 1941, well aware of the conflict in Europe but with little awareness that this would directly affect my future plans. The suddenness of Pearl Harbor realigned the atmosphere in tranquil Charlottesville. Some voluntary programs of preparedness with first-aid instruction resulted in a *New York Times* Sunday rotogravure photograph of me applying a sling to a fellow student.

I became a registrant, number 140 in a pool of 241, at my local draft board, and in the late summer of 1942 I voluntarily enlisted in the V-1 Navy program in order to permit my continued full-time no-vacations pre-medical education. I applied to several medical schools and in January 1943 was accepted at the medical schools of both the University of Virginia and the College of Physicians and Surgeons of Columbia University.

Upon receipt of my acceptance to medical school, I was advised by the University to apply for a commission as an Ensign. This Navy probationary commission category allowed V-1 reservists to remain on inactive status until their start in medical school. This seemed like a good idea, so I applied in late February or early March 1943. Shortly thereafter, the Navy announced that on July 1, 1943, members in the V-1 program would be either transferred to active duty as Apprentice Seamen in V-12 to continue their education or be returned to the supervision of their local draft boards.

I was surprised that by July first I had had no word regarding my probationary commission. Expecting that this would arrive shortly, I accepted the transfer in status. I donned my uniform with its 13-button broad front pants and became familiar with close-order drill, vigorous physical exercises, and military regulations, and continued my required premedical classes.

A Letter from BUPERS

An even greater surprise was in store for me. On August 5, 1943, a letter came from BUPERS—acronym for United States Navy's Bureau of Naval Personnel—saying that I did not meet the criteria for permanent appointment as a naval reserve officer! No reason was given, and neither the University nor I were able to obtain any explanation for this decision.

Obviously this put a major crimp in my long-standing plans and desire to go to medical school. Needless to say, I experienced more than a little emotional turmoil. There was apparently nothing I could do except continue my studies and await my transfer to some boot camp, pending further assignment.

Some time during the following week, on my way through the duty office of our dormitory, I caught sight of a recently posted letter from the Bureau of Naval Personnel dated July 27, 1943. This letter stated that anyone who had been accepted to medical school prior to July 1,

1943, who was found not to be eligible for the Navy program, was eligible for discharge. With this in hand, I requested an interview with Captain E. M. Williams, Commander of our V-12 Naval Unit.

"Why do you need to see the captain?" asked the yeoman at the office.

"I want to apply for a discharge," I answered.

The yeoman could not comprehend this (I wasn't dressed like Corporal Klinger in MASH). When I showed him the two letters, he shook his head in disbelief and sent me in to Captain Williams' office. In less than a week Captain Williams authorized that my request for discharge be forwarded through channels. The bureaucratic process then took off. On September 11 the initial discharge approval was given but my actual separation was delayed for a variety of reviews until October 11.

Back to School

For the remainder of the War, I was a civilian student under the jurisdiction of my local draft board. I was given a series of deferments, and after completing my premedical work at Virginia matriculated at Columbia University College of Physicians and Surgeons. Medical-student life during this period was identical to that prior to the War, save that there was no interruption between semesters or class years. The program was heavily demanding and I had little spare time; still, I found time to participate in extracurricular physical activities (basketball) and intellectual challenges (bridge) as well as working part time for the medical-school bookstore.

At the start of my junior year in June of 1945 I began working every other night in *The New York Times* medical department as one of the "night emergency physicians." Sleeping quarters, access to the cafeteria, and a small stipend were provided by the newspaper; in return, I examined new male employees and was on emergency call every other night. Each day I rode the subway back and forth from 168th Street to Times Square. Fortunately this was an express and my direction of travel was opposite to that of the heavy traffic, so I usually had a seat both ways.

With the cessation of hostilities in August of 1945, medical schools throughout the country had to work out a return to their pre-War class scheduling. At Columbia this was accomplished by extending our senior year by six months, resulting in our graduation occurring in June of 1947 rather than December of 1946.

Throughout this period I obtained no explanation for the Navy's refusal to educate me as a physician. It was not until 1999 that, under the Freedom of Information Act, some very heavily redacted documents were obtained. My case was settled at the recommendation of W. L. Moise of the Bureau of Naval Personnel, Office of Naval Officer Procurement in Richmond, Virginia. On July 15, 1943, Moise wrote:

> In view of the detailed investigation report of the applicant's father's connection with the enemies of this country it is the opinion of this Director that on the assumption of giving the Navy the benefit of the doubt in any such case the application in question should be rejected.

I had suspected that the reason for the Navy's action lay in their concern that my father might be a pro-German sympathizer: he was employed as the Executive Vice President and Director of Medical Research of a pharmaceutical company of German origin that had been seized by the Alien Properties Custodian. Even though my father was the *only* member of the senior management not relieved of his position, the Navy exercised a caution in my case.

Bob was born and raised in the suburbs of New York City. After medical school he moved to California, where he married Libby Toll, a third-generation native Californian. Following postgraduate training in Internal Medicine at the UCLA West Los Angeles VA Hospital, he was appointed a Trainee of the National Heart Institute, followed by appointments at the USC School of Medicine. After the Korean conflict he served two years in the Army as a Medical Officer at Fort Leonard Wood, Missouri, and was discharged as a Captain. With three children and no job, he started as an internist and cardiologist in Arcadia, California. In 1986 he and Libby moved to Prescott, Arizona. They lived there until coming to Kendal at Hanover in 2004.

Wartime in Europe and South America

The Early War

~

Rachel Lowe Aubrey

I<small>T WAS A BEAUTIFUL</small> S<small>EPTEMBER MORNING IN</small> 1939. Living in England, we were vacationing in Toller Porcorum, a little village in Dorset. My sister, Hanna, and I had gone for a morning stroll and then secretly played with the house cats: Mother, phobic about cats, might become ill just hearing the word.

We returned to the old farmhouse, the smell of Sunday's roasting mutton wafting out. Mother and Father were already at the house radio, ready for the eleven o'clock news.

After the familiar chimes of Big Ben, the BBC announcer intoned: "This is London." Then Prime Minister Neville Chamberlain solemnly read his declaration of war with Germany.

I looked around; Father's face was ashen, Mother was crying, Hanna seemed confused. Fighting back tears, I knew I must be strong. On Monday morning I slipped out to the store and bought two forbidden items, a pale pink lipstick and some clear nail polish. I would wear both for many years, like an invisible shield. I was almost eighteen.

My father, Adolph Lowe, again had reason to worry. If Germany were to invade England, as was widely feared, he and his family would be deported back to Germany and probably killed.

Frankfurt

Earlier, in 1933, when my father was a tenured professor of economics at Frankfurt University, and a known liberal, he had been placed on Hitler's first list of academics to be "dismissed as dangerous to the Third Reich." Close friends—Paul Tillich, the theologian, and Karl Mannheim, the sociologist—were on the same list.

Immediately after that list was drawn up, my father, realizing that our Frankfurt apartment was being watched, had us sleep in a hotel. A few nights later, Hanna and I were told we were going on vacation. We crept through the dark streets to the station and found an empty compartment on the train. There was a tense moment when the conductor came, the morning paper in his back pocket. Had he already read that all Jewish passports would be recalled today? He looked us over a long time, shook his head, punched the tickets, and then quietly closed the door.

Geneva

We got off in Geneva, each of us with one small suitcase. Since we could not afford a hotel, Mother, Hanna, and I were taken in by the Salvation Army, to stay in their Home for Troubled Girls, while Father left to look for a job, anywhere in Europe. The officers were very caring; at night I heard them pray for us. Hanna and I were enrolled in a strict French school, where relapsing even briefly into German would bring the slap of a ruler. After a few months, our French became quite good and we could keep up in class.

Then Father phoned from England: "Stop speaking French, learn English, we are moving to Manchester," where he had just found a low-level academic job. Mother hired a teacher; I hated the sound of English vowels and tried to boycott the lessons, to no avail.

We had been in Geneva eight months; I was eleven, Hanna was eight.

Manchester

We arrived in Manchester on Christmas Day 1933, soon to be enrolled in a Girls' Day School. Speaking either German or French was forbidden; even at home we now spoke only English, once our parents' secret language. Wearing the school uniform helped us fit in, but for Mother and Father adapting to English life was more difficult. In 1938 they managed to bring out Father's elderly parents, to live with us. Some food items—sugar, meat, and butter—were already rationed. We were urged to "dig for victory" and to eat parsnips from the garden. The grandparents would not touch margarine, so we gave them all our butter rations. My first after-school job was as taste-tester for a large margarine company; most of the samples tasted rancid. Grandmother, a gourmet cook, once burned our entire meat ration, straining an already difficult relationship with Mother.

The political situation was tense. Chamberlain's appeasement policy had failed to create "Peace in our time." At night there were frequent air-raid alarms, during which we were supposed to put on our gas masks and go to the designated shelter. My grandparents hated the shelter and would not wear their masks, clinging to the supposed safety of our apartment. I also hated my mask, proclaiming I would rather die of mustard gas than slowly choke to death. With everyone in the shelter, I would slip back under the stairs and listen to short-wave radio. Once I tuned in Furtwängler, conducting Beethoven's Fifth, in Berlin.

The high-school years in Manchester were happy. I spent a lot of time with Otto, my best friend, whose family had also managed to leave Germany. Though in different schools, we often did homework together, cooked up chemistry experiments, and went on hikes. We also made music, Otto on our house organ, I on my recorder. In 1937 both of us graduated from high school; too young for college, I spent a year volunteering in a Manchester slum and taking singing lessons.

London

In September 1938 I started on a three-year bachelor's degree at Kings College, London, living with a family friend. During the War years female refugees were allowed in only two professions where there were shortages: nursing and home economics. I took a lot of science, though I really wanted to study psychology. Political meetings, concerts, and a course at the London School of Economics gave me a real sense of independence, but when war was declared the College was evacuated to Cardiff, considered safer than London.

Cardiff

We were billeted with Welsh families and were to attend classes at Cardiff University. I met Pamela, my red-haired, freckled, and very Scottish roommate, at the London bus stop. She dreaded her first time away from home and quickly cast me in the role of older sister. I envied her mathematical skills, having twice flunked my math exam. Soon we were arranging our room to allow each some privacy, and then we began to explore the neighborhood.

We would have little time for cultural activities: the academic program was very demanding. After classes and labs I spent many hours in the library. The calm of night was often pierced by the warbling of air-raid sirens. Pamela would sit up, rigid with terror, unable to speak; I would hold her until we heard the moaning of the all-clear. At least once there was the thud of exploding bombs, and in July 1940 the Germans finally hit South Wales. Anticipating an air-raid often kept me awake. Also, I was deeply worried about Pamela. She made it through the Blitz but at War's end was hospitalized for an acute psychotic episode. Thanks to excellent care, she eventually recovered.

I had come to love Cardiff, my studies, and singing with the University Chorus. Then Father suddenly appeared, to announce we were all moving to New York, where he had accepted a tenured professorship. I was shocked; we had all just been naturalized British. With only a year of college left, I had planned to find a job and help win the War. After a heated argument, Father made a thinly-veiled suicide gesture, leaving me no choice.

Otto had been studying engineering in Manchester but, early in 1939, was interned as an "enemy alien," as were thousands of other European-born men, nearly all of them refugees. I went to see him in the internment camp. He was briefly let out of the wire enclosure; we hid behind an old barn and hugged goodbye, with him comforting me. As I slowly walked away, I felt pierced by the eyes of many lonely men. In 1942 the camps were closed, and Otto volunteered for the Pioneer Corps. His name anglicized to Roger, he carried out many secret missions, then served with the Army of Occupation in Germany. We remained lifelong friends.

Passage to America

September 1940 was a difficult month. The Blitz had begun. Back in Manchester we were packing and waiting for a ship. A little pocket diary that I kept still documents daily air-raid alarms; from August 24 to September 25 there were up to four a night, sometimes two a day. In the September 15 Battle of Britain, over 400 people were killed in London. Invasion seemed imminent. I felt numb and confined, the glorious freedom of my life gone. Hanna was also home again, having survived three difficult billets. We did not make the first ship, the *City of Benares*, which went down with hundreds of British children on board. Many friends thought we were on the *Benares*, and security precluded our telling them we were safe.

On September 23 we boarded the *Scythia*, an old Cunard liner, in Liverpool. It was to be in a convoy of three, but the ship next to us was torpedoed and could not leave. Very slowly, the two ships struggled across an angry September ocean. Many passengers were seasick. I tried to stay on deck, preferring it to our hot cabin. Walking around, I saw Ben Gurion, and Hanna recalls seeing H. G. Wells.

Before we set sail, there had been the mandatory life-boat drill. The ship's sirens were deafening, and the clumsy orange life vests almost impossible to manage. Mother, slowed by illness, needed a lot of help. Five days into the crossing, the ship's alarm went off again. Hastily we struggled into coats and life-vests. Father's ashen face spelled danger; Mother looked scared, Hanna surprisingly composed. All passengers were sent to the lowest deck, where we sat, closely huddled together, for many anxious hours. It was terribly hot, but we could not take off our coats. I was terrified: none of us could swim. Then there came a loud boom. Someone screamed, "We've been hit!" The *Scythia* twisted and turned but managed to stay afloat.

We celebrated Hanna's 16th birthday on board. Mornings at eleven, bouillon was served; I can still hear the sound of the gong.

On October 3 we finally pulled into New York Harbor. I was on deck to see the Statue of Liberty but did not rejoice. The whole voyage felt wrong. I had deserted my best friend, and my adopted country, in crisis. The immigration people were nice to Father: he was coming in as an out-of-quota academic. But then the officer looked at my passport:

children over 16 were not allowed on this quota. I barely cared; the officer was just confirming I should not have come. An old family friend, at the pier to meet us, finally persuaded immigration to give me a student visa, promising I would enroll in college immediately.

New York

It was very hot and humid in New York. We spent the first night with friends, Hanna and I sleeping on the floor. Missing the boat's motion, I finally got sick.

The next day we went to the New School for Social Research, where Father would be teaching. In a tall white building on West 12th Street we met Alvin Johnson, the man who single-handedly rescued many endangered academics from Germany and Austria. He was very kind; though I had not yet completed my undergraduate work, he suggested I audit courses in the Graduate Faculty: this would satisfy immigration. Lunch was in the cafeteria, dominated by Orozco's powerful murals.

Hanna, too young for college, enrolled in secretarial school; she would later graduate from Connecticut College. I began auditing a class with Max Wertheimer on Gestalt psychology, which he had founded, and another with Rudolf Arnheim, on the psychology of vision. American-style dating was new to me; I was shy with several graduate students who were eager to show me New York. Unfamiliar with the expected good-night kiss, I fit the parody of a professor's daughter.

We heard that Smith College was offering two scholarships for refugee girls. I had hoped to stay in New York, but even so I did apply and, to my surprise, was accepted as a second-semester Junior, to start in February 1941.

College

It was a lonely long ride to Springfield, Massachusetts, then a change of trains to Northampton. A senior met me at the station, amused by my British accent, which would never quite leave me. We sat on the floor of my room to unpack the steamer trunk. When I pulled out my new Jaeger cardigan, she quipped: "We don't wear such things here, we only wear baggy sweaters." At dinner I saw she was right. I put away the cardigan, bought some cheap yarn, and knitted myself a white bag.

I rarely listened to the news and was shocked when Pearl Harbor was attacked. We assembled in John M. Greene Hall, where Hans Kohn, the Czech-born historian, spoke movingly about recent events. A 1933 German refugee, he fully understood what was happening. To me this "new" war did not feel real; it seemed to lack any civilian involvement, such as rationing, blackouts, and air raids. I focused on my studies and began to think about graduate school. Getting a Ph.D. in clinical psychology seemed financially impossible; then I heard about the Smith School of Social Work, and applied. I had completed all my course work and made the dean's list, when someone discovered I had never passed the required swimming test, because of emotional scars from my first childhood swimming lesson. A specially convened faculty meeting finally decided to let me graduate, so I was able to enroll in the School of Social Work.

By the time the War ended I had completed my M.S.W. and was working in New York. In 1947 I married a young academic, and we left New York, to study and teach at several American universities. We also lived in Stockholm, Sweden, and in Ankara, Turkey, both of us doing research. Our two children enjoyed an early exposure to different languages and cultures.

Rachel was born in Berlin and lived in Switzerland and England before coming to the United States in 1940. Trained as a clinical social worker and certified psychotherapist, she served for many years on the faculty and staff of Columbia University. She specialized in issues of transition and loss and in working with international students. Rachel came to Kendal at Hanover in 2001.

Death of the *Graf Spee*

Ana Mayor

THE *ADMIRAL GRAF SPEE*, a pocket battleship designed to outrun any vessel she could not outgun, was one of the most famous German naval warships of World War II. In 1939 she was sent as a raider to the Atlantic Ocean, where she sank nine Allied merchant ships. The Royal Navy assigned a number of hunting groups to track her down.

On December 13, 1939, as manager of the *Time* and *Life* magazine office in Buenos Aires, Argentina, I had the rare privilege of eye-witnessing the battle in which the *Graf Spee* was engaged by one of these British Admiralty hunting groups. This was the first major naval battle in World War II, and it took place at the mouth of the Rio de la Plata, between Buenos Aires, Argentina, and Montevideo, Uruguay.

Our New York office had recently sent us another correspondent to cover our part of the world—one Sherry Mangan, a charming Communist who, instead of a briefcase, carried a Harvard green baize bag over his shoulder, a memento of his student days there.

On that December morning, when we got word over the local wires that a naval battle was going on in the Rio de la Plata right under our

(Courtesy of Roke, Wikimedia Commons)

very noses, he and I rushed off to a tall tower on the shore overlooking part of the action and climbed to the top.

Sure enough, there sat the *Graf Spee*, just off the coast, waiting to pounce on Allied shipping. Heading for the mouth of the Rio de la Plata, she was spotted by one of those British search groups: the heavy cruiser *HMS Exeter* and two light cruisers, *HMS Ajax* and *HMS Achilles*. While we watched through our binoculars, the British ships engaged the German ship right there in the Rio de la Plata estuary.

As soon as she was in range, the *Graf Spee* opened fire on the *Exeter*, turning her into a floating wreck. Meanwhile, the *Ajax* and the *Achilles* continued raking the larger ship with their lighter guns, creating damage serious enough that the *Graf Spee* broke off the action and headed for Montevideo, a neutral port, to make repairs and to bury their dead.

Bursting over what we had witnessed, we came down from our tower and rushed back to Buenos Aires to file our story.

It continued to unfold for several more days. Uruguay permitted the *Graf Spee* to remain in port for the period specified by international treaty, plus 72 hours, but required that she leave by December 17 or else be interned for the duration of the War. The captain, Hans Langsdorff, seeking orders from Berlin, was instructed not to allow internment and was offered three alternative choices. Of these, rather than what he saw as risking the lives of his crew, he chose to scuttle the ship. He sailed her to the limit of Uruguayan waters, and the crew was taken off by Argentine barges. The *Graf Spee* was then blown up, and sank.

Captain Hans Langsdorff had very much wished to stay with his ship, but his officers had talked him out of it, saying he was needed in seeking amnesty for the crew. Back in Buenos Aires, he was taken to the Naval Hospital. But once he learned that the lives of the crew were to be spared, he wrapped himself in the *Graf Spee's* battle ensign and, as a symbolic act of going down with the ship, shot himself.

In after years he was honored by both sides in the battle for his honorable conduct and for faithfully fulfilling his duty and maintaining his personal code of honor and decency on many occasions throughout his long career.

(Courtesy of Maritime Quest)

Admiral Graf Spee *seen in late 1936 or early 1937*

Postscript. "The grey hulk of…the *Admiral Graf Spee* was last seen sinking into the waters off Montevideo more than 70 years ago," reported the *Times* of London on March 20, 2010. "Today plans to raise the Nazi pocket battleship…are causing an international row" between Berlin and Montevideo. In 1985, a Uruguayan businessman obtained salvage rights and spent many years and millions of dollars in the operation, only to be challenged by the German government, who hope to reclaim the wreck in order to prevent the ship's artifacts —symbols of the Nazi regime—from falling into the hands of neo-Nazi enthusiasts and becoming commercialized.

Ana was born in Buenos Aires, Argentina. She is fluent in Spanish and English—and gets along in French and German. She worked for Time *and* Life *magazines in Buenos Aires and in New York. In 1945 she married Brantz Mayor, who also worked for these publications, a widower with four children under the age of 12, to which they added two more. They lived in Mount Kisco, New York, and later went to Europe (Paris and Munich), where Brantz worked for The Boeing Company for ten years. In 1972 they moved to Hanover and in 2003 came to Kendal at Hanover, where Brantz died in 2005.*

England Under Siege

~

Pamela Scoffin Phipps

W HEN ENGLAND DECLARED WAR ON GERMANY on Sunday, September 3, 1939, the air-raid sirens went off. My father was in the bathtub and scrambled to get dressed and find out what was going on. I was in church and was equally mystified. The congregation paused but then continued with the service. When church was over, we all went home to listen to Neville Chamberlain on the wireless. At the time, a single plane flying overhead was enough to send us into a panic. No one knew what to expect. Were we going to be invaded? Was the plane a scout for the Germans? It turned out to be one of our own, but the worry continued. Germany and Russia were invading Poland and soon to follow were the Netherlands and Belgium. Was England to be next?

I lived with my parents in Bromley, a suburb of London in Kent. At 17 years of age, I had completed a course at a business college and qualified as a shorthand-typist. After taking a Civil Service examination, I was temporarily working as a secretary at the Lever Brothers head office in Blackfriars in London. When the results of the examination became known about three months later, I was asked to report to the Admiralty Headquarters in Bath, where all naval operations had been evacuated. My secretarial job at the Admiralty was with Naval Stores, which handled supplies of everything for ships from ammunition to food.

Bath suited me well, as I had relatives near there. Later, my parents moved to Wiltshire, so I was not too far away from home. The railway provided a good enough service for me to travel to and fro, a journey of about 40 minutes. When the worst of the bombing raids took place between September 1940 and May 1941, passengers sometimes were transferred to busses to go round a place where a bomb had destroyed the line. Bath itself was also bombed.

Later, when Hitler turned most of his air force against the Soviet Union, I was transferred to London at the time that part of the Admiralty moved back to Whitehall. One section of offices—including Naval Stores, where I worked—was in a building in New Oxford Street, with shops on the ground floor. If we had an air raid, we would go to the basement and make ourselves as comfortable as we could with our own blankets. The Underground was nearby but was too crowded and noisy. After a midday raid at lunchtime, one young married couple did not return: the Tottenham Court Road restaurant where they were eating had been bombed.

During this time I was also a volunteer fire watcher. The Germans were dropping incendiary bombs that landed on rooftops and contained a material like napalm that could not be extinguished with water; standing on the roof, we were supplied with buckets of sand to put out the fire. Fortunately, I never had to cope with a bomb of this kind.

Also at this time, I volunteered at the canteen for service men from all branches except for the Americans, who had their own canteens. Between the explosive bombs, the fire-watching, and the canteen, I got very little sleep.

In the last eight or nine months of the War, the Germans began sending unmanned V-1 and V-2 rockets over London. The V-2s were especially frightening. Because of the way the sound carried, you heard the explosion first and afterwards the whistle of the missile's journey.

My parents, who were in a suburb, had an iron table in the dining room which was so heavy that the only way to move it was to take it apart. Although it was supposed to protect them from bombs, they did not use it much. Their neighbors, who had what was called an Anderson shelter in their garden, invited them to use that underground room whenever it became necessary. A school friend, fire-watching at our parish church, was killed when the tower received a direct hit.

Rationing was quite severe. There was plenty of bread but very little butter, sugar, cheese, eggs, meat, or fish, among other things. When I was in Bath, I had friends who owned a poultry farm. They supplied us with eggs when they could, for which we were very grateful. Peanut butter was introduced as a substitute food, but most people disliked it: they had not been brought up on it, and they found it unappealing. Our diet was mostly potatoes and cabbage. Fresh vegetables were hard to get, although some people had access to allotment gardens near their homes.

Clothing was also rationed, but I can't remember much about that. I do remember that I had an uncle in the tailoring business who made me a coat from a blanket.

The War in Europe ended in May 1945, and I continued to work for the Admiralty. Early in 1946, two girls each were chosen from the Admiralty, the Air Ministry, and the War Office to go on loan to New York City to work for the United Nations. I was one of the two from the Admiralty.

We had a very rough sea voyage in early March. When we arrived in New York, we were amazed to see in the shops all the goods that were not available at home. But we had been allowed to take only £50 out of the country, and our pay at the United Nations was low, so we could not afford such things.

With another girl, who had come on the same ship, I was assigned to live in the apartment of a widow on East 71st Street. We shared not only a room but a bed, something neither of us expected nor liked. And no food was allowed in those quarters, so that for the first time in our lives we had to eat breakfast in a drugstore. However, because the U.N. Military Staff Committee office was in the Henry Hudson Hotel on West 57th Street, we could at least have a pleasant walk through Central Park to get to work.

An English friend of mine who had married a GI was living in Washington state. I told her that I regretted accepting this job—life was proving so rough. Three weeks later, I received a letter asking me out to dinner: my girlfriend's husband had written to a friend of his in New York, saying, "For God's sake, take the poor girl out and give her a square meal."

The New York friend was Harry Phipps, and he and I were married on November 6, 1946.

Pamela Scoffin and Harry Phipps' wedding took place in Denver, Colorado, where Harry, Regional Comptroller for the U.S. Plywood Corporation, had relocated. They later lived in Seattle, Washington, and in Portland, Oregon, before going overseas. Pam worked for the Joint U.S. Military Mission to Turkey while they lived in Ankara for two years. They then moved to the U.S. Air Base in Chateauroux, France, before returning to the United Kingdom for eleven years of retirement. Harry's interest in Quakerism brought them to Kendal at Hanover in 1991, where Harry died in 2006.

A Child in Norway Under the Nazis

~

Agnar Pytte

Agnar Pytte, right, with brother Peder, 1940

I WAS PLAYING WITH MY BROTHER PEDER IN A FIELD near our house in
Norway on April 9, 1940, when we looked up and saw the sky filled
with airplanes. I was seven years old and Peder was eight. We had never
seen so many airplanes. We tried to count them and couldn't. We ran
to the house. The planes were headed for Oslo, we learned.

It was the beginning of the Nazi *Blitzkrieg.*

A few days later, friends of my parents who were Jewish came from a
town south of Oslo to stay with us for a short time. They, like everyone else,
had heard about *Krystallnacht* and the terrible persecutions of the Jews in
Germany. If there was a chance that the Nazis might take over Norway,
they did not feel safe in their home. In those early days, they made it safely
to Sweden. (*Krystallnacht* was the night of November 9, 1938, when Nazi
storm troopers and Hitler Youth began a two-day pogrom, trashing and
looting Jewish shops and synagogues all over Germany.)

Norway, which had hoped to remain neutral, was in turmoil for
about two months. Germany wanted naval bases that would break the

Allied blockade and help her invade England, and she also wanted the iron ore that came out of Narvik, a city far to the north near the coast. The British sent ships to try to stop the invasion of thousands of German troops, but the English were in a weakened condition, and the operation was not the success that either Norway or England had hoped for. Nonetheless, the Nazis were held back long enough to allow the Norwegian parliament to take a hasty vote for a government in exile and also to allow King Haakon VII and his family to escape to England on a British ship.

The British withdrew on May 28, 1940, and Norway surrendered to the Germans on June 10, after holding out against the *Blitzkrieg* longer than any other European country.

During this time Neville Chamberlain resigned and Churchill became Prime Minister. Of course I learned all that later. I was too young at the time to be aware of anything except the anxieties of my parents and the stories they told.

While Norway was struggling, thousands of young men took to the sea and sailed out of the fjords to England. The parts of the Norwegian navy and air force that had not been lost also went to England, where they could organize a resistance operation. Men were trained as pilots and as parachute troops.

And this is where my family came in. My father owned an extensive tract of wooded land in the mountains, where he ran a lumbering business. Our family of six consisted of my mother, my father, and four boys. We lived in the town of Hvittingfoss on our farm, which was called "Pytte" and had belonged to the family for many generations.

After the Germans took over the government, my father became active in the resistance. The Nazis confiscated all guns and also all radios: they did not want people to know about the progress of the War. However, my father had a radio that he kept hidden in the attic, and every night he went upstairs to listen to the BBC. Messages would come through in code. One phrase I remember is, "The wolf will howl tonight": that meant that British planes would fly over the mountains in the dark and look for signal fires set by my father and his friends. When the pilots saw a fire, they would release parachutes carrying men, weapons, and explosives. The men on the ground would be ready to help the parachutists and to take them and the things they were carrying to a safe hiding place before dawn. Of course this was very dangerous work, and I worried constantly that my father would be killed.

Because we grew most of our own food, no one could keep track of whether we were consuming extra rations; also, once a week a man who sold fish came to the house with his truck. So we did not experience the food shortages that were common in most of the country.

My older brother Peder and I slept upstairs in a large room that had two extra cots. Quite often, men would arrive and stay for a night or two, sleeping on the cots and usually hiding guns under their pillows. After a few days, they would disappear. We children were told that if anyone asked, we were to say that they were servants.

Then later on, we would hear that a bridge had been destroyed or a train blown up.

Heavy Water

After the War was over, I learned that what many considered the most successful sabotage attack of the entire War had taken place not far from our house. Near the town of Rjukan was a factory that produced heavy water (deuterium oxide), something that the Germans needed to build a nuclear bomb, and this was the only plant in Europe that was making enough of it to be useful for weapons.

British planes flew Norwegian commandos into the mountains by night to try to destroy the plant. After two failed attempts and incredible hardships endured by the saboteurs, and after an American bombing raid that was only partially successful, a final attempt at last succeeded in landing ten commandos, who, with inside help, planted explosives that disabled the production facility.

The Nazis decided to remove the heavy water that remained. They loaded barrels of it onto a railroad car to be taken at night by ferry across Lake Tinnsjø west of Oslo. A skilled team of saboteurs succeeded in planting a bomb timed to explode when the boat was over the deepest part of the lake. The heavy water was lost.

I never knew whether my father had any part in that operation.

One night I heard noises outside and got up to look out the window. I saw a group of people hiding boxes in the yard and burying a lot of their equipment under a large pile of sawdust. Someone had had a fire nearby, perhaps just a harmless barbecue, and the pilots had mistaken it for a signal fire; so, the men and the boxes had been dropped in the wrong place. Two of the parachutists had landed on the far side of the nearby river and been captured. I was very upset.

Twice the Nazis came to search our house. I will never forget the terrifying sight of the German soldiers standing near the door in their dark uniforms with guns and bayonets while their confederates went through the house. Neither time did the Germans find the radio in the attic or any other incriminating evidence.

One time my father was driving when he was stopped at a German road block. In a carrier on top of the car were guns. The Nazis searched the inside of the car but found nothing. This narrow escape added to my anxieties.

I had friends in school whose families were refugees from Finnmark, the northernmost section of the country that shares a border with Russia. Late in the War, the Russians had invaded, and my friends had come south. They could not wait to get home again, and I wondered why they were so eager to return to a place where it was winter for nine months of the year and very, very cold.

Toward the end of the War, the Germans became less threatening. They knew they were not on the winning side. I remember a couple of soldiers coming around and asking for an *okse*, which is Norwegian for 'ox.' Their pronunciation was not very good, and we were bewildered, until it finally turned out that what they wanted was an *øks*—an 'axe.' We actually had a laugh together over that one.

On May 8, 1945, while I was playing soccer, someone bicycled onto the field and shouted, "The War is over!" Peder and I immediately rushed home. My mother was weeping with emotion. I was 12 years old, and we were all alive and safe. The tensions we had lived through for so many years began to melt away.

The formal end of the War in Norway took place at Akershus Castle in Oslo on May 11. The pictures show a grim German commander, in dress uniform with medals, surrendering to a slight, young, bare-headed but erect Norwegian official dressed in what appear to be Army fatigues. As I look back now, this seems to symbolize the strength of the tenacious resistance over the Nazi terror.

Soon after the end of the War, my father received a certificate of commendation from the king for service to his country.

Ag attended the gymnasium in Kongsberg, spent a year at Phillips Exeter Academy in the United States, and later attended Princeton University. After earning a Ph.D. at Harvard, he spent much of his career at Dartmouth teaching physics and holding progressively higher administrative positions, ending as Provost. In 1987, Ag and his wife Anah moved from Hanover, where they had raised three children, to Case Western Reserve University in Cleveland, Ohio, where he served as president for 12 years, before retiring in 1999. The Pyttes came to Kendal at Hanover in 2009.

Invasion and Escape

Jean Kann Sonder

Jean with her brother Don in 1939

MAY 10, 1940, THE HAGUE, NETHERLANDS. At approximately 5:00 a.m., on a beautiful spring morning, gorgeous blue sky, I was awakened by a noisy "ack-ack, ack-ack." The sound was from antiaircraft guns at a Dutch army encampment a few blocks from our house. I, a little past my 11th birthday, got up to look out my window and over the balcony to see the family—my parents, my nine-year-old brother, my four-year-old sister, and our two servants—gathered one floor below outside my parents' bedroom. So I made my way down there.

The sky was full of parachutes, mostly above the other side of the city. It took us a while to realize we were under attack by the Germans. There had been talk of this for months, but we had hoped, and some had chosen to believe, that, just as in World War I, the Germans would bypass our country to the south through Belgium. Apparently not this time. It took a while for things to sink in, but eventually my mother, realizing that with all that racket none of us could go back to bed, decided that we might as well eat breakfast. Not that I was hungry. We ate, got dressed, and then were told not to venture above the main floor in case of air raids. Buckets of water were filled and placed on each floor, and the bathtubs were filled with water.

The rest of the day passed in a daze for me. I remember going to the store with my mother to buy strips of paper and helping her paste them on the windows to prevent them from shattering in case of explosions. Sometime during the day my parents must have listened to the radio and realized that the whole country was under attack and that there was heavy fighting in the east. There were frequent air-raid alerts, at first announced by church bells. We retreated to the basement for safety during the alerts, but, after the first attack, there were no planes in our area. Soon we didn't know if we were under alert or in the all clear, even after they got the sirens working to differentiate between the beginning and end of a raid. This situation continued throughout the day, and my father decided that we had better all bed down in the basement, as that was the safest place in the house. The servants dragged down mattresses and bedding and just managed to fit all seven of us on the floor with almost no walking space left. I hardly slept that night, afraid I might not wake for an alert. The next night my mother had had enough of that, and we were all given sleep medicine.

And so things went on for several days. We slept in our clothes and used only the toilet and small sink on the main floor. After a few days we children were taken upstairs one by one and given a very necessary sponge bath. Because the phone was cut off, our servants went off one at a time on their bikes to find out if their families were OK. They were. Similarly, my aunt biked over to tell us her parents and my father's parents were not harmed.

At one point my mother took my sister and me out on the street to play jump rope on the sidewalk, but a Dutch soldier soon came along to warn us that we should go inside. There was danger, not apparent to us. About the same time, we saw Dutch soldiers chasing some men across the flat rooftops of the houses across the street. It was only years later that I figured out what must have been going on. A German family had moved into the house next door and appeared to be running a pension. Their two children, the same age as my brother and I, had accepted an invitation to come over and play, but only once; as soon as they found out we were Jewish, any further invitations were refused. Now, I believe the pension was just a front—that it was actually a "safe house," where parachutists could find civilian clothing to enable them to merge into the general population. The rooftop chase probably had something to do with that.

After several days, there was a very long air alert, probably two or three hours. During this alert my parents were gone on some errand, and when nothing happened as time went on, the servants left us kids in the basement while they went about their business. This didn't reassure me at all, but the alert did end, and my parents came home. They had had to hide to avoid a shootout between Dutch soldiers and a few of the remaining parachutists. (Most of the parachutists had been mopped up almost as soon as they landed.)

Later, we heard that the city of Rotterdam, Holland's most important port, had been heavily bombarded. The Germans were threatening to hit Amsterdam and The Hague next unless the country surrendered. And so came the news: despite the fact that Holland had fought bravely and shot down over 100 German planes, the country would surrender. The royal family and high government officials had left, and the country was to be under Dutch military rule until the Germans arrived. I was so upset I wanted to cry. I headed for the bathroom to do so in private, only to find my mother there ahead of me for the same reason.

We had just been through a five-day war, a lightning-fast war—the *Blitzkrieg*!

Deutschland über Alles

My grandparents, with one of their servants, had arrived at our house to spend the night, and the place was being turned upside down to accommodate them. My grandfather was very afraid of German looting and atrocities and felt unsafe in his large house. As a precaution, he had directed that his collection of wine be flushed down the toilet. He also immediately sold the family business, a small bank that had been built up over generations, in order to get the Jewish name out of it and thus keep it safe from the Germans.

My family, too, was worried. A few days earlier my mother had called in the dressmaker and had her create an American flag, which now hung in front of our house. (My mother was born in the United States and was therefore American as well as Dutch by virtue of her marriage to a Dutch citizen.)

In the middle of all of this, one of my uncles suddenly arrived. I had answered the doorbell and turned to let the family know he was there. As I said his name, he hushed me; he was very much afraid, afraid that he would be immediately arrested by the Germans. He was a writer for a small publication, and apparently his anti-German feelings were well known. My father calmed him down and reassured him, and he went home. But a year or so later he was arrested, interned, and transported to Sachsenhausen concentration camp, where he succumbed. Apparently he was a wartime hero, for there is a street named after him in Amsterdam.

But the enemy arrived very peacefully. By mistake—we should never have been there—my brother and I were out on an errand with one of the servants as the German motorcade arrived. There were hundreds of small trucks, each with a bundle of wood tied neatly behind, followed by untold numbers of motorcycles. But the streets were empty—none of the roaring welcoming crowds the Germans would have liked to brag about. The city had turned its back. Doors and windows were closed, the curtains drawn. Only a single woman was on the street giving the Nazi salute.

We spent that night back in our own beds, my grandparents having gone home, but it was not the quiet night we had anticipated. The Dutch army spent the night destroying as much military equipment as possible to prevent it from falling into German hands. There were constant explosions. Except for the first morning, it was far noisier than it had been during the War.

There were of course immediate changes in our lives. We were put on German time, which was probably just an example of German efficiency but felt like an insult to us. This meant that in the fall it didn't get light until late, and so school started at 10:00 a.m. instead of 9:00 a.m., and our lunch hour was shortened from two hours to one. There was a curfew after dark, so dinner guests had to spend the night.

Far more important was that all contact with England or unoccupied France was cut off. My father went on half salary, our car was sold, and in the fall one of our servants was let go. All news was censored; listening to the BBC was forbidden. Hollanders who had fed and nurtured German boys back to health from the starvation in Germany that followed World War I were appalled to see them return as enemy soldiers.

I learned in a hurry what propaganda was, for the tone of the newspapers changed overnight. Now we were told that we were part of the great Aryan race, fellow Aryans, and that we should be proud of that, proud of the fact that Germany had conquered most of Europe and sent the British packing. Occasionally we found a blank space in the newspaper, surrounded by a black border: that represented a story that was killed by the German censor.

Listening to the BBC

We children were warned by our parents, and also by a teacher, to watch what we said in public, as the Germans were encouraging people to tell them what they heard or saw of anti-German behavior and tricking the younger children at school into revealing that their parents listened to the BBC. German nationals were especially asked to do so. One of my grandfather's employees, a woman who had been with him for years, reported that he had listened to the British radio. My grandfather had to appear in court and was fined. He then promptly fired her.

The Germans bragged that they would be in England by fall. Indeed, we did see many barges (no doubt either confiscated from the owners or paid for in the hated German currency), lashed two by two, presumably to carry invading soldiers across to England. But those barges suddenly disappeared. It seemed that there had been a staging area in Belgium, and the barges were launched from there. But we never heard about that. What we did hear were rumors of badly burned bodies washing up on the beach. There was no official news from the Germans, except that suddenly it was next summer when England would be conquered. This incident was never reported in the Allied press, but Churchill's book mentions a German commando raid that was repelled by pouring oil on the water and setting it afire.

Meanwhile, we heard about those who had lost friends and family during the War: soldiers killed in combat, Dutch nationals overcome in the bombardment, some undone by the stress of the five days and suffering strokes, or whatever. One cousin arrived in The Hague by bike in such bedraggled shape that she was immediately offered a bath. She had spent several days in bombed-out Rotterdam trying to care for an injured boyfriend until she could get him into a hospital, where he died. My great uncle and his wife, he Jewish, she not, committed double suicide. The house where my Brownie troop met was turned into a hospital, and we met outdoors until late fall. Other refugees from Rotterdam were housed on the grounds of the zoo, which of course no longer had any animals on exhibit. In the fall, my brother's Cub Scout troop was merged into the Hitler Youth, and he had to drop out.

It was of course a depressing time for Hollanders. Families and friends seemed to become closer, as we valued what we did have. There was a feeling of heaviness, a sense that things could only get worse, and a pervasive anxiety, fear of an unknown future, and the knowledge that it would be a long time, if ever, before the country would be free. And it was that loss of freedom, of nationhood, of civil liberties, that was heavy. Our laws were valid only insofar as the Germans allowed. Our parliament became a rubber stamp, and the Germans were free to do whatever they wished. Our homes were no longer safe. We could be arrested at any time, ordered to house officers, to turn in our bikes, and worse. If one entered a house and saw a tea cozy sitting over the telephone, it was a warning that the phone might be tapped, that there had been an uninvited visit by the telephone repair man. Our food rations were shorter every month, as was the amount of coal we could buy. But the bread, now adulterated with sawdust because of a shortage of flour, was delicious. We wore heavier clothes to school, and by December the teacher interrupted our desk work every so often for setting-up exercises—much needed—to get warm; my hand would cramp around the pen. Recess now became long walks to get our blood flowing warmly. Adding to the insult were the rumors that the stores of food and other necessities laid in by the Dutch government were being transferred to Germany with signs on the railroad cars that said "From Thankful Holland."

Shortly after the invasion I saw the German girl from next door wearing a Nazi arm band. I wanted to spit at her but didn't dare for fear of Nazi repercussions. Hollanders were angry. It seemed to me that morality was turned upside down. It was suddenly OK to lie, to cheat, to hurt, to murder—and worse—if the victim was a German. Early on, the driver of the vegetable truck confided to our cook, "We got two more last night." Two more German soldiers knifed in the back in the dark and the bodies dumped in the canal. (After the War the canals had to be cleaned out.)

On a trolley one day, I found myself sitting down while several older Dutch women and a German soldier were standing. As soon as I realized what had happened—that the soldier had offered his seat to the women, who had refused to accept it—I became very embarrassed and couldn't get off fast enough. We sang patriotic songs in music class, dating from the Eighty-Years' War against the Spanish over 300 years earlier, but everyone knew the enemy was not the Spaniards but the Germans. The dumbest boy in my class was suddenly the class hero when he came in with a broken arm, sustained when he was hit by a flower pot during a brawl with Nazi sympathizers. And this group, the NSB (National Socialist Bond, the Dutch Nazi organization) was active and vocal.

My brother and I were half an hour late one day coming home from school, as we had been held up by a parade of these people and could not cross the street. I was afraid that next year in secondary school, when German would be one of the required languages, in all honor I would have to flunk it, when learning it would be so much easier. Above all, I was petrified when I thought, probably very unrealistically, that I would be asked to perform some sort of secret errand for the underground.

Our planned summer excursion to Norway was of course cancelled. My father arranged a sailing trip on Holland's canals for us instead, although my four-year-old sister was left behind. The agreement was that we were not to read any newspapers. We were to have a complete vacation from bad news. It was a real vacation and, as yet unknown to us, our last. While we were gone, a planeload of Americans was allowed to depart for the United States. It was just as well that we missed that, as my mother was not ready to decide whether to stay or go.

Enjoying the Blackout

Meanwhile, the night sky was gorgeous, with an almost total blackout from Spain and Vichy France to Eastern Europe and north to Sweden. I spent hours watching the beauty from my bed at night. "The moon was a ghostly galleon tossed upon cloudy seas." One night I saw a cat-and-mouse hunt between a searchlight and a plane darting in and out of the clouds. I never heard any gunfire, so I assumed that either the British plane escaped or it was a drill for the Germans.

Finally, just before Christmas, all "Aryan" Dutch were ordered to get picture IDs—but not yet the Jews. After the holidays, one of my schoolmates was forbidden by his family to walk to school with us. Another had to switch schools because, as a Jew, he was no longer allowed to ride the trolley to reach ours.

Then I visited an aunt in Rotterdam. Traveling there by train, we passed through the bombed area of the city: block after block of neatly cleared rubble. The destruction was total except for the cathedral, left standing apparently intact in the center of all the ruins. But except for the sight of the destroyed city, all memory of that visit was erased by the announcement that my mother, my siblings, and I were leaving for the United States shortly.

Departure

There had been discussion of this for weeks while my mother, as an American, tried to make arrangements to return to what was, for her, still home. At first there were strong family objections. My grandparents were convinced that we would be better off remaining where we were as an intact family instead of going to the United States, where my mother had no means of support, although she had some family there. They refused to believe that, as Jews, we were in any great danger.

My mother had spent the fall making untold numbers of visits to the American Consulate and the American Legation in order to get back her American passport, which she had let lapse because it was cheaper to travel on a Dutch passport. But now she had to reestablish her citizenship, which appeared to be in doubt and at first was denied her. Finally, a very meticulous official walked into the room, looked up the precise wording of the law, and then asked her for the exact dates of her various return trips to the United States. My mother, with her excellent memory, could supply the dates and so prove that she had returned often enough to retain her citizenship. On that hung our lives.

Then there was the matter of getting exit visas to leave the country. At first these too were denied us. Ultimately, it took direct interference from the American government to gain permission from the Germans for an American citizen to return home with her three minor children. Although my younger sister was an American citizen, my brother and I, by some freak in the law, were not, and were given non-quota immigration visas. Then it took time to arrange the trip, the transportation, and the visas for the countries through which we would travel.

My father spent the remaining time stuffing my brother and me full of Dutch culture—visiting museums and historic sights. He also taught my brother, as the temporary man of the family, how to carve

Jean's father, Johan Kann

meat. Just before we left, he gave my brother the house key to take with him. That spoke volumes of unsaid words. My brother carried that key with him on his belt for about a year before putting it away.

Back at school after the holidays when my classmates heard I was leaving for the States, I suddenly found myself in the center of a circle, with all the girls skipping around me chanting "Jean is going to America!" It was a wonderful sendoff, as the next day I was sick and did not return to school. I was happy about that, since I had not wanted to leave. In a patriotic fervor, I thought that now I would be able to stay home with my father; but the family made short shrift of that. The doctor gave me a penicillin shot, calling it horse medicine, as it was still relatively unknown, and I was well enough to leave. Before that, one of my classmates, accompanied by her mother, came to visit me, surprisingly, as we were not that good friends. But it gave her mother, who had been a schoolmate of the royal princess, an opportunity to ask mine to convey a message to the princess. (It was of course dangerous for anyone to communicate with the royal family directly: all mail was censored.)

That was not the only message my mother carried. One of our relatives with connections to the Dutch underground asked her to convey a call word to facilitate radio contact with the British. (There were messages broadcast from England to tell those left behind, at the very least, that their loved ones had crossed the Channel safely.) My mother, of course, could not write any of this down, so she chose as the call word her own name, Elizabeth. After we reached the United States, she contacted the writer Hendrik Willem van Loon, who presumably passed the word on to England.

So that day came. We were up in the dark to catch an early train. It had snowed, and we would not be able to play in the snow. The train took us to Berlin. It seemed that all international travel, regardless of the destination, now had to go through that city, and ships crossing the Atlantic were available only from Sweden or Portugal. We spent what felt like hours at the Dutch-German border for passport checks, customs, and so forth, while German school kids on their lunch hour wandered curiously around the train, carrying their book satchels strapped to their backs. (I came to hate those practical schoolbags. Many years later, while we were in Italy, when our girls wanted to buy such school bags for their own use, I at first resisted.)

In Berlin we were met by one of my father's business associates, who escorted us on the many errands we had to do there: to mail back the picnic basket the cook had so lovingly packed for us with cucumber sandwiches and lemonade (in January!) because she knew we loved them, to the proper office to get food ration stamps, and more. It was my first subway ride, marked by periodic dousing of the lights, as the train traveled briefly above ground in the blackout, and finally we reached the hotel. Our accommodations were first class, as we happily spent as much money as possible: before we left the Continent, all remaining funds would have to be deposited at a particular bank, where they would be at the Germans' disposal. And there was plenty of food, while we had been short in Holland.

Early the next morning, we boarded a Lufthansa plane for Barcelona, Spain. The flight took all day, making many stops across France. My mother was relieved to find another American on the plane, a State Department courier named George Kennan (later ambassador to the Soviet Union). Arriving in the late afternoon, we boarded a sleeper train for Madrid, where we spent the following 24 hours.

Late the next afternoon we were off again, bound for Lisbon, Portugal, this time without sleeper accommodations, although we did have a compartment to ourselves. The train also carried a large number of Spanish troops in carriages between us and the dining car, which was blocked by a locked door. The only way to get there was via the station platform when the train stopped. Refusing to accept the situation, my mother dragged us through the troop cars, stepping over and around the soldiers, only to find that the door was indeed locked. So back we went. Fortunately, the soldiers were good-natured, and we had no problems returning to our compartment to await the next stop in hunger.

We had several days before boarding the ship that was to take us on the final transatlantic part of our journey. Upon checking on our reservations, my mother found that they had been cancelled because the fares had not been fully paid; so, she cabled an American cousin, who sent the money. Then, with the help of George Kennan, we were given a first-class cabin for all four of us. He had noticed a forgotten piece of luggage at the airport in Barcelona and put it with his, to be returned to us on the ship, a small vessel meant for travel in the Caribbean but carrying twice the usual number of passengers. Dormitories had been built all around the dining room, and we were very lucky to have one cabin with four berths and a bath. Because of wartime conditions there were huge illuminated American flags painted on the sides of the ship. Opening the porthole was forbidden. The lack of much-needed ventilation became a problem as the voyage went on.

After about a week we reached Bermuda, where we spent most of the day on deck in the harbor, because we were not permitted on shore. We could feel the lessening of tension, especially since, after the January crossing, it was a balmy day. But the next day, after we left Bermuda, it turned cold again, and by the time we reached port at Hoboken, New Jersey, it had snowed.

America at Last

At Hoboken we were met by what seemed like a delegation. My mother had sent a number of cables alerting friends and relatives to our arrival. She had absolutely no idea of what would happen after we landed. But one of my father's brothers was ready for us. Working for Philips Electric Light Company (now Royal Philips Electronics) in the Netherlands, he had been in contact with his German coworkers and knew better than most what was coming. Accordingly, he had picked up his family, left for the United States one month before the invasion, and was working for Philips in New York. He expected that some members of his extended family would make it out of the occupied country and had rented a large house in New Jersey, so he was now prepared to shelter us. And there we went. The very next morning I found myself in an American school.

As I walked in after lunch, I was greeted enthusiastically by one of the boys, who said, "Aren't you glad to be here and isn't this the biggest and best country in the world?" I stood there dumbfounded—no, I was not glad to be here, I would have preferred to stay in Holland, and I didn't think the United States was the biggest country (wasn't China bigger?), and how would I know after less than 24 hours on shore which was the best? Of course that was not the enthusiastic positive response that he had expected.

The Duration

In the fall of 1941, my mother moved us into a two-bedroom apartment in New York, where she had gotten a job. There the culture shock of New York City and living in a one-parent family with only part-time help hit us. We were often alone and left to cope as best we could with the reality of living in a strange city and attending a large overcrowded city school with rigid rules and teachers who were overloaded and who seemed uncaring. In a sense, I lost my identity. I had lived and gone to school where my family was known, and suddenly I was a nobody. Because I spoke the language without accent—having grown up bilingual—I was not even known as a refugee.

What could we do but settle in for an indefinite future? Pearl Harbor and the subsequent declaration of war by Congress gave us a ray of hope. While we recognized the shock to Americans, for us it meant at least a chance that Europe would eventually be liberated from the Germans. But it also meant that all communication with friends and family in occupied Europe was totally cut off.

Some news did filter through. We learned a lot from a monthly magazine for Dutch expatriates. Occasionally there were short visits from friends and acquaintances who had escaped by means not divulged (for safety reasons for those left behind) and who brought us what news they could. From family in England we learned more. One of my father's cousins there worked for the British secret service and somehow made occasional secret trips into Holland. I still wonder how. She spoke Dutch, as well as English and German, and used the opportunity to check on various family members. Her news reached us via her sister at Oxford, who was one of a group of Jewish scientists spirited out of Europe by the British and Americans. We learned that my grandparents had been interned, at first in Holland, where they could still receive visits and food parcels. Then they were deported to Bergen-Belsen and later to Theresienstadt along with the "Barneveld Jews," those who had had some sort of social or political status and therefore received somewhat better treatment.

My grandparents were allowed to ride in a passenger car, rather than being jammed in the usual freight or cattle car, and in the barracks were given a "room" of their own. My grandfather had had a colostomy years earlier and had always had a woman to help him take care of it. She went with them and, I believe, was allowed into the nearby village to purchase some food. Nevertheless, both grandparents died of "natural" causes during the last year of the War. We actually had a letter from them once via the Red Cross, which did visit one of the camps, saying that they were glad we were where we were and that they were looking forward to summer (probably 1944), hoping to sit in the sun and feel better.

Earlier, perhaps in 1942 or 1943, a man whom I did not know came to see us in New York. He had been part of a group of ten people, my father among them, who had made careful plans to escape to England by boat. They had gotten as far as the beach in the dark when an unidentified plane triggered the use of a search light. They were seen boarding the boat and, of course, arrested. There may have been some sort of a scuffle. It seemed that some jewelry was later found in the sand. My father was put in jail, apparently treated very badly, and then deported "to the East." The man who told us the story had planned to go with the group until it was realized there was no room for him in the boat.

A year or two later we received a letter from Switzerland with more details from a cousin, active in the Dutch underground, who had been aware of the whole operation. This cousin, an M.D., luckily had left three days before the Nazis came for him. He and his fiancée, whom he had not been able to marry because he was half Jewish, walked to Spain, where they were turned back by the Nazis at the border. They went on to Switzerland, where, because of his underground connections and his work with UNRRA (United Nations Relief and Rehabilitation Administration), they were admitted. He wrote us that my father had managed to throw a letter out of the train as he was being deported. The letter had been found and delivered to him at great risk to the messenger. My father wrote that he had been badly mistreated while in prison and was suffering from hunger edema. The rest of the message was never divulged to any of the family; it was considered too disturbing.

On the whole, the "duration" seemed to last forever. The long, dreary wait in unpleasant schools and a dismal apartment in a noisy neighborhood was broken only by summers at camp in the country.

Until V-E Day.

Joyfully, my siblings and I started to celebrate, but my mother, who joined us later after coming home from work, seemed somewhat subdued. She had long suspected what she soon found out: that my father had not survived. His name had turned up on a list of French prisoners of war who had died. Years later a Red Cross death certificate listed him as having died of typhus at Auschwitz-Birkenau the day after his arrival.

Aftermath

The War might have been over, but news of friends and family filtered out slowly. Some of our belongings had been saved, even though a German family had been living in our house. My father had stored the rugs and two antique cabinets in the bank building, and the silverware with friends who had the same initials. The rest of our belongings disappeared when the German family left. We did receive financial compensation, but it was years in coming.

The letters that arrived on thin paper scraps brought further news. Although all eight of my cousins were sheltered from the Germans, they had lost their parents. The mother of one set of cousins, although not Jewish enough to face deportation, nevertheless was taken away and died because she refused to reveal the location of her daughters. And we learned of the cousin, an M.D., married to a non-Jew and already a grandfather, who was able to save himself from deportation by agreeing to be sterilized.

The stories go on and on. More harrowing is the experience of one more distant cousin, who spent the time "underground," fleeing from house to house, sleeping in 30 different beds. Her mother was also "underground" when she had a stroke and died in the hospital. The daughter had the very dangerous task of getting into the hospital to replace her mother's false ID with the real papers so her mother could be buried under her own name.

One of my first cousins, a blond boy, was about 13 when he and his father were picked up in a *razzia*. The Germans would cordon off a whole block and arrest the able-bodied men for slave labor. Recognized as Jews, the father and son were held in jail for a week before deportation. The father spent the week planning with the boy how they might escape. Indeed, on the train an opportunity arose, and they jumped the train. The father, determined that his son would escape, waved his hat to distract the guards' attention, and he succeeded. The boy hid in a canal and, after the train left, made his way to a hut for railroad workers, where he was helped and eventually sent home. The father, however, was shot, hit in the knee, and reloaded on the train. He ended up in the "hospital" at the camp where my grandparents were being held before he recovered, only to be sent on to his death.

Also, it seemed as if my father had left a message of some sort. While in jail he had had long conversations with one of his prison-mates, a man who survived the mistreatment and apparently felt strongly the importance of conveying the substance of these conversations. I was supposed to write him after the War but never did: the task was more than I could do alone. I was faced with my mother's new marriage to an American who had never crossed the Atlantic and who wanted to hear nothing of our European experiences. The message did reach me years later, and even then I could barely take it, but I did get the essence of it: that my father had had a high opinion of his elder daughter.

These experiences and stories are definitive for me. They have determined my values, influenced whom I married, and affected how I brought up my children. They have made me who I am.

Jean was born in the Netherlands in 1929 and emigrated to the United States in 1941 after the War started in Europe. Raised mostly in New York City, she attended public schools, Queens College, and the University of Illinois for an M.S. in biochemistry, with additional study in physiology. She married Edward Sonder in 1953. They lived briefly in Iowa, then moved to Oak Ridge, Tennessee, where Ed worked as a physicist at the National Laboratory, while Jean worked part time and did volunteer work while raising two daughters. They moved to Kendal at Hanover in 2006.

Flight from Bulgaria

~

Joan Bliss Wilson

In this family photo, Joan is seated on right

My father's family had been involved in the Middle East ever since my great grandfather went to Syria as a missionary in 1856. Ten years later, in 1866, he founded the American University of Beirut. His name was Daniel Bliss and he was the first president of the University. His son, Howard Bliss, was the second. My father, Huntington Bliss, Howard's son, was born and grew up in Beirut. After graduating from Amherst College, he taught at the St. Louis Country Day School in Clayton, a suburb of St. Louis, but, like others in the Bliss family, he wanted to continue in the family tradition of teaching in the Middle East. He was therefore delighted to be offered the opportunity to teach at the American College in Sofia, Bulgaria.

It was 1938 when he took his wife and three daughters to Bulgaria. I was seven years old, and my two sisters were younger still.

We sailed from New York on the Italian luxury liner *Conte de Savoya*. For me the most memorable happening on the ship was the movie *The Chocolate Soldier*. It was a musical, and my favorite song from it was "My Hero." I loved it so much that I learned to play it on the piano, and I still play it today. The only stop on that trip that I remember was at Naples, Italy, where we visited the ruins of Pompeii.

Our house in Bulgaria was on the edge of the campus, which was surrounded by a fence. Outside the fence was a field, and in the distance we could see Bulgaria's capital city, Sofia. After the War in Europe began in 1939, we watched the Bulgarian soldiers training in the field. Our new Chevrolet was taken from us that year to be used by a Bulgarian general, but otherwise our lives continued pretty much as usual.

My first year in Bulgaria, I attended a German school in the city, but when we were car-less, I changed to the grade school on the campus attended by the employees' children. It was a one-room schoolhouse with four grades and one teacher. There was one other student in my grade and perhaps 10 in the whole school. The language of instruction was Bulgarian, so by this time in my youthful academic career, I'd had first grade in English, German, and Bulgarian.

The war activity seemed far away. Every morning my parents would listen to the 8:00 a.m. news on BBC radio, and I'd aim to get to breakfast about 8:15 a.m. so I could avoid hearing it. Initially the fighting was mostly in the western part of Europe. Hitler had invaded Russia in June 1940, and as time went on the German armies were getting closer and closer to Bulgaria

Because the Bulgarians had seen what happened to Hungary and other countries in Europe when the German *Blitzkrieg* was launched against them, the Bulgarians capitulated without any fighting. In the spring of 1941, I remember going into Sofia and watching the German soldiers marching on their way south to attack Greece. Sofia was bombed twice. Once when it happened at 2:00 a.m., I thought it was thunder, but my father said it was bombing, and we went outside and watched from our back yard. We could see a few planes and hear the explosions, but it didn't last long. I don't believe there was much destruction, but it was frightening. I don't know who was doing the bombing.

There was a lot of talk among the adults after Japan bombed Pearl Harbor in December 1941 and the United States declared war on Japan, Germany, and Italy. I was unaware of any changes in our life until one day my parents told us that we were leaving to go back to the United States. It seems that all Americans had been given the option of going either to the States or to Istanbul, Turkey. A plan had been formulated to exchange Germans living in the United States for Americans living in Europe. Three round-trips were planned.

Thirteen of us left Sofia in a sealed railroad car in May 1942, on the same railroad line as the one used by the famous Oriental Express. We passed through parts of Yugoslavia and Hungary, and I remember that we stopped in Vienna, where we got off the train and stayed in a hotel. I think it was there that some German officers looked through our luggage and questioned us. I was ten and a half at the time. They found some Bulgarian fairy-tale books that I had taken with me. When they questioned my father about them, he referred the German officer to me, and I think I translated some of the stories for him. At any rate, they let me keep the books.

The hotel was very grand, but because of the War, food was scarce. All we had was potato soup, and our guide had to use some of her own food stamps for our dinner.

Our railroad car went on through Switzerland and southern, then "Vichy," France. I remember we stopped in Madrid, Spain, and again stayed at a hotel. My father went to a bullfight, but we girls weren't allowed to go. We finally reached Lisbon, Portugal, and lived in a hotel for a few weeks while waiting for our ship to arrive. We went daily to the zoo, where they had a lovely section for children.

The exchange boat was a Swedish ship called the *Drotningholm*. This was to be the second of its three round trips, but it turned out to be its last. We had an uneventful crossing of the Atlantic. At night we sailed with all our lights on so the U-boats would see that our ship was from a neutral country.

On July 3, 1942, we arrived in New York. The dock was crowded with a sea of faces of friends and relatives waiting to greet the refugees. As we stood at the rail looking out on the sizable crowd, my father suddenly exclaimed, "There they are!" People nearby were amazed that he could identify anyone in that mob of people. My father pointed to two bright yellow handkerchiefs being waved by my grandfather and uncle; then he showed us the yellow handkerchief he had in his hand. It had been a family custom of many years to use such handkerchiefs to signal relatives at departures and arrivals.

Unfortunately, we were not allowed to leave the ship until July 6.

All the passengers had to be questioned to be sure there were no spies on board. We heard that a man was caught carrying $10,000 in the hollowed-out heel of his shoe.

We returned to St. Louis. My father was welcomed back at the St. Louis Country Day School, but he was anxious to help out in the war effort. He was accepted into the OSS (Office of Strategic Services), predecessor of the CIA. He spoke both Arabic and French, and they sent him overseas, first to Egypt and then to Italy. He was away until the end of the War, while my mother, my sisters, and I remained in St. Louis.

My father would never talk about his OSS experiences except to say that his Jeep in Egypt was named *Alice* after my younger sister. I'm proud to say that after the War he and my mother went back to the Middle East, where he taught English to students in Istanbul, Damascus, and Beirut.

Born in Flushing, New York, Joan spent her growing-up years in five different countries, going to eleven different schools in three different languages. After college graduation, she married Tom Wilson. They lived in Princeton, New Jersey, for 40 years, where they brought up their three children. Since they moved to Kendal at Hanover in 2001, Joan has continued her interest in early music, reading (mostly mysteries), swimming, and travel. However, Joan and Tom have their best times with their children, their children's spouses, and their eight grandchildren. One grandchild is married, so his bride has become their ninth grandchild.

Home Front

DOMESTIC DETAILS

Jane Atwood Barlow

WORLD WAR II FRAMED MY YEARS in high school. As I look back, my most vivid memories are of a few dramatic events and of how the War affected my immediate family and friends.

On Sunday, December 7, 1941, when I arrived at the meeting of the teenagers' group at our church at 6:00 p.m., I found my friends heatedly discussing the Japanese attack on Pearl Harbor. I was the only one who had not heard about it. By the time I got home, my parents had learned the shocking and devastating news. Untold numbers of men and ships had been lost. Having focused on the War in Europe, we found the attack a total surprise. None of us knew what it would mean. President Roosevelt's serious but reassuring tones rolled out of the radio. I was immediately struck by the thought that my father might have to go into the Army. When he told me that because he was over 35 the Army would not want him, I felt enormous relief.

When I was entering seventh grade in 1939, I had stood in front of my family's art deco tabletop radio and listened to the news that England had declared war on Germany. It was the first day of school, and I had walked home for lunch. I knew the news was important. My father assured my two younger sisters and me that the War was a long ways away, and we did not have to worry that the occasional airplane overhead was going to drop a bomb. Propaganda about the United States' effort to help England ("Bundles for Britain") was everywhere. And of course the propaganda was all positive. It never occurred to me, then or later, that Germany might win.

Once the United States entered the War, my father became an air-raid warden. We sealed the windows in our basement with black cloth stuck down at the edges with some kind of dark tape, gathered flashlights and batteries, stored food and water downstairs, and piled extra blankets and pillows in a corner. When the fire siren went off to warn of an air-raid drill, my father roamed the neighborhood using a flashlight with a blue-covered lens to look for houses where lights were showing.

Soon the nearby firehouse was in use for rolling bandages. I joined a group of girls and older women, who sat at long folding tables. On our heads we all wore triangles of white cloth with a red cross in the front, tied at the back of the neck to ensure that no stray hairs escaped into the bandages. The bandages themselves started with squares of cheesecloth that were then folded and refolded until they ended up as two-inch squares, probably surgical sponges. The woman in charge was extremely strict about precise folds so that all the bandages were exactly the same size. More than once I had to redo my efforts.

Besides rolling bandages, my mother knitted various articles from yarn supplied by the Red Cross: scarves, balaclava helmets, and mittens, all in heavy khaki-colored or navy blue wool.

Gas rationing soon came along. Every car had a square "A," "B," or "C" sticker affixed to the lower right corner of the windshield. At the time, we had two cars, a 1941 Dodge and a 1938 Chevrolet. Until after the War was over, all the automobile factories were converted into plants that made airplanes, tanks, jeeps, or other matériel needed for the War, and new cars simply were not available after 1941. Portraits of Rosie the Riveter, with her kerchief-tied head and ever-present smile, made an appearance. I even knew one girl who left her private high school to work in a factory.

My father went to work at the Division of War Research at Columbia University in New York, which had a contractual relationship with the Office of Scientific Research and Development headed by Vannevar Bush. A gentle soul who probably would have found himself totally unable to go into combat, my father was nevertheless enthusiastic about contributing to the war effort. There was no ambiguity either at home or elsewhere about the morality of the War: Germany and Japan had to be brought to "unconditional surrender."

Because my father's work was centered in New York, New London, and Washington, D.C., the family moved to Larchmont, a Westchester town with convenient rail transportation to all those cities. We left our Albany, New York, suburb at the beginning of the summer of 1943.

Toward the middle of August, Mother managed to persuade the Larchmont rationing board that we could save food and contribute to the war effort if she and the children visited her sister's family, the Arkleys, who had a vast "victory garden" in Burlington, Vermont. The board granted a small extra allowance of gasoline for the trip. When we arrived, we joyously piled into the Arkleys' new house, and Mother and Aunt Marion rolled up their sleeves and plunged into preserving the harvest.

Two weeks later we returned from Burlington with jar after jar of green beans, beets, carrots, tomatoes, corn, and other vegetables; there may also have been some fruits, such as berries or applesauce. These all helped during the following winter, when the impact of the War on our daily lives became clear even to us youngsters. It was clearest in the acute shortages of food.

Rationing Food

Rationing had begun. Meat, especially beef and other red meat, was expensive and hard to get; such meat went to the troops. We occasionally heard of steak obtained on the black market, but just how the black market worked was a mystery. Meanwhile, chicken became more common. Butter was in short supply, perhaps a half pound a week per family. To make up for what we lacked, we bought margarine that came in one-pound plastic bags with a pea-sized round orange capsule in the center. We squeezed the capsule through the wrapping until it broke, then kneaded the bag until the contents turned yellow and looked—but did not taste—like butter. My mother had to cajole us into kneading the margarine, a job that was long and incredibly boring.

Canned goods and other food were doled out in the grocery stores by ration books. It took a certain number of coupons to buy various kinds of food. Sugar and eggs were also rationed, and women traded recipes for cakes and cookies that did not use those precious items. Bananas disappeared, as did such other tropical fruits from overseas as pineapple. Frequently what we wanted was not available. Once we had lobster for dinner—an expensive treat, but it was only because there was no other meat or fish in the store.

My new school was very different from the WASPy community I had come from. There were students from refugee families, some of whom spoke a different language. Others were living with relatives because their parents were in war zones. Some had single parents because their fathers were in the service. And some even quit school in their senior year because they were so eager to get into the War.

We saved empty cans, washed them, and removed the bottoms so they could be flattened and turned in to a collection center. Whether they were really recycled or not, I don't know. I do know that many iron objects such as fences or gates in public places were removed and sent to factories to be used (we were told) for building planes and tanks. All but one of the cannons from the War of 1812 that we had played on as children in Battery Park in Burlington were contributed to the war effort.

We saved fats and turned them in, too, to a central collection office, although I'm not sure what purpose they served. One year President Roosevelt, who was not universally popular especially in my Republican family, suggested that all the fat from the Thanksgiving turkey be saved, making him the object of much derision: any good housewife knew that turkeys had to be basted with extra fat.

The first Larchmont house turned out to be very hard to heat, a serious matter because heating oil was also rationed. At the end of the school year in 1944, that house was sold, and we moved to another one where we could stay in the same schools, although we were somewhat farther from the railroad station. The stairway to the second floor in the new house opened from the living room, and one of the first things Mother did was to make a large, heavy monk's-cloth curtain to hang at the top of the staircase to keep the heat downstairs.

We walked everywhere: to school, about 20 minutes; to friends' houses, often a long distance away; to the "village" (as downtown was called); and to the park on the shore of Long Island Sound, a good 45-minute walk. Sometimes we saw adults sitting on the benches scattered around the park gazing out toward the water with binoculars. They were somewhat suspect. Were they spies? Were they watching for the submarines that were rumored to sneak into the waters of the Sound? Or were they simply bird watching?

When we took the bus or the train to Mamaroneck, New Rochelle, or "the City," we sometimes saw young men in civilian clothes. We wondered why they were not in the service. Were they 4F, meaning they'd been classified by the draft board as unfit for some reason? Were they draft dodgers with influential fathers? Occasionally they wore a pin in their lapel that marked them as discharged veterans, and then we could only wonder where they had been and what they had seen.

The Gold and Blue Stars

We knew, or knew of, a few young women whose husbands had gone off to War and been killed. One or two had babies and were living with their parents. In the window of their houses was a small "service flag," about the size of a sheet of paper. These had red borders and a gold star in the center of a white field if the serviceman had been killed. If the flag showed a blue star, it meant that the family had a son or husband in one of the armed forces.

As I grew older, I became more aware of overseas events. We listened to Churchill's inspiring speeches and sometimes to Hitler's rants in incomprehensible German. In each case, the emotion came through. Flickers of fear ran through me when the Allied army was trying to march west across North Africa. Fear turned to elation when British forces turned back the Germans at El Alamein. On D-Day, June 6, 1944, when U.S. forces invaded France, the principal called an assembly, and we listened silently to the news broadcasts in the crowded school auditorium.

In November of 1944, Roosevelt was re-elected for a fourth term. The day after the election, our social studies teacher stood up after we were all seated in class and announced in a resonant voice, "The Republic is dead." The local newspapers seized on his statement and called for him to be fired. I was sufficiently shocked to write and circulate a petition asking that he be retained. I thought he was entitled to his opinion, and most of my classmates agreed. He stayed.

On a sunny afternoon early in April 1945, I was outside our house after school when a friend shouted across the street, "Roosevelt is dead!" I ran inside to listen to the radio and learned that he had died in Warm Springs, Georgia, where he often went to exercise and bathe in the warm water. The photographs that I see now show a very ill man, but I don't remember anyone at the time remarking on his frailty.

The country turned toward the War in the Pacific and the savagely depicted "Japs." My father began pinning maps to the wall in the breakfast room, where we ate most of our meals. Like most of us, I had little knowledge of the geography and found it difficult to follow the island-hopping strategy of the Allies.

I graduated from high school and went off to a summer job as a counselor at a girls' camp on Lake Champlain in Vermont. My family moved to Silver Spring just outside Washington, D.C., where my father's job continued under the auspices of Johns Hopkins University. In early August, while I was at the camp, we heard that the United States had dropped an atomic bomb on a city in Japan called Hiroshima, causing unbelievable destruction. Three days later, a second atomic bomb landed on Nagasaki, another city we'd never heard of. About three weeks after that, representatives of the Japanese Imperial Government signed surrender papers aboard an American battleship and General MacArthur accepted them.

The War was over. The camp leaders planned a service in the outdoor tree-lined chapel. We heard about the jubilant celebrations in cities all over the world, but we marked the day quietly. I wondered what the newspapers would find to write about when they had no more war news.

Throughout the War we heard almost nothing about the Jews. There were occasional rumors about concentration camps, but, as I realized much later, Roosevelt had decided not to bring what is now known as the Holocaust to the fore. Anti-Semitism throughout the country was strong, and he believed it would be difficult for him to rally support for admitting Jews into the States. I had many Jewish friends in school, but I cannot recall any discussion of the situation. Also, we heard only vague rumors about Japanese-American citizens from the west coast being sent to camps in the midwest. They were never called concentration camps, and we knew almost nothing about them.

In watching recent television programs and reading books about the War, I am appalled at how little we teenagers were aware of the broad picture. Statistics of losses, whether they were troops, ships, or towns, were never printed in the newspaper or broadcast on the radio. Of course there was no television, and the only visual images we saw were the carefully controlled newsreels. The propaganda machine was very efficient.

Until long after the War was over, none of us realized what a major turning point it was in our lives. For my generation, there is only one War. Events happened before The War or after it. And that is true to this day.

After graduating from the University of Vermont, Jane Atwood took an M.A. at Cornell and became an Assistant Dean there. She married Mark Barlow, who worked in progressively higher levels of administration at Cornell, Wesleyan University, and, before retirement, as head of St. Mark's School near Boston. As their three children grew older, Jane became an archaeologist, gradually earning a Ph.D. at Cornell, excavating in Cyprus, and publishing or co-publishing three books and numerous articles. The Barlows came to Kendal at Hanover in 2008.

A Fortuitous Encounter

~

Barbara Gilbert

Barbara with her husband John in 1943

MINE IS A HAPPY STORY! My husband, John E. Gilbert, M.D., was the pathologist with the 121st Evacuation Hospital, attached to Patton's 3rd Army—supposedly within five miles of the troops, though not always able to keep up with them. In the spring of 1945 they were racing through Germany, "liberating" several POW camps as they went.

One such time, John went to Admissions to learn what was happening and who might be there. Seeing a handsome young man in a Canadian Air Force uniform, he went over to talk with him.

"Where are you from?" John asked.

"St. Anne de Bellevue—nowhere you've ever heard of," replied the young soldier.

"As a matter of fact," said John, "I graduated from McGill Medical School, and isn't St. Anne's where the Agricultural College is?"

"Yes—and I'm Bruce Britain; the Dean of the College is my father!"

John went on to tell Bruce that he had met Dean Britain when the

266

dean came to Douglas Hall, the men's residence where John lived while at McGill, to speak at a dinner. (John was probably too modest to say that he was the president of the Residents' Association and, as the host, had sat beside the dean at dinner and introduced him as the speaker.)

At the hospital, Bruce told John how he had parachuted from his burning plane and broken his ankle in the fall but was otherwise just fine. Unable to run and find a place to hide, though, he had been taken prisoner and sent to the now-liberated POW camp.

Back in his quarters, John wrote me a V-mail telling me all about this encounter. I was living in my dad's apartment in Montreal while John was overseas, and the letter was delivered while we were eating breakfast.

"We must let Bruce's parents know about this right away," was Dad's response, and I immediately put in a call to the dean's office.

At first, the secretary was sort of snippety; but when she heard why I was calling, she suddenly burst into tears of joy. Bruce had been missing in action for several months, and they didn't know whether he was alive or dead. The dean was away, in Vancouver, she told me, but could she tell Mrs. B. the good news and have her call me? Of course I said yes.

Within a very few minutes, Mrs. Britain called, almost hysterical in tears and laughter—she was so happy to learn her son was alive and well! After hearing me read John's letter, she thanked me and asked if she might get in touch with her husband, in Vancouver, and have him call me and hear the letter too. Again—of course I said yes.

A few minutes later Dean Britain called. I read the letter to him—now an ecstatically happy father who had just learned for the first time, after months of agony, that his son Bruce was alive, and in fine shape, and in the hands of the American Army, where he would be looked after and brought home in safety.

While I was talking with the dean, I reminded him of how John had once introduced him as speaker at Douglas Hall—the same John who had written this letter with the wonderful news about his son. Dean Britain said he remembered John very well: "A delightful fellow—thank him from the depth of our hearts."

I have never forgotten the joy I was able to give those proud and happy parents. Bruce arrived home safely about six weeks later—the War in Europe was over!

Barbara Brooks Gilbert grew up in Montreal and attended McGill Medical School, specializing in pediatrics. She married classmate John Ellis Gilbert the week after their final exams. After John's three-year service in the U.S. Army Medical Corps, they settled in Northampton, Massachusetts, where John was chief of Pathology at the Cooley-Dickinson Hospital, and raised five children. Ever since they moved to Thetford Center, Vermont, in 1972, Barbara has devoted herself to child protection work, especially prevention of child abuse, for which she was given a Distinguished Service award from the University of Vermont. The Gilberts came to Kendal at Hanover in 1991. John died in 2005.

THEY ALSO SERVE

Marion Weathers Grassi

Marion and Joe 1939

WHILE STANDING AND WAITING, those on the home front worked to support the war effort. Some of these unsung heroes of World War II were the wives or parents of servicemen. Parents often took in the children of refugees or others who were unable to care for their offspring. While they became involved in many programs to support the war effort, they were living with rationing, censorship, and little or no knowledge of where their servicemen and women were.

People wrapped bandages, gave to the Blood Bank, served on volunteer boards, sent clothes via Bundles for Britain, and knitted scarves, hats, and gloves for servicemen. Women filled in at factories as the workers went to war, and volunteer groups provided day care for their children. There were plane-spotting schools followed by schedules of volunteers for plane identification; there were blackouts and air-raid warnings.

My mother, a widow with seven children, responded to the War in Europe by taking in two children from London, through a distant family connection, when the British evacuated many children from the city to escape the bombing by the Germans. These children, ages two and six, stayed with her for eight months before the father was able to collect them. My mother, who had had a chauffeur before the War, also took a course on how to check her car engine, recognizing and identifying problems. I don't believe she had ever raised the hood before that.

In 1939 Joe and I were married. He had a secure job as we were coming out of the Depression, working for a company whose specialty was marine insurance, underwriting ocean cargo and hulls. With the advent of the War in Europe they became extremely busy, spending long hours rewriting policies to fit the new circumstances. We had one child and lived in an apartment in New York City.

With the bombing of Pearl Harbor, our world soon changed. My five unmarried brothers all entered the service; one was a Marine, one was a medical service corpsman, and three were pilots. Though Joe was very nearsighted and had a child, he too would eventually be eligible for service. With that hanging over us, we made arrangements to move into my childhood home, with my mother, in the New Jersey suburbs.

Rationing of scarce commodities changed everyone's life style. It was not easy, but we soon learned to adapt. Everything was secondary to the war effort. Gas rationing came first. Our household had an "A" card because our needs were minimal. Those whose jobs depended on the use of a car were allowed more gas—a "B" card. Woe be to the person with a "B" card whose car was seen parked at the golf course on the weekend! Soon families found that shoes were rationed. Our daughter was learning to walk, and although we had coupons to cover the need for shoes, we found socks in short supply.

It was rationing of food that presented the most adjustments. Meat, butter, coffee, and sugar were the scarcest items. There were minimal fresh vegetables in the markets: there was no one to grow them, so we soon planted "victory gardens" and preserved the resulting crops. My mother collected food stamps from our help and then parceled out each one's share in an individual container. One was heard to mutter that "us working girls must eat to do our jobs." With enough people in our household, we sometimes saved up coupons and could have a roast on special occasions. After it was eaten, we would render any fat which had been saved from the meat scraps. The aroma of the melting fat was so reminiscent of the tasty roast that we would moan in memory of that rare treat.

No sacrifice was too great for those with family members in the service. To our disillusionment, those with no military members often managed to get all the red stamps they wanted on the black market or through illegal connections.

Joe and the *Red Gauntlet*

Officer training was out of the question for Joe because of his nearsightedness, and with a family there was need for a higher rate of pay than he could get as a noncommissioned soldier. Lykes Lines, a freighter company that was a customer of his insurance company, was involved in transatlantic shipping for the war effort, so he managed to get a job as purser, where he could use his math skills. When he went into the Merchant Marine in the spring of 1944, he was assigned to the cargo ship *Red Gauntlet*. Pregnant with our second child, I went to Baltimore to see him off, not knowing where he was going.

There was much emphasis on secrecy, with signs all over reminding people not to talk about where they thought their military members were: "Loose Lips Sink Ships." I had no idea where Joe was: the mail was strictly censored. I would get occasional letters with no indication of where they came from, and his address, in turn, was just c/o Lykes Lines; I would write letters and wonder if he would ever get any of them. He could write about his fellow crewmen, though, and once wrote me that he was taking a "load of potatoes from Maine"—innocent-sounding enough but hardly potatoes. When our son was born in October, Joe got word of it somehow and wrote from the Firth of Forth in Scotland.

One day while Joe was overseas, I returned home to learn that the representative from the Red Cross had come bearing a telegram with the bad news of the death of one of my brothers, Prentice, in a raid over Germany. He was the Captain of a B-17 bomber and had been stationed in England with the 8th Air Force. A squadron of bombers had flown over Frankfurt, where they were attacked by German fighter planes, and he had received a direct hit in the cockpit of the plane. His crew broke formation and sped to England, hoping to save him, to no avail. Letters from his crewmen followed, filled with sorrow and appreciation.

It was only after Joe came home at the end of the War that I finally knew of his whereabouts, his sailing destinations and routes. His load of "potatoes" (munitions) had gone by convoy across the North Atlantic.

One port was Antwerp, which, at the time of the Battle of the Bulge in December 1944, was under frequent attack by German V-1 and V-2 rockets. Joe had a very close call there. He needed a haircut and had heard there was a barber on a freighter three piers down, so he started out for his haircut. He had stopped to talk to a crewman on another ship, and when he got to his destination the ship was gone—blown up by a direct hit while he was on his way to it.

At the end of the War in Europe, the *Red Gauntlet* was ordered to Calcutta. On the way, in the Suez Canal, they passed ships loaded with troops heading home, who yelled at them, "You're going the wrong way!" They landed in Calcutta, unloaded, and gave the crew shore leave. When they were due back, Joe saw an angry mob, with clubs and stones, pursuing a crew member who had gotten drunk and ridden a sacred cow. He made it aboard with a wound on his head. Joe knew he could not get the injured man to a hospital safely, so he took out his first-aid gear and sewed up the wound as best he could.

The War in the Pacific was now over, so they headed for home, around the Cape of Good Hope, up the west side of Africa to Dakar, and thence across the Atlantic to Caracas, where they took on a load of bauxite, and finally to the United States.

One by one, our own boys returned home. We were all very conscious of the huge gap left by Prentice's death. One brother, the Marine, had taken part in the battle for Iwo Jima, and another had been in five invasions as a medical service corpsman. By 1947 our postwar paths were set and we each went our separate ways. Our servicemen never really talked about their experiences, which gave a new poignancy to that part of their lives we never could be a part of.

Marion ("Wiggy") Weathers Grassi (Smith 1937) and Otto Joseph Anthony Grassi, Jr. (Princeton 1936), both from the New York suburbs, met in their early teens sharing summers in Sunapee, New Hampshire. They married in 1939. After the War, Joe returned to his old job underwriting marine insurance. They raised two children in Scarsdale, New York. Joe died in 1962. Wiggy came to Kendal at Hanover as a founder in 1991 to be close to Sunapee, where she continues to spend summers with her family.

THE DEFENSE OF AMERICA

~

Midge Rogers Guise

WHEN THE NAZIS MARCHED INTO POLAND IN 1939, then kept right on going to overwhelm France, Denmark, and the Low Countries, there was nothing left between them and me at Chatham but the great Atlantic. What could prevent U-boats from surfacing off Cape Cod's barrier Outer Beach and discharging flotillas of rubber rafts which armed soldiers could carry over the sand to relaunch into Pleasant Bay? The possibility was acutely real to me at age 11, and I knew what I was going to do about it.

Our summer house, perched on a high sandy bluff, was marked by a stately 40-foot flagpole overlooking Pleasant Bay. Close by at the edge of this great lookout point was a well-camouflaged little depression, actually a secret rendezvous we kids called "Sleepy Hollow." I had already figured out that I could lie there hidden, propped on elbows with my brother's .22 rifle at the ready, and watch if any of those rubber boats were dragged across the beach and into the Bay. If any raft paddled within range I would shoot holes in it and sink it. I worried about having enough ammunition if there were more than five or six boats. And if they reached shore and started to climb up my steep bank, I'd scramble down the back side, run across the salt marsh, jump the creek, and disappear into the woods beyond. Eventually I would alert the Navy and the Coast Guard in town. I might be a heroine.

In Chatham there were lots and lots of Navy and Coast Guardsmen, perhaps because the primary radio receiving station for the North Atlantic and European Theater of War was located there. Up to 5,000 men filled the Old Harbor Inn, the Mattaquasson, the Hawthorne, Wayside, and Chatham Bars inns. Uniforms were everywhere, as were jeeps and small trucks with Navy insignia on the doors. I got to know some of these men when my brother joined the auxiliary patrol to monitor the harbor entrance from a commandeered yacht. Many 17-year-old boys volunteered to do that the summer before they were drafted.

I also knew some of them from picnicking on the Outer Beach and visiting with the walking patrols from the Old Harbor Life Saving Station and the Orleans Coast Guard Station. These men carried pistols, radios, and binoculars, and usually had a dog as well. On four-hour cycles, they walked towards each other from their respective stations. Where they met was our chosen spot. They would stop and visit with us, we'd give them cookies, and then they would jog off to reach their stations in the allotted time. I was spellbound by their stories of U-boat sightings, flotsam and jetsam picked up on the beach to analyze, and talking to their headquarters. I could see for myself black oil on the beaches.

Along with all these servicemen came some warlike regulations. Each person in town got fingerprinted, photographed, and issued an I.D. tag. Mine was a steel-link bracelet, which I was ordered to wear. We were also ordered to be off the beaches and the water by 6:00 p.m. I remember one time when we got becalmed while sailing and the Coast Guardsmen came rowing after us. Did they really think 11- and 12-year-olds were threats to our national security? Many of these servicemen were from Iowa and Nebraska and didn't row all that well either!

I remember also our difficulty in blacking out our huge old summer house full of windows, sitting so high on a windy hill. We had installed the recommended black-paper roller shades and the twist tabs to hold them tightly down the sides of the window frames. We decided to declare the living room with its picture window off limits after dark, since we really couldn't black that out. Mostly we stayed in the kitchen or out on the porch in the fading evening light. We had become very used to the accommodation by the summer of 1943 and recognized its importance from the government posters proclaiming the risks of disaster visited upon our merchant marine men from U-boat sinkings. (We later learned we lost up to 43 ships a month in the North Atlantic!)

We felt the danger too, especially when my dad had sailed from Norfolk, Virginia, to Oran, Africa, to set up a general hospital during the North African campaign; we had worried so much during the long intervals between his V-mail letters. We had become used to gas rationing and a national speed limit of 35 m.p.h. in order to save rubber on tires. We had a large "victory garden," sailed to the poultry farm in South Orleans, and walked to town for groceries or to go to the movies.

*Pleasant Bay, Chatham, Massachusetts, as viewed from
Midge's house. The barrier reef shows just below the horizon.*

One day I was in the kitchen with my mother, deep in our annual jelly-making. It was terribly hot. The four-burner Glenwood kerosene stove, the stewing, steaming apples, the boiling beach plum juice, and the kettle of sterilizing jars conspired to keep us perspiring even in our bathing suits. It took two of us to keep up with all the simultaneous demands of our mass production. I was on a cooling-off breather at the window when I noticed the two naval officers below.

"Mom, come here. There are two officers outside." We hadn't heard them, and I couldn't see any vehicle around.

"Oh, dear." Mom tightened as she looked out the window. "One of them is a Commander. What in the world do they want?" We watched as they walked around the house. Then suddenly Mom froze.

"Oh no, is it Horatio?" she gasped. Stepping determinedly to a door, she called out, "Can I help you, Sir? Do you have word of my husband?"

The men seemed to ignore her. They continued to poke around the house, looking here and there. We followed from inside, moving from room to room and window to window.

"Please, Sir, tell me if you have word of my husband?" she pleaded.

"Ah, no Ma'am, is he in the service?" Mom visibly relaxed. And now at last she had their attention.

"Yes.... he is in North Africa. He's a surgeon with the 6th General Hospital." Then to me, "Midge dear, run get my raincoat to put over this disreputable old bathing suit."

While I did so, she returned to the kitchen and moved the pots off the stove. I saw her try to stroke the loose strands of her hair back in place, but they didn't behave. She found the men again, back under the kitchen windows, and invited them in.

"Thank you, Ma'am, in a minute." The Commander talked on a radio. The other officer made notes on a clipboard, then finally met us at the door. A long interrogation followed regarding the history of the house and our occupancy, activities, and any technical equipment, photographs, or maps we might have of the area. It made me nervous. I saw that one man had a gun in a holster and handcuffs on his belt. Were we suspect?

"Well, thank you, Ma'am," the Commander finally allowed. "I'm sorry to have worried you, but you were reported signaling eastward out to sea on four separate occasions this month. I think you are aware that U-boats are sighted quite frequently off these shores?"

"Oh, yes," I piped up excitedly, "One went through the Cape Cod Canal and sank a freighter in it. We saw the freighter. The soldiers stopped us and looked into our trunk for guns."

"Yes, well, here it's the fishermen who we find running out to the German subs. They signal at night with headlights from some especially prominent hills. We believe they may be trading local maps and photographs of the area for money. Sometimes our auxiliary patrols find food or oil hidden under their decks in the fish holds. Now, may I come in please and check your blackout shades?"

The men finally left with a handshake, a thank you, and an armful of our family photograph albums, which they said would be returned at war's end.

That night in bed I thought once again how we really were on the front line of the defense of America, and I reviewed the integrity of my strategic position in "Sleepy Hollow," the .22 rifle, and my escape route.

Midge Rogers grew up near Boston, spending summers at Chatham on Cape Cod. She attended Winsor School and Middlebury College. In 1950, she married David Donnan and raised three children in Boxford, Massachusetts, and later Columbus, Ohio. There she married Gordon Guise and was deeply involved in schools, inner-city child day care, and much other volunteering. As a grandmother, she physically rehabbed three stately but totally trashed 1900-era inner-city town houses. Gordon died in 1995. Woodworking, tennis, and sailing draw Midge to Chatham annually. She entered Kendal at Hanover in 2000 with her soul mate Bob Van Horn, who died in 2002.

Mary with husband John in 1945

IN FEBRUARY 1944, AS A YOUNG NEW ENGLAND-BRED BRIDE who had never been west of Ohio, I found myself in the heart of Kansas. Hays, Kansas, to be exact, a small town where tumbleweed blew down the main street and the natives talked proudly of their one claim to fame: Wild Bill Hickok had been their first sheriff. My new husband, John, had just received his gold bars as a Second Lieutenant and was assigned to Victoria Air Force Base, just outside Hays, one of several bases training B-29 crews prior to their departure for Asia.

A small town has problems when faced with a sudden influx of outsiders, but Hays was doing its best to accommodate the families of the men at Victoria. We considered ourselves extraordinarily lucky to find an apartment.

Well, to be honest, a room.

It had once been a sleeping porch, a long narrow room with windows along one side. Furnishings were sparse, and the bed—which in the daytime could be lifted up against the wall, though the wheels stuck out, creating small, uncomfortable protrusions to be avoided with care—reached to the window wall when in use. This meant that to get from one end of the room to the other in the evening, you had to crawl over the bed.

A dark closet, a step below the room, was the kitchen; it managed to accommodate a small stove and a small refrigerator. No cabinets. It being wartime, all pots and pans were Pyrex. That was fine until one evening when I was cooking cauliflower and the pan exploded, sending boiling water and hot flowerets of cauliflower all over the room. Luckily I was not in the closet/kitchen at the time.

We shared a hall bathroom with two other couples who had accommodations much like ours—though we seemed to have more than our share of windows. We liked our windows, but the near-constant Kansas wind rattled and shook them so we rarely had a quiet night. Oddly, when we left Kansas some months later, I had trouble sleeping and tossed and turned at night, missing my creaking and shuddering window panes.

Our grocery store was named "Grass's." After my first request for help, as I eyed a bin full of peas—"How many of those pods do I need to have enough peas for two people?"—they knew they had a neophyte on their hands. Every time I entered the store they had something waiting for me. Since Hays was surrounded by farmers with many children, Grass's had rationing coupons to spare. "Now tonight, Mary, you're going to have a T-bone steak, and this is how you'll prepare it." We ate better during our months in Kansas than at any other time during John's years in the service.

My feeling of playing house in Hays was interrupted by my first bridge game at the Air Base. I was invited to have lunch and a friendly game of bridge by a fellow military wife who shared our house. My partner at the bridge table was a colonel's wife. A friendly, appealing woman at lunch, she became a fierce bridge player. Everything that went wrong was my fault. I was certainly not a great bridge player, but being the one always at fault finally became too much for me, and I suggested that, since she had played the hand under discussion, perhaps it wasn't all my fault. The colonel's wife looked startled. One of the other women immediately jumped to her feet and dragged me with her to the ladies' room.

"Mary, you *never* disagree with a colonel's wife!"

"But she's been nagging at me all afternoon."

My friend shook her head firmly. "Never mind. Just remember that you must never disagree with the wife of an officer who outranks your husband."

The true seriousness of my new life became apparent when I saw the first crashed B-29 at the end of a runway at the Base. The smoldering remains of the huge silver plane brought the War home. It also brought a clearer understanding of why the pilots we met and drank with distrusted the new plane: the men we knew at Victoria would be in the first group of B-29s to go overseas. The enormous, lovely-to-look-at, uncamouflaged airplanes had been rushed into service before all the mechanical problems had been resolved. We did not know then about the huge numbers of B-29s that would fall from the skies even before they reached their bombing destinations. At a later date one group of 111 B-29s, on their way to bomb Japan, lost 17 planes to mechanical failure during the flight from their base in Guam to Japan. Nor did we even dream about the kamikaze attacks our pilots would endure over Japan as Japanese fighter pilots crashed their planes into the B-29s to bring them down. Though I certainly had concern for the well-being of our new friends, I was enormously grateful that John was not a pilot.

One bright, sunny morning in late spring, after John had left for the Base, there was a knock on our door. When I opened it I found a tall, handsome, full-bird colonel. He smiled, "I want your apartment. I've been at Victoria for almost a year and I've not been able to find an apartment so my wife can join me."

"But we're still in it!"

Another smile. "You won't be for long."

Of course he was right.

That evening Johnny came home: "You won't believe the orders I got today."

"Ah, yes. I know. Where are we going?"

John was ordered to go to Florida for further training, and I planned to return to my parents for the six weeks we would be separated. As we said goodbye to each other at the railroad station, I was in tears. We'd only been married a few months and I dreaded the separation. Minutes after John's train departed, I found myself embraced by an older woman. She led me to a sheltered corner of the platform, patted my shoulder, and wiped a tear off my cheek as she said, "My dear, he'll be all right. He'll come home to you." I cried for a moment on her shoulder and then realized, with shock, that my new friend thought John was going off into combat. My tears stopped and I stammered my thanks for her sympathy, too embarrassed to tell her I only faced a short separation. My comforter probably went home thinking she had done her wartime duty; certainly I got on the train feeling a little more mature than I had earlier in the day.

On to Louisiana

Eventually I joined John again—in Alexandria, Louisiana, at a B-17 Air Base. This time we had the whole second floor of a big, shabby house on a tree-lined street in the residential part of the city. The apartment had high ceilings, scratched and stained furniture, two big rooms plus a large kitchen with a white enamel table in the center where a good southerner taught me to create pralines by throwing them at the table. We also shared the apartment with a seemingly endless host of over-sized cockroaches who claimed the bathroom and kitchen as soon as the lights went out at night.

Our landlady, Mrs. O'Neal, had an elderly black woman, Lettie, who came in daily to take care of the house. Our days were full of Mrs. O'Neal's complaints about Lettie, and we often heard her loud scoldings. It troubled us. Then, one day, Mrs. O'Neal told us, with tears in her eyes, that Lettie had had a stroke. The tears surprised us, but we were even more surprised when we found Mrs. O'Neal spending much of each day cooking soups and puddings to take to Lettie every afternoon. We had daily reports on Lettie's health until, finally, Lettie returned. The scolding recommenced.

We decided we were too northern to understand.

By April of 1945 we had a baby daughter. On the 12th of that month I was reading a book and listening to music on the radio when the radio suddenly went dead. After a silence of several seconds, an announcer said, "President Roosevelt has died. I repeat. President Roosevelt is dead." There was another silence and then the music resumed.

In a flash the world changed. The sun was still shining through the window, creating a beam of light across the floor, and small Patty was still cooing gently in her crib. To this day the streak of sun and the contented sounds of a baby lock that moment into my memories. But the reactions in Alexandria were far more dramatic. People were crying on the streets. They stopped each other, even total strangers, to share their sorrow. History seemed to pause for a moment as everyone worked to understand and accept that their leader, who had seemed somehow immortal, was gone.

John remained in the Air Force for another year, and then we started over—he to find a job, I to be a housewife and mother. But those first years of our married life marked us, even as they marked our whole generation.

A native of Hanover, New Hampshire, Mary graduated from Skidmore College, married John Jenkins, and spent the first 15 years of marriage caring for four children. She then became president of a local League of Women Voters. This led to offices in local government in Westport, Connecticut: Planning and Zoning Commission; RTM (Representative Town Meeting), where she was the first woman moderator; and the Board of Finance. Time out for a two-week grant from the West German Government to study German women in politics, and two US-USSR Bridges for Peace exchange trips to the Soviet Union. Mary and John entered Kendal at Hanover in 1999.

"Loose Lips"

~

Marcia Auerbach Khatri

IN THE SPRING OF 1944, when I was 15 years old and living on a farm in Vermont with my parents and sister, my father, George Auerbach, left the farm to travel by train to Los Angeles. Although he had thought that he and my mother would be able to manage a farm and leave behind the work they had been doing in the movie industry—my father wrote screen plays, my mother was an actress—it hadn't been easy. So he was on his way back to Los Angeles with a new screen play that he had recently completed.

Not long after he left, I came home from school one day and found my mother in a state of agitation. Two black limousines, bearing Washington, D.C., license plates, had driven up to the farm, and several men had poured out of the cars and proceeded to search the house and barn. My mother was even more disturbed because the neighbors had been driving slowly by our farm all day, craning their necks to see what was going on.

There had been much gossip at our expense ever since we moved to the farm. They called us "city folk" and looked at us with a great deal of suspicion. We were different. It didn't help that my mother wore blue jeans and high heels to the grocery store—which caused considerable interest, as well as many *tsk's* and shaking heads.

We had a huge antenna in our back yard that my father installed because our radio reception was extremely poor. Neophytes at farming, we also caused smiles as our neighbors watched us.

One disaster almost became local lore. My mother's first purchase, on our arrival in Vermont, was a washing machine. With horror she discovered that we had no electricity. The washer was returned and the money spent to buy a horse that, quite logically, was named Bendix. My father thought the bigger the better—so Bendix was huge. The first morning after his arrival I woke to noise, confusion, and lots of people milling around the stable. Bendix had fallen through the stable floor! The poor horse was suspended on the floor, his legs dangling below him in the stable's dark, low cellar. How to get him out? Eventually the stable roof had to be removed, and Bendix—unhurt, but clearly unhappy—was hauled up and out with a huge derrick.

As the War intensified, the town's suspicions, fed by our strangeness, my father's British accent, his German name, our California life style, the antenna, and our ineptness as farmers, developed into a belief that my father was a German spy. Aware of their suspicions, he had given a speech in the Town Hall calling the charges absurd and adding that his wife's ancestors had fought in the American Revolution. It didn't matter what my father said; the men in the black limousines confirmed the suspicions. The townspeople believed the visit meant that military authorities had come to investigate.

My life really changed after the limo visit. I had been elected president of my class, but after the limos no one would attend class meetings; a teacher told me, "Marcia, no one will come any

George Auerbach

more." I had been an airplane spotter—a position I was very proud of—and they told me I could no longer do that. Worst of all, my friends no longer called to invite me to various events.

It was not until we moved back to Los Angeles, late that same summer, that my father told us the following story that explained why we were visited by black limousines containing agents from military intelligence.

On arrival in New York City, in early May, with several hours to kill before his train departed for Los Angeles, my father went to the Harvard Club. At the bar he began a conversation with a high-ranking officer in uniform who, he realized, had already had many drinks. The general told my father that he had just returned from England and, in a slurred, half-drunken voice, began to talk about the preparation of troops for the coming invasion. As he reeled off many details, my father became anxious about the information the officer was revealing. He finally asked the general if he was staying at the Club. Learning that he was, he escorted the general to his room.

When my father boarded his train for the West Coast, he continued to worry about the general telling a complete stranger so many details about an invasion scheduled to take place soon. He was too restless to sleep, so he went to the club car, where he joined a card game with two young men. He was surprised that the young men were not in uniform: they seemed to be about thirty years old. He asked what they did, and they said they worked for the government.

My father then told them that he had a friend who had told him a story about a high-ranking officer in the Army who had casually revealed a lot of details about his unit; the friend, he said, had asked my father what he should do about it. My father asked the government men what advice he should give his friend.

At once the two men stood and told my father he should join them in their compartment. They were alone in the club car, and my father became nervous and said he didn't think he would do that. They then showed him their government identification and insisted that he follow them. When they reached the compartment, they wanted to know more about the friend, and my father admitted that he was actually the one who had had the experience. He told them everything the general had told him. One of the agents disappeared, but the other stayed with my father for the entire trip, never letting him out of his sight. On his arrival in Los Angles, an agent remained with him until after the D-Day invasion. My father was not allowed to make phone calls or write letters. He was totally guarded at all times.

Soon after his arrival in Los Angeles, he read in a newspaper that during the days he was on the train traveling to the West Coast, the officer he had talked to at the Harvard Club had committed suicide in a Washington, D.C., hotel room.

My father was a writer with a great imagination. He loved to tell stories of all kinds—and often exaggerated. So, was this story true? We'll never know. But the men in the black limousines who examined our house and barn and bombarded my mother with questions were very real.

Marcia spent her childhood in Beverly Hills, California, where her mother acted in film noir *and her father churned out movie scripts. In the late 1930s the family moved to a Vermont farm. The unsuccessful venture lasted only five years. After the University of Chicago and Katherine Gibbs School, Marcia worked for the theatrical producer of Arthur Miller's and Lillian Hellman's plays. Marriage and an autistic son precipitated an effort to learn all she could about autism. The development of a medical vocabulary led to an editing job at a medical textbook publisher and a final happy marriage to an Indian doctor. He died in 1995. Marcia came to Kendal at Hanover in 2004. Her son died in 2009. Marcia died in 2011.*

PARALLEL REALITIES

~

Sally Todd Nelson

W<small>HEN THE</small> W<small>AR BEGAN</small>, I was in high school, so the war years were the years in which I grew up. One by one, the boys I grew up with went off to fight. Their letters and stories allowed me to share their experiences and made the War shown on the radio and in papers and magazines a parallel reality to our own daily lives.

Everyone I knew was in the Navy, and I spent the War writing letters. At first, it was just fun and exciting. The boys were in boot camp and wrote funny, complaining letters with Sad-Sack-type cartoons of oversized uniforms on undersized sailors, and we wrote long letters with S.W.A.K lipstick kisses on the backs of the envelopes. Then we sent little blue-gray V-Mail overseas letters to the Pacific, which made their way to PT boats, Pacific islands, and all the ships at sea. You could communicate a lot despite the censor. The boys I knew well were telling amusing stories about Japanese torpedoes just missing them, but I knew it was real, and not funny.

During the War, Columbia University trained naval officers, and at Evensong at Riverside Church the nave was filled with the midshipmen singing: *Eternal Father strong to save, Oh hear us when we cry to thee for those in peril on the sea.* And I thought of all my friends at sea.

In New York we went to dances at school, and at Riverside we went to parties in people's homes. At these, we met boys in the Navy on leave or in training. At Columbia, we met a lot of the midshipmen. They had not yet been exposed to the War, and they felt grown-up; they were funny and confident, and they flirted. One boy I danced with asked the name of my perfume, and when I told him it was Elizabeth Arden's *Heaven Scent*, he smiled and said, "You certainly are." I danced with an English sailor at a party in the school gym; it was a slow dance near the end of the evening, the lights were low, and the singer sang: *And a nightingale sang in Berkeley Square.* And I felt a tear on his cheek.

In the subway we smiled at groups of Russian sailors who were stationed at the Brooklyn Naval Yard. At parties we heard what it was actually like to be escorting a convoy with supplies for England across the North Atlantic and for Russia on the Murmansk Run, and for how many minutes one could live in the cold Atlantic water. I knew a boy who had gone ashore in the second wave on Iwo Jima; the second wave lacked the benefit of surprise, and most of his buddies died. My sister and I wrote to a childhood friend, the son of our mother's college roommate, who was on Tinian Island, where going out in the open meant facing Japanese snipers. His letters to me were later used by the Navy as evidence for giving him medical benefits: once home, he still could not go out of the house to work or school.

Our lives changed. My grandparents had planned to send each of their grandchildren to school in England for a year, but that all ended on September 1, 1939, when, instead of being in England at school, I looked at the pictures of people digging trenches in London's Hyde Park. My aunt's wedding to an Oxford classmate was put off because her fiancé was now in the RAF, flying in the Battle of Britain. Those were the flyers that Winston Churchill spoke of when he said, "Never have so many owed so much to so few." My aunt and her fiancé never married; by the end of the War they'd lost too much time together.

My father had been in the 7th Regiment of New York in World War I and had fought in the battle breaking the Hindenburg Line. Each day, he read the *Herald-Tribune* on his way to work at the Bell Labs, listened to the radio when he got home, and, after supper, listened to the radio with Rosalie Allen singing cowboy songs while he waited for the late news. He had maps on which he followed the progress of the War. At our dinner table, you could not leave until we had all finished—not only the food, but the discussion. We talked about the War, the Nazis, Stalin, the concept of democracy and the Greek origins of the word, our treatment of Japanese-Americans, Churchill, history, and so on.

I had read Jan Valtin's *Out of the Night*, in which he described in horrifying detail the Gestapo torturing and killing his wife. When I was younger, I wasn't aware of much about the terrible things of the world and I was shocked to discover them. My friend Lois had met a sweet midshipman from Nebraska who wanted to marry her; one Saturday night he suddenly realized that she was Jewish and immediately dropped her. My school had foreign diplomats' children, and my friend Atya was Czech. Her father was in the United States during the War, but his brother was in Moscow and took part in the Czech coup d'état and probable killing of Jan Masaryk.

Life of the everyday sort went on. We lived a normal family life, but there was the parallel reality of the letters from the Pacific and the news in the papers, in the newsreels, and on the radio. There was meat available from the butcher as long as you did not want to know its weight or its cost per pound. Gas was hard to get, and we had given up the car.

Dancing Fast and Slow

My friends and I lived our own parallel reality. In the daytime, we all wore white bobby socks, saddle shoes, penny loafers, wool skirts, Peter Pan collars on our blouses, pearl necklaces, and cardigan sweaters. In the daytime, we were still kids and we went to school. After school, and after Riverside Church on weekends, we went over two blocks to our favorite drugstore and soda bar, where we played the juke box and danced and ate sundaes, chocolate malts, root beer sodas with chocolate ice cream. We danced fast numbers. I could swing my legs up across the front of a partner and around his back, because I had been a dancer. I loved *Don't Fence Me In*, *Chattanooga Choo-Choo*, *Sentimental Journey*, *The White Cliffs of Dover*. At dances, the bands alternated fast and slow songs, but every dance ended with the lights down as they played *Stardust*.

On the weekends, in the evening it became a different world. We wore high heels and rayon stockings: silk had disappeared, but even rayon was scarce, and sometimes we rubbed brown stain on our legs instead. Night life was really exciting during the War. I was a sailor's girl, an adult, out on the town. Although I was young, if I accompanied a man in uniform—himself perhaps only 18 or 20—we could get theater tickets, or get into nightclubs at the head of the line; we were welcome everywhere. Sherman Billingsley of the Stork Club gave me a little wooden stork for my birthday. At Armando's, they gave me a bottle of French perfume for Christmas; the pianist always played my favorite song when we left. Maxine Sullivan, between her shows at the Blue Angel, came and sat with us as she used to years ago with my parents at the Village Vanguard. Josh White sang *Strange Fruit* at Café Society. We went to Nick's in the Village to hear jazz by Bird, PeeWee Russell, and Eddie Condon. We saw every show on Broadway. At the Pierre, I finally learned to eat escargots, lobster, and mushrooms.

The parallel dimensions of our lives were clearly reflected in magazines. In *Life* magazine, for example, wartime tragedy and home-front frivolity were side by side: bombed cities, island-hopping invasions, a naked Chinese baby crying alone in the rubble; Betty Grable in a bathing suit, Rita Hayworth kneeling on a bed in a black lace nightgown, and teenagers in bobby socks dancing the Lindy Hop. It was a strange balance of things side by side; we went to parties and danced, joked and flirted, and had a good time; then, late in the evening going home, the nice boy I had been dancing with sat on the hallway steps with me and told me how he had felt looking at the bodies of his friends on the beach of Iwo Jima.

But it was especially the movies that colored our feelings and experiences with the patina of romance. It was easy to go to movies because it was a bargain, especially at Saturday matinees: 10 cents for under 12 years, and only 25 cents for older than 12. You saw an A feature film, a B film, cartoons, an installment of a series (I liked *Tarzan*), previews of coming attractions, a travel film in color, and the "News of the World in Review." During the B film, if there was any kissing, we squared our Hershey wrappers on our knees and loudly popped them. In the newsreels, we saw all the things we had read about in the paper: Chamberlain coming home from Munich having sold out Czechoslovakia; the King and Queen walking through the rubble of bombed-out London.

The emotional and romantic impact of the movies on us was enormous. We thought that the movies echoed the way we felt about the

War, although in fact, of course, they were teaching us how we *should* feel. They showed us a romantic war. People were always getting on trains and leaving. *Brief Encounter*, though not a war film, showed the romance and the departure of wartime. Later, I saw *Mrs. Miniver*, and it was like our lives, happy everyday events, and then watching from afar the miracle of Dunkirk when all the little fishing and pleasure boats crossed the Channel to bring the soldiers safely home. On a cold, snowy night I was walking with a deeply unhappy boy. It was too cold to stay out walking, so we went to see *Casablanca*—maybe the most romantic film of lost love ever made, and politically romantic as well. Emotionally, it is a great war film.

Of course, when we talk about the parallel lives of teenagers during the War years, the phrase embraces our young military men as well. Wars are largely fought by kids. We take them at 18, show them how to use weapons, and send them off to fight other kids. It is exciting for them and, until the actual fighting begins, romantic as well. "Join the Navy and see the world"; and they learned from the movies that the guy in uniform always got the girl. What could be more enticing, especially if you are in a sexy uniform that makes you an instant adult, with all adult pleasures suddenly available? But their other world—the world my friends and I knew secondhand from news reports and letters—was the one in which they got to die.

Finally, the War began to wind down and then it ended in Europe. Then the bombs were dropped on Japan, and the War was over. My parents and I had a drink at Times Square and watched the crowds. Dickens' lines seemed applicable to our War, too: "It was the best of times; it was the worst of times." That day, with the entire Square full of sailors, and all of them joyfully kissing girls, it seemed the best of times.

Sally was born in New York City and lived in New Jersey and New York. She went to Buxton School, graduated from Horace Mann-Lincoln High School, went to Middlebury College and to graduate school at Wesleyan and McGill University. Sally married and had four children. After teaching English at various high schools in the United States, she moved to Montreal, where she taught for 40 years at Dawson College and McGill University. In 2008, she retired and came to Kendal at Hanover.

Marriage in Wartime

Trudie Colson Nicholson

Trudie and Howard Nicholson

S IOUX FALLS, SOUTH DAKOTA! Where on earth was that? Howard
Nicholson and I had become formally engaged after a college court-
ship at Oberlin. Now, six months later—in September 1942—the Army
Air Force was sending him to Sioux Falls to receive training to become
a radio operator. South Dakota was many, many miles from where I
was teaching in Albany, New York.

By December, we had decided we wanted to get married before he
might be shipped overseas. My Christmas vacation would be our first
opportunity, and I agreed to travel to Sioux Falls if I could get travel
accommodations.

Space for traveling civilians was scarce; most trains were reserved
for troop movements. I was extremely fortunate to be able to get a coach
seat on the New York Central Albany-Chicago train in their special
coach for women travelers. I planned to spend a night in Chicago with
my college roommate and, the following day, start the long 36-hour
trip to Sioux Falls. It was important that my train arrive in Sioux Falls

before 11:00 p.m. because Howard, who had classes from 11:00 p.m. to 7:00 a.m., wanted to meet me and take me to the private home where he had been able to rent a room for me.

With traveling plans completed, I went home from Albany in early December to visit my parents in Brooklyn. There was both sadness and gladness in that visit. For many reasons it was impossible for them to make the long strenuous trip to South Dakota, but, sad as they were to miss their daughter's wedding, they didn't want to interfere with our happiness.

Very soon after I returned to Albany from this visit, I received a phone call from my father. To my amazement he had followed me from New York to Albany and was in the Albany railroad station. Could I come and meet him immediately before he took a train back to New York? My parents had found my precious, very-difficult-to-obtain tickets and train reservations on the dresser in my bedroom! I couldn't believe it. My father had raced to catch up with me only to arrive in Grand Central Station just as my train pulled out. He had been nervous about entrusting the tickets to the mails, since only a few days remained before my departure, so he decided to deliver them in person. My trip was not starting very propitiously!

On Tuesday, December 15, with my primary school classes over until the new year, I arrived at the Albany railroad station with an enormous, very heavy suitcase full of clothes to please a new husband, Christmas presents for Howard, and the heavy warm apparel I'd need to cope with South Dakota's sub-zero weather. When departure time was announced, I was surprised to see very few other passengers waiting to board. I walked down the platform, dragging my heavy suitcase as I looked for an open car—but I couldn't find one. I began to panic. How could I get on the train? I saw a trainman farther down the platform readying his lantern to signal the engineer that the train should leave. I screamed at him, "No! No! I must get on!" He walked toward me, banging on the doors of several cars until a porter finally appeared and opened one of them. I climbed on and found myself at the rear of the long train, far from my reserved coach near the front. I have no recollection of who or what occupied the various cars that I passed through, lugging my cumbersome suitcase, but I do know that when I finally sank into my seat in the ladies' car I was trembling with total exhaustion.

I could not allow myself to get too excited as the train started westward. It was only Tuesday, and I would not be in Sioux Falls until Friday evening.

As I left Chicago after the visit with my roommate, my excitement began to build. The afternoon passed; the night passed; Friday morning went by, then the afternoon—I began counting the hours. I repeatedly checked the time of our station stops on my watch. Our train was due in Sioux Falls in the early evening. We were running behind schedule, but not enough to cause concern.

Then we arrived in Sioux City—and stopped. It was a long delay. I began to realize that we wouldn't reach Sioux Falls before 11 p.m. I was right: it was almost midnight on Friday evening when we finally pulled into my final destination. I had been sitting in that train seat for 36 hours. My spirits sagged as I got off the train knowing Howard couldn't be there to meet me.

On the platform I looked around, hoping that by some miracle Howard might be there. Then a young soldier appeared beside me and asked, "Are you Trudie? Howard asked me to meet you and take you to your room. He'll call you as soon as he can in the morning." He then took me to 900 West 10th Street, which was to be my home until the first of the year.

Early in the morning the ladies who owned the house called me to the telephone. It was Howard, calling from the Air Base. He had just finished his night classes and would soon be having his "dinner." He'd then get his "'night's'" sleep for the next eight or nine hours. We were very excited that we'd soon be seeing each other. He told me that he and the clergyman who would marry us had decided the ceremony should take place on December 20 at 6:00 p.m., in the choir instead of the sanctuary.

It was then December 19; I had lots to do.

Howard had ordered flowers for me, but since he couldn't leave the base, I had to pick them up myself at the local florist. Our rings were waiting at another shop, and I was to meet with the minister. The Linahans—two maiden ladies and one widow in whose home I was staying—took a genuine interest in the coming marriage and shared our excitement. They sent me to the local bus, and I went into town to complete our wedding arrangements. I don't know how I protected my flowers from the sub-zero weather as I walked about town; I fear they were not at their best on Sunday. I picked up the rings and met with the clergyman. I had brought a copy of our favorite Oberlin hymn, "Still, Still with Thee," and told the minister of my hopes that someone would play it for us at the wedding.

The day passed quickly, and in the late afternoon I left Sioux Falls on an Army bus to go to the Base and meet Howard for the meal that was my dinner and his breakfast.

Our first meeting since my arrival was exciting and joyful. We had a good, though not private, visit in the recreational hall, and then I went back to my room to await my wedding day 24 hours in the future.

Sunday, December 20, arrived. It was not especially sunny, but it wasn't raining and it wasn't snowing; it was just extremely cold. In the morning I went to the church where I would be married that very evening. It was strange sitting alone in the pew, not knowing anyone, and wanting to tell everyone, "I'm getting married here later today."

After the morning service I walked to a cafeteria in the YWCA for my lunch. As I neared the counter, one of the waitresses said to me, "Oh my! Your ears are frozen." "They can't be," I said, "I'm getting married this afternoon!" I knew this was a complete non sequitur, but it was foremost in my mind and I had to tell someone.

Getting to the Church on Time

My time was dragging, but Howard was having a very frustrating, even panicky, time at the Air Base. He had arranged for a special pass to leave the Base for our wedding, but arriving at his unit's headquarters to pick it up, he was told that there was no record of his leave and no pass. He carefully explained his situation and, fortunately, after some deliberation, the lieutenant on duty signed a pass. And Howard was able to pick me up and get us to the church on time.

The choir looked beautiful in the low lights; a young serviceman was playing our Oberlin hymn; and, most surprisingly, there were seven guests in the choir pews—the three Linahans, devout Catholics; the Episcopal Bishop of South Dakota and his wife, alerted to our marriage by the headmistress of the Episcopal School in Albany where I was teaching; and a couple who had learned of the ceremony from friends of Howard's mother in Montclair, New Jersey. Including the organist, the minister, and Howard and me, there were eleven of us there to celebrate our special occasion.

Now, some 68 years later, we love to recall that hectic, confusing, and altogether wonderful time.

Born in Brooklyn, New York, Trudie graduated from Berkeley Institute and Oberlin College, where she met her husband, Howard. She taught primary school classes while Howard served in the United States Air Force, and later became a housewife and mother to their son while Howard attended graduate school and became a professor of economics. Trudie was always an active volunteer and enjoyed reading, writing, and traveling. Howard and Trudie are enjoying their retirement in Hanover, an area Trudie has loved since her years of camping on Lake Fairlee in Vermont. She and Howard came to Kendal at Hanover in 1991.

Looking Through Barbed Wire

~

Lafayette Noda

BEFORE I CAN WRITE ABOUT THE WAR, I need to talk about the situation for Japanese-Americans in America and my life as a Nisei—a "second-generation" Japanese-American. I was born in California. My parents were among the Issei ("first generation") who immigrated here from Japan. We were nine children, growing up during the hard times of the Depression. Father put in vineyards and planted peaches and almonds. When we lost our land in 1929, he started a trucking company.

Before I was born and all the years I was growing up, there was a lot of prejudice against Japanese-Americans as a class. We were called "the Japs." The public in general didn't want the Japanese in California. There was a feeling of competition with us, certainly economically in farming, but also in the schools. We Nisei wanted to excel and do well in school and in our work. We felt this drive, and our parents also tried to instill in us the determination to succeed.

There weren't opportunities for the Japanese in those days, and it was tough. With few exceptions, jobs were closed to us. Some Nisei who graduated from colleges or universities went back to the farms and worked with their parents. Others opened service stations or shops of various kinds, like the laundries run by our Issei parents in the past. It was hard for us Japanese to be considered part of the business activity of the American scene. We weren't accepted.

I wouldn't say that I could really have a dream for myself in the middle of all that prejudice. I aimed for an education and to excel in it, as our parents encouraged us to do. They expected that we boys would go on but that our sisters would marry.

My father's ideals could be seen in the background of his aspirations for us. He hoped that Japan, an old country, would contribute something to young America. He wasn't aggrandizing Japan; he just wanted Japan, with its old traditions, to give something to this country. He thought that, if in no other way, at least his children should do something for America. That's why he named us boys for great men in American history: my oldest brother Andy for Andrew Jackson, Patrick for Patrick Henry, Grant for Ulysses S. Grant, and me for the Marquis de Lafayette.

I went to the University of California at Berkeley because it was a public university and tuition was cheap. I had to pay only $29 a semester. It was very easy to make enough to pay for college in those days. Most of us Nisei earned our way. We worked as "school boys" or "school girls," doing housework and chores for white families in exchange for room, board, and living expenses.

At Berkeley, I majored in chemistry. This probably would have led to a job in some company if I hadn't been Japanese. Still, given my background in agriculture, I thought I might have a chance at an opportunity if I minored in fruit products—the development and control of the production of food. Chemistry would be very useful in canneries, for example, and I hoped I might find a technical position.

When I graduated from Berkeley, I didn't think there were many possibilities for using my studies in the San Joaquin Valley, so my thoughts turned to the orange-juice business in southern California. I went down to Los Angeles and contacted juice-manufacturing companies, imagining they might need chemists to help them develop new juices. My plan was naive, I suppose. Japanese weren't accepted, but I kept trying to find a job. My sister-in-law later told me she heard about me long before she met me: I was known as someone who biked all over Los Angeles looking for a job.

Finally, as a last resort, I found a place in the Central Valley at a canning company near Modesto. I was put in the cannery's control lab and worked with tomato products. The requirement for market production was to concentrate the tomato to a thickness that met government standards. This was rather arbitrary, involving how many seconds the tomato concentrate would stand up when a cylinder of paste was blown out of a can. I had a job, but anyone could have done it, and it was just for the summer.

In the fall, I went back to L.A. and looked again. I kept trying, though there was nothing hopeful and I was torn. My father had an accident and couldn't really run the farm, but my older brother was there. I didn't want to go back to the farm. I didn't want to just be a farmer. I wanted to be more.

Finally, I met someone in the Irrigation Department at UCLA who had a grant from the Avocado Association to study the maturation of avocados. He said he would take me on, and I found a school-boy position with a bachelor who gave me room and board. I helped with the avocado research and enrolled in the masters program in organic chemistry at the university.

Pearl Harbor

On December 7, 1941, I was biking to the lab from the place where I school-boyed. I saw a colleague, a graduate student. He'd stopped for me once before when I'd had a bike accident. This time, he said, "Japan bombed Pearl Harbor." I just couldn't believe it. I couldn't believe it. Japan? Japan bomb Pearl Harbor?

I went to the lab and of course all of the radios were on and everyone was talking about Pearl Harbor. Things changed fast after that. The identification of the Japanese intensified. People focused on our black hair and the shape of our eyes. Requirements were instituted. There was a curfew for us Japanese, and travel restrictions: we had to stay within a few miles of home. The government froze our bank accounts, and then later we could only withdraw a certain amount of money at a time.

My family was on the farm in the San Joaquin Valley in a little place called Cortez, but I decided to stay in Los Angeles, even when there was talk of an "evacuation," a removal of all the Japanese from the West Coast.

In February 1942 President Roosevelt issued Executive Order 9066 authorizing the "internment" of all West Coast Japanese—the Issei and the American-born Nisei. In L.A., we were assigned certain times to appear at designated places. We were told to bring only one suitcase. One suitcase was hardly able to take care of all my clothes, but it was possible. I didn't have a lot.

I went to a bus depot, as ordered. Army soldiers who were there herded us into buses. They took us to the Santa Anita racetrack and told us to get off. The Army had made temporary barracks at the track and organized them around central places for eating and for toilets. There were guard towers and barbed wire around the entire site.

In a Horse Stall

I was put with a group of bachelors who were treated as one unit. We were given one horse stall, which was still obviously a stall, with horse manure on the walls. It smelled. We carried four straw mattresses to our cots. We had to just make do in the horse stall, sleeping and living there and getting our meals at the eating place. We existed. We just got along.

The Japanese as a whole had a *shikata ga nai* attitude about this whole situation. *Shikata ga nai* means "there is nothing you can do about it." You can't do anything. You have to accept. I felt that way.

The *hakujins* (white people) in general were not sympathetic. Some few were, though, and they tried to be helpful. They were limited in what they could do, but they sent letters and asked us if we wanted anything by way of clothes, paper, supplies, other things.

It was really quite something to have the *hakujins* come and help. There was a man named Patrick Lloyd who was a true friend. I had met him while I was at UCLA. He lived a simple life, sharing his possessions with those who needed them. It was quite a chore for him to go from Pasadena, where he lived, to UCLA, in West Los Angeles, but there was a period when he was able to do that. He was a Quaker, a pacifist, who came just to meet with us students. We would come with our paper-bag lunches and we would talk about anything on our minds.

Before the War, Patrick Lloyd had helped me in every way he could as I searched for jobs and tried to just get along in life. While I was at Santa Anita, he reached out to me. There were restrictions. He had to apply to come visit and there were limitations regarding the number of visitors and the time they could stay. I remember walking to the part of the fence where we were allowed to meet visitors. I looked through the barbed wire to talk with him.

It was wartime, and people were caught up in the War. I felt hopeless about it. There was nothing I could do about the War. *Shikata ga nai.* But Patrick Lloyd was very understanding and sympathetic—a good Quaker. He was always trying to help. Even in the middle of war, he was a true friend. I felt I could rely on him. He always showed up.

When I was in Santa Anita, Patrick Lloyd, the Quakers, and some people from other religious bodies who felt that war was wrong were really the encouragement and hope.

War and killing and fighting are not good. They're entirely destructive. The Quakers say that there is that of God in everyone, and I agree. I think that there is goodness in everyone. If we search, we find the good, even in our so-called enemies. If we look, we do find that our enemies are humans, like us.

When I was in Santa Anita, I never gave up. I just felt that there was hope in people. People are good.

Lafayette was eventually moved to the Heart Mountain prison camp in Wyoming. He later rejoined his family, who were imprisoned in Colorado. Through the Quakers, he left the camp during the War for Pendle Hill, a Quaker study center in Pennsylvania. Lafayette earned a doctorate in biochemistry from Stanford University and had a long career as a Professor of Biochemistry at Dartmouth Medical School, where he served as the school's first Asian-American department chair. With his wife Mayme, he became a blueberry-and-Christmas-tree farmer after his retirement. He and Mayme got their Kendal at Hanover apartment in 1991. Mayme died in 2006. A lifelong Quaker, Lafayette was 94 when he wrote this essay.

A Sad Lesson Learned

Sonia Landy Sheridan

IN 1941 BROOKLYN, NEW YORK, the area from Fort Hamilton in the north to Bensonhurst in the south bordered Gravesend Bay, the entry to the New York ports. At night it would be pitch dark on land, for blackout was strictly enforced by neighborhood volunteer wardens. During the day one could see that the entire length of the area bordering the bay was lined with rocks. One could sit on the rocks and watch the supply ships and battleships streaming in and out of New York City. Had I not been a 16-year-old girl, I would have enlisted and been on one of those boats. As it was, my view of World War II was primarily from this vantage point on land.

I say that I would have enlisted because I was a member of a Bensonhurst youth group that was largely concerned with social issues and we were bitterly anti-fascist. Four of us were fast friends and we all considered ourselves artists. There was Phil, a sculptor; Irwin, a painter; Herbie, the star artist in Lafayette high school; and myself. As soon as the three boys were of age, they enlisted. Phil joined the Navy; Irwin chose the Army; and Herbie became an Army parachutist. So while they went off to war, I went to college. From that point on, our experiences were worlds apart.

While I went off to Hunter College to major in art and French, with a war major in drafting, my three friends were living the War with their bodies, minds, and lives. Not until the late years of the War would I realize how different our lives had become. Yet I wanted to make a contribution. So in my 16th year I collected balls of tin foil and made posters supporting the troops. On weekends one could find me in front of *The New York Times* building on 42nd Street and Broadway shaking a collection can and shouting, "Give to the war effort! Give to war relief!" It usually took only a short time to fill up a can with nickels and dimes.

In my 17th year, when I was still very much a teenager in spite of a year in college, a Bensonhurst girlfriend asked me to accompany her to the New York Public Library. She was to meet a French sailor there, and she needed someone to translate for her. When I got to the library steps, I saw that her French friend had a friend with him. During the rest of that year, I spent all my free time with him, not really understanding the implications of his being a seaman on the battleship *Richelieu* belonging to the French Vichy government. The young man was a splendid 19-year-old and of fine character; moreover, he was French and wrote poetry.

When at the end of the year the *Richelieu* left New York City, friends told me that I should not have been with a Vichy service person. At an older age his character would have mattered more to me than his service on a Vichy ship. As it was, my friends easily convinced me that now that I was 18 I should join the Free French Canteen on 42nd Street and 2nd Avenue, a version of the American USO but for French de Gaullist servicemen.

Joining the Free French canteen required a letter from one of my French teachers confirming that I was indeed a Hunter student, spoke French, and was 18 years old. Thus I spent the third year of the War dancing with French servicemen and regularly meeting such celebrities as Charles Boyer. I learned a lot of colloquial French and slang, much to the chagrin of my other French professor, a former member of the Comédie Française, who wanted us to be deeply entrenched in Molière and Racine. But I thought that I was at least no longer with Nazi collaborators.

I still was doing my college work, and I took many life drawing classes. I thought that my work was very good and was anxious to share it with my artist friends upon their hoped-for return; I had always suspected that they did not quite share my opinion of myself as artist.

Since I was still living at home in Bensonhurst, I was able to keep in touch with information about my artist friends. Sadly, I heard that Herbie had been killed while parachuting into France. His war experience was very short; he must have been just 18 years old. Then one day Irwin's mother told me that her son was lying wounded in an Army hospital, while Phil wrote to me that he was wounded and in a Navy hospital. The War was over for both of these young artists.

The first time I saw them upon their return, they were walking arm in arm. This was unusual for them. They told me that since each had lost an opposing eye, together they were one visual person. Now as serious as these young artists were, they were still from Bensonhurst—and anyone who has ever seen a WW II movie knows that the wise-cracking private was usually from Bensonhurst, as was Danny Kaye. As they walked together, Phil and Irwin sometimes met guys who had not gone to war. When they saw Irwin's face covered with blue shrapnel and a missing eye, one would make a nasty crack such as, "Are the big ugly heroes without eyes back?" Irwin would say nothing, but would pluck out his artificial eye and shove it in the guy's face.

My lack of actual war experience may be why I did not understand what happened when I proudly showed Irwin a poster that I had recently made. I wanted to let him see how I had progressed as an artist. With years of life-drawing experience, I was able to paint an image of a very handsome soldier thrusting his bayoneted rifle towards the viewer. This was an unfortunate lack of sensitivity on my part, for when Irwin saw the poster, his face turned angry with disgust. I vaguely remember that he said, "I find that kind of thing very distasteful!" All I recall of that is my horror at having shown him that image. As the years went by and I pursued my work as an artist, I always had that image of Irwin, his face covered with blue shrapnel, one missing eye, and his look of dismay that I did not understand what war was about.

During the waning days of the War, as I was about to graduate, I went to a college counselor in response to an enlistment call for servicewomen. The counselor dissuaded me from enlisting and suggested that I go on to graduate school. In retrospect, I must have been strongly influenced by what happened to my three artist friends—for I agreed with her.

For all of my remaining productive years as an artist, I often had Irwin in my mind, for he showed me that the finest painting was not art if the emotion was false. I never returned to live in Brooklyn. I lost track of Phil and Irwin, so I do not know how they managed as artists, each with only one eye. Phil, as a sculptor, needed two eyes for depth perception, and Irwin's shrapnel-filled head posed a serious danger to his life.

Sonia was for many years artist/professor in The School of the Art Institute of Chicago. Her work is in permanent collections there at the Art Institute, as well as in the San Francisco Museum of Modern Art; the National Gallery of Canada; the Fundacion Telefonica, Madrid, Spain; the Tokyo Metropolitan Museum of Photography; and other institutions. Dartmouth's Hood Museum of Art accessioned 634 of her art works into its permanent collection. The Daniel Langlois Foundation of Montreal accessioned her media art work and records of her pioneering program Generative Systems. She was a Guggenheim Fellow and three times National Endowment for the Arts grantee. She and her husband Jim came to Kendal at Hanover in 1993.

INTERNING THE JAPANESE

Elizabeth Toll Stragnell

FOLLOWING THE GREAT DEPRESSION of the 1930s we were comfortable in our WASP community in Southern California. Events occurring in Europe were shadows on a distant stage, having little effect on our lives. My grandparents had decided against their long-planned trip to Germany for the XI Olympiad, fearing what Adolf Hitler might have in mind. They read the *Los Angeles Times* and were aware of his rise to power, but chose not to dwell on his antics.

My mother, a single parent of four, was too busy with us and with school and town activities to take on Hitler. It is my impression that my family was fairly typical of the time and place in feeling isolated from the War in Europe.

We rode the school bus morning and afternoon and looked forward to the adventures of each day, forming neat lines as the bus approached, boarding to join youngsters from the first stops: the Anglo, Mexican, and Japanese families who lived in unincorporated county territory abutting San Marino. The Nisei, second-generation American-born Japanese, were the quiet ones sitting sedately on the school bus—the ones with the straight black hair, the shy looks, the perfect grades, the strange names. We knew that their first names were Shezui, Shigeko, and several others I've long forgotten, but if we knew their last names we could not have pronounced or spelled them. Their families ran a large chrysanthemum nursery that kept them totally occupied. The children had nursery chores after school each day and attended Japanese school all day Saturday. They were not allowed to socialize with us in any way. They were reserved, and quietly polite. How little we knew them!

On September 1, 1939, Hitler dropped bombs on Poland and sent his troops to invade that country. As well as changing the lives of untold millions of people, the news of that invasion ruined my 14th birthday. We went through the motions of Labor Day *cum* birthday, but the usual festive spirit was missing; our thoughts dwelt on the Poles as well as on our own servicemen and what might happen to them should we get into the War, as many thought we should. As folks closed summer places for the winter, we couldn't help but wonder what the future held for us and who might be missing from the next years' gatherings. But the War was still far away.

South Pasadena

These feelings of unease stayed with us for several years as we followed the actions in Europe, prayed for Allied soldiers, sent Bundles to Britain, watched snippets of the War in Europe as shown in Movietone News, but the War seemed very far away. The demeanor of our Japanese acquaintances remained unchanged; they were shadows in our midst. We advanced into the high school in South Pasadena, riding the "Big Red Streetcar" instead of the school bus, the Japanese sitting sedately, the Anglos intermingling as before.

Here in South Pasadena we found another kind of Nisei teenager, active in sports and student-body activities. They had American names. "Bill" Yamanaka was a football hero and junior class president. "Pat" Nomi was involved with Bengals (a school service club), Scholarship Society, and office activities; she aspired to be a nurse. Both Pat and Bill were members of the Honor Society and maintained 4.0 grade point averages and hoped to attend Stanford, USC, or Pomona.

For our sophomore class party in June of 1940 we had selected Wagner's, a swimming-pool complex in Pasadena. As we lined up to pay our fee, Bill Yamanaka was denied entrance because of his skin color; our Mexican classmates would be next. The teachers fussed and sputtered with embarrassment. The Anglo students, each and every one, raised such an uproar that the pool attendant went in search of the manager. We were finally placated with an offer to have our party in a private pool which was part of the complex, at no extra fee. He stated, "The pool will be emptied, cleaned, and refilled overnight." Cleaned of what, we wondered. We learned about bigotry that day; we also learned the satisfaction of standing up for the victim.

It was nearly noon on Sunday, December 7, 1941, when we heard about the Japanese bombing of Pearl Harbor. A paperboy was shouting the news in our almost rural neighborhood; this had never happened before. Suddenly, the War which had seemed so remote from us just weeks ago was right on our doorstep. Our Japanese were absent from school on Monday and for some days after that. Could they be afraid of us, and of how we might react to this act of aggression from their homeland? Were they in physical danger? There were rumors that the Issei, the Japan-born Japanese, planned to return to Japan after saving enough money to live comfortably at home. Quite unfairly, we regarded them with some suspicion and fear, fear which increased as the Japanese army and navy took more and more territory in the Pacific and even shelled the Santa Barbara area from a mini-submarine. We did not hear until the War was over that many loyal Japanese served in U.S. forces in the European Theater of Operations.

Santa Anita and Manzanar

We had mixed emotions when we heard that "our" Japanese were to be interned at Santa Anita racetrack in stables or in crude wooden shacks before being taken to an internment camp at Manzanar, California. Only a few miles north and west of Death Valley, this parched location boasted similar characteristics: scorching heat, salt flats, volcanic rocks, and sand dunes. It was a great contrast to the verdant surroundings of the San Marino area, where many of the Japanese men and women had worked as gardeners. I'm not sure whether it was the severity of the War in the South Pacific that vindicated our fears and comforted us, or the diversion of finishing high school and starting college that took our minds off of the harsh living conditions of the Japanese.

After graduating from Pomona College, I worked at the Mayo Clinic in Rochester, Minnesota, for a short time. A laboratory accident there put me in St. Mary's Hospital for surgery. Imagine my surprise to find that Pat Nomi, the Nisei who had been my schoolmate in South Pasadena, was the OR nurse! It was a pleasant surprise for me to see a familiar face, and she also seemed pleased as she greeted me warmly. She told me that she had been sent to college to study nursing, and that life was good. In 1947 I returned to San Marino to live with my mother and attend the Huntington Memorial Hospital School of Medical technology in nearby Pasadena. Pat Nomi was working there also—a nurse in the Neurology Service.

On neither occasion did we speak of what must have been a dreadful experience at Santa Anita and Manzanar. As I have matured, I wonder how I could possibly have been so unfeeling. I do not know how many Japanese came back to the San Marino area, nor what happened to the thriving chrysanthemum nursery. I do know that these innocent folks suffered much because of our fears and because the people in power in our government did not think through the ramifications of incarcerating these gentle people in such a humiliating manner. They were suspect, but they were also in mortal danger from people who would "punish" them for the bombing of Pearl Harbor, of which they were totally innocent. However, I am also aware of the very real fear we felt, fear of folks who had kept themselves separated from our culture, fear of people who looked different, fear of the unknown. I suspect that there is no complete and final answer to the matter of "interning the Japanese," just opinions aplenty.

Libby is a third-generation Southern Californian. After graduation from South Pasadena High School and Pomona College, she trained as a Medical Technologist at the Huntington Memorial Hospital in Pasadena, California. She and her husband Robert raised six children in nearby Arcadia, where he practiced Internal Medicine and Cardiology for nearly 40 years. They came to Kendal at Hanover in 2004.

The War Comes to Vermont

Betsy Bankart Sylvester

IN LYNN, ON THE MASSACHUSETTS COAST, the early spring mornings in 1939 were chilly and dark at the hour when the shortwave broadcasts came from Europe, but it was the news that was truly chilling. Already Germany had annexed Austria and now Hitler wanted to take over the industrial fringe of Czechoslovakia, where a few Germans lived. I remember the angry voice, clearly threatening even before the translator put the words into English. We lived with foreboding, the heaviness of problems beyond control. Hitler got his way in exchange for his promise of no further territorial acquisitions; Chamberlain's tired voice told us of "peace in our time." Six months later the Nazis invaded Poland. England and France bestirred themselves in the country's defense, and the War began. Badly.

My father had come at the age of four with his family, including seven brothers and sisters, from Bradford, England, to Rochester, New Hampshire, where his father hoped his skills with woolen textiles would provide a better life for his family. The Bankarts held anything English in high esteem. England lay at the family's emotional core.

Then bombs began to fall on London. Residents slept every night in the subways, not knowing whether they would have a home to return to in the morning. I remember a newsreel of Princess Elizabeth, nearly four years younger than I, and her little sister Margaret, standing staunchly, symbolically, with their parents. So when the *Boston Evening Transcript* announced a plan to bring over 500 children to be evacuated from London and its nightly air attacks, it was entirely natural for my parents to volunteer to host two children. The *Transcript* offered to check on family background and circumstances, endeavoring to match the life style of sending and receiving families in order to help smooth the evacuees' adaptation.

A group of children arrived in Boston on July 25, 1940. They all were housed for a time at Wellesley College, while the Wellesley president wrote all the parents about their safe arrival and the host families were notified. Just before Labor Day my parents picked up two brothers, Alan and Graham Ardouin, aged nine and eleven, who stayed with us until shortly after V-E Day in 1945. They were picture-book British schoolboys in gray flannel jackets and shorts.

There was barely time in the excitement of newness to enroll them for the opening of the Swampscott Public School. After one day of classes, my mother sensed something wrong. Graham was hiding his embarrassment at being the only boy in his grade wearing shorts. She took him immediately to the local department stores and hemmed new trousers overnight, and all was well thereafter. I do not know whether the boys suffered homesickness, for they settled into our lives quickly. They turned out to be fun, interesting, exasperating, wonderful, normal kids.

The Ardouins' arrival precipitated a number of changes. First, the two young women from Nova Scotia who, as our housekeepers, were receiving room, board, wages, and training from us, quit; my mother then had to deal with meals and running a rambling five-bedroom house. We all had to take hold of any job, indoors or out—or else. Second, my parents sold that house, rented a more manageable place, and, as they had previously planned, began looking for a place to retire.

My father, a loyal Dartmouth alumnus and college football star, wanted to return to the scene of happy youthful days. He and my mother found a "handyman's special" on a narrow dirt road, a short walk from the Norwich Inn; we moved in, and some local handymen put in rudimentary plumbing, wiring, and heat. My mother, my sister Debbie, and I painted most of the inside and furnished it from nearby auctions, where the merchandise was well broken in, not attractive to dealers. The house was a great place between school and camp for the English boys, and for me as well, during vacations from school and college.

When the Pearl Harbor attack came, it unified the nation. Isolationism was no longer a possible stance. Airplane factories and shipyards expanded, and automobile factories changed their assembly lines to build the countless war machines needed. A shortage of workmen to fill all the new jobs meant that even women were employed in heavy manufacturing. "Rosie the Riveter" posters recruited the labor pool. Petroleum was essential to run the tanks, ships, and planes, so gas rationing was mandated. As a result our errands out of town had to wait until a need was really pressing. What a lark it was to drive the five miles to Lebanon! At the top of the hill near the present Centerra we would turn off the engine and, with enough initial speed, could coast almost to Densmore's brickyard, located on Hanover Street near the Lebanon High School.

Road Signs Down

All the road signs were taken down, lest Axis infiltrators find their way into innocent Vermont towns from busy rail stations such as Lewiston (Norwich) or Kendall (Pompanoosuc). We were not bothered by the signs' absence because, in a practical—though not existential—sense, we knew where we were. Best left unspoken lay the scary thought of spies slipping across the border from Canada or landing from a sub on a not-very-distant shore.

Air-space surveillance began. Deb and I trained as plane spotters with a group of other local citizens. We learned to identify the silhouettes of our fighters and bombers, as well as British, German, and Japanese planes. We believed a sneak air attack was a real possibility. Our post was a hut near the top of Meetinghouse Hill, the highest accessible hill in Norwich, and our weekly shift was three hours. We were all sworn not to divulge the code, "Dingwall," to be used when the telephone operator asked, "Number, please?"

Although the sky-watching network specified teams of two, I was, of necessity, alone on duty one day. The atmosphere was serene, with a sole Piper cub practicing lazy S-turns near the White River airport.

Suddenly, the roar of engines. A dark shape flashed over the tree-tops and vanished. In that split second I could catch sight of two engines but no other distinguishing marks. I rushed to the phone, impatient for the operator's voice. Dingwall was busy. And another roar overhead. No chance to see the plane because I was in the hut, willing the phone to work. For the rest of the shift I alternated between the phone and the open air, trying to reach Dingwall, its line constantly busy with calls from other spotters.

I felt I had failed my country.

The Unlikely Truck Driver

My mother had decreed that we would raise food to help the war effort, beginning with our own garden, expanded greatly by her renting a hill farm she had found with one of the real estate men. She organized volunteers from the military training programs at Dartmouth to help farmers on Saturdays. She would drive over to Hanover in the morning and bring the gang of workers across the river, dropping them at various farms. At barely 100 pounds and just over five feet, she was incongruous driving the big old dump truck we had inherited, and the men loved her.

Since gas was scarce, a ride to town was a treat. When we returned, my sister and I seized the opportunity. After our grubby work we took speedy showers and put on summer dresses. Those young volunteers seemed quite stunned by our Cinderella transformation.

Lighthearted though low-key moments did occur. I still remember helping pick the Austins' huge crop of green beans up at their house, the brick one near the top of the Elm Street hill. The rows were long, our backs were constantly bent, and the bushel baskets grew heavier as we picked and as our backs tired, but we could talk and joke. We enjoyed the change of scene and the fulfillment of doing needed work with companions.

Our own vegetable gardens flourished, providing for the table all summer. But we craved protein. Meat was rationed. Our "red points" did not permit meat more than once or twice a week, and part of the time we had two growing boys to feed. In our suburban innocence, we thought that raising chickens sounded easy; so, soon several dozen adorable, fluffy chicks arrived by mail and were settled into a makeshift pen in a warm corner of the kitchen. Within a few days replacing the newspapers under them no longer stifled the stench, and we had to contrive a suitable home for them, with heat, in the yard.

I was not fond of chickens; they seem brainless and neurotic. But pigs were another matter. Our one pig, Ralph, named for an ex-boyfriend of Deb's, ate up garden leftovers and gave us no problems. That success made us enthusiastic. At the Hanover garbage dump/pig farm, now site of the town Public Works, we bought about 15 small piglets, though often it seemed like more. Tending them daily made me appreciate them. Pigs are not "dirty." I believe they are the only domestic animal that, on its own, chooses one area as a toilet. True, they enjoy rolling in the mud, but, since they do not sweat, the mud cools them and prevents sunburn.

In 1943 the U.S. troops invaded Italy at Salerno. My sister enrolled in the Red Cross and was sent to Italy. My father, increasingly beleaguered in the grocery business by wartime shortages of merchandise and help, was rarely able to join us in Vermont. I took a summer job at the *Lynn Daily Evening Item* and kept house for my father in Massachusetts.

The months in Vermont were over, but they remained in my mind as an oasis in the harsh war landscape.

After graduating from Smith College, Betsy spent several years in work connected with skiing, including editing the original, infant Ski Magazine *when its headquarters were in the Upper Valley. She became a New Yorker by marriage to "Mike" Sylvester. When their two children were old enough to look after themselves, Betsy went to work at the Brearley School, serving there in various capacities for more than 20 years. The family continued its allegiance to Norwich, Vermont, and spent many vacations with the Bankart family. Betsy and Mike entered Kendal at Hanover in 1998. Mike died in 2004.*

FOOD WAS MY WEAPON

Jane Willits Mead von Salis

I WAS VERY YOUNG DURING THE WAR YEARS, and I watched my brother in the Navy sailing off to the Pacific and my brother in the Air Force going to England. Both brothers advised me to stay in school and not do anything foolish like joining the military.

I heeded their advice, but I did want to do something during summer vacations to help our war effort. Our summer home was in northern Westchester County, New York, still rural at that time. When we arrived there in the summer of 1942, my sister Betty and I set out to devise ways we could help win the War.

We spent a lot of time scouring the woods, collecting tin cans, metal scraps, and once even the zinc lining of an old-fashioned wooden ice box; in those days there were no plastics to discard. We dutifully delivered our findings to the local collection center. But that hardly sufficed to make a dent in what I perceived was our potential usefulness.

I realize now that I never had a very clear idea about how my efforts would help win the War. I am sure I was responding to the posters, slogans, and other propaganda about the need to conserve, avoid waste, be self-reliant. One of the ubiquitous slogans was "Use it up, wear it out, make it do, or do without." Also, "victory gardens" were widely praised and encouraged. So Betty and I embarked on what became our main effort during every following summer until victory: the production of food.

I persuaded my father to have a 20-by-40-foot piece of our meadow plowed up for a vegetable garden. It took me a lot of work to dig over the sod, rake the surface soil, and finally plant seeds—but what satisfaction it was to see straight rows of beans, corn, and carrots appear! Then, in the heat of summer, came hours of hoeing and weeding. I got everyone in the family to help—Mother, sister Betty, sister-in law Marianne, and visitors. It was a hot summer, but fortunately the lake was nearby and we could cool off with a good swim.

I remember selling corn to Mrs. Faunce, who complained that there were worms in the ears. How could one complain, I wondered, about a worm, when the goal was winning the War? She wanted quality; I wanted to defeat the Nazis, who we expected would invade us at any time. Indeed, we were sufficiently alarmed over the possibility of an attack by enemy paratroopers that, in the summer of 1943, several of us teen-agers received instruction by the local firemen in shooting a .22 rifle. Just where we thought the planes would come from, and be able to drop paratroopers, eludes me now, but at the time we took it very seriously.

When the vegetables were ripe, Mother drove us to the central canning center in Bedford Hills. The local women from neighboring towns gathered to wash, sort, and fill Mason jars, then boil the sealed jars. Everyone took home her share to help tide us over the winter.

By the summer of 1943, I had my junior driver's license. I persuaded the local dairy farmer to let me drive his pickup truck, loaded with cans of milk, to the pasteurizing plant once or twice a week. I felt very important as I drove home with a precious load of cases filled with bottles of rich milk, covered with ice and a heavy tarp. The milk had wonderful cream on the top of each bottle. In fact, Mother could scoop off that top cream—and, with some effort, whip it into delicious whipped cream.

And I must not forget the chickens! School ended early in May one year, and with my saved allowance I bought twenty-five baby chicks—

actually twenty-six but, sadly, one died. They were dear little yellow fluff balls, peeping happily as I fed them fine chicken feed. As they grew, I had to have help making a chicken-wire fence, the bottom edge dug into the ground to discourage foxes and weasels. The chicks spent a happy summer, neither they nor I realizing how difficult the end of their story would be. The day came when I had to take an axe and end their lives on a sturdy chopping block. It was tragic when one or two of them slipped out of my grasp and ran around the barnyard—the proverbial headless chickens.

Here Mother's expert help was invaluable. Her mother had kept chickens—a big surprise to me, since I knew my grandmother only as a gentle little 80-year-old grandma in a rocking chair. Mother showed me how to dip the chickens in hot water, suspend them on the laundry line, and pluck their feathers. After cleaning them, cutting them up, and packaging them, it was time to freeze them. Twenty-five little fryers to freeze. But in those days there were no home freezers, so we had to beg for space in a commercial freezer locker—at least that's what I thought. It occurs to me only now, as I write this many years after the fact, that Mother must have had to pay rental for the space. Well, even if it was a costly project, it was worth it: production of food was a crucial part of our war effort, and that was the most important thing.

Summer was finally over and I went off to school, proud of my contributions toward winning the War. The following year, magically, the War ended!

Jane was born in Brooklyn, New York, in 1926, and raised in Scarsdale, New York. She graduated from Smith College in 1948. After graduation, she worked at the U.S. mission to the United Nations in New York until her marriage to a Swiss national, Gaudenz von Salis, in 1952. During the next 24 years, while they raised three children, the von Salises lived in the United States, but in 1976 Jane and Gaudenz moved to Switzerland. He died in 1997, but she continued in Switzerland until 2004, when she moved directly to Kendal at Hanover.

THE HAND OF DESTINY

Constance Haaren Wells

DURING WAR TIME, OUR INDIVIDUAL PLANS for running our lives have a far lower priority than the nation's needs for running the War. But does Fate play a part too?

I grew up in Garden City, Long Island, and when the Japanese attacked Pearl Harbor on December 7, 1941, I was midway through my junior year at Connecticut College for Women in New London, Connecticut, with no plans for any particular connection with our armed forces.

My best friend, Larrie, was planning a June wedding; her fiancé, Dick, was training at the Naval Air Station in Jacksonville, Florida, where he learned to fly OS2U catapult-launched planes that were capable of landing on land or water. Right after he got his wings, he hopped on a train for New York to prepare for his wedding. His seatmate, a member of the squadron, was a tall, good-looking guy named Dan Wells.

As the two of them stepped off the train in New York, Dick learned that one of his four ushers had responded to Uncle Sam's call and was no longer available for the wedding, leaving Dick one usher short. He turned to Dan: "Can you help me out?"

"Well, first I'll need to go home to Hartford and see my folks." He did—then showed up at the rehearsal the day before the wedding.

And that's how I, the maid of honor, happened to meet Dan, the fourth usher—on the eve of the wedding. Was it destined?

The wedding took place in New York City at the Little Church around the Corner. Afterwards, Dan and I, with another couple from the wedding party, had dinner together at Café Society. We lingered there until 3:00 a.m.—and the next train the Long Island Railroad could offer was the 5:00 a.m. milk train. So, with what I later found to be characteristic resourcefulness, Dan excused himself from the table and soon returned to announce that he had located a taxi and made a deal with the driver to deliver us, for a set amount, to our various houses out on the Island. The four of us stretched out across the seats of the taxi and sang all the way home.

Next day Dan departed for his post, the Naval Air Base at Norfolk, Virginia. As soon as he got there, though, he found his orders had been changed: by a great stroke of luck (or *was* it mere luck?), he was to report to Floyd Bennett Field in Brooklyn ("they didn't know what else to do with me," he explained modestly). This airfield just happened to be within easy distance of my home—which was far more interesting to us than the fact that just five years earlier, in 1938, it had been Douglas ("Wrong-Way") Corrigan's take-off point for his "accidental" flight across the Atlantic.

Dan's duty involved patrolling the east coast for signs of enemy submarines. When he reported there, we began dating regularly, and by November—not long after I had started my final year at college and only five months after we had met—we got engaged. In view of the uncertainty of wartime, we decided not to wait until June. In February, we interrupted my college semester long enough to get married and go on a honeymoon, a skiing trip to Pico Peak in Killington, Vermont. My "trousseau" consisted of a beautifully matched skiing outfit: jacket, pants, cap, gloves, scarf à la Lanz of Salzburg.

It was a glorious time, only partially characterized by a few small inconveniences.

Dan, who was rather reserved by nature and disliked calling attention to himself, didn't want anyone to know that we were newlyweds. So we could hardly protest when we found that our accommodations were a small space with two narrow bunk beds and a long, cold, out-door walk to the facilities.

Another inconvenience for him was that I needed to write thank-you notes each evening for our wedding gifts—necessary, I insisted, before I returned to the hallowed halls of learning and midterms.

And then one evening back in the lodge, while I was trying to get warm, I backed too near to the pot-bellied stove and singed my beauti-ful new skiing clothes. "Oh-oh," groaned Dan, seeing my scorched rear view, "the honeymoon is over."

Back from our wedding trip, we parted ways once again—Dan to Floyd Bennett Field, I to finish my senior year. Even so, we were just a train ride apart. Sometimes he would come up to my campus; we'd rent a room downtown, and I would trudge up the hill to class in the morning. Or, I would use one of my precious cuts from class in order to escape early and meet him in New York.

At last, after graduation in June, we were able to live together as a married couple in an apartment in Brooklyn—with maid service, no less. Then on December 7, 1943, two years to the day after Pearl Harbor, Dan received orders to report to the naval base at Martha's Vineyard, where he was trained to fly carrier-based single-engine TBM Avenger torpedo bombers. Our home there was a converted pearl shop with a mammoth coal-burning stove for cooking and a closed-off back stair-way, which the heat from the stove never reached, for a refrigerator.

California

Dan's next tour of duty took us to California. He flew to San Diego with the squadron, while I drove across the country with Marv Anderson, a squadron-mate of Dan's, and his wife Shirley. We were all to meet up with Dan at the Naval Air Station in Oakland; but when Marv checked in, he found orders changed. Within a few hours we heard planes ap-proaching, and his finely attuned ears recognized them: "Hey! Those are *our* planes!"

Sure enough, they appeared, flying in formation, and began peel-ing off for landing. I got the thrill of my life watching them: I didn't know *which* plane Dan was piloting, but I knew it was one of them.

The squadron was to be based at Long Beach, so with two other couples we set about the formidable wartime task of finding a place to live, in nearby Bellflower. Nothing was available, and we were reduced to walking up one street and down another knocking on doors: "We need a place to live temporarily. Could you rent us a room?"

And three families, all on the same street, actually did.

There, for a while, the six of us carried on a normal life, like peacetime suburban couples: husband goes off to work in the morning and comes home at six in the evening. We shared shopping, cocktail hours, dinners, parties, life in general. We were like a family. And we wives all got pregnant.

Suddenly, one black day Dan came home looking quite different from his usual relaxed self. One of our "family" had been killed that morning in a crash takeoff during a routine training flight.

From that moment, war deaths were no longer a matter of cold, impersonal statistics; they were an immediate personal reality. They could happen right here on the block to one of our own dear husbands. We now saw the War in a whole different light.

Dan was to accompany the body home by train later. Meanwhile, I drove back east with La Veda, the bereaved wife, to their home in Des Moines, Iowa. During that car trip we became especially close friends. She was so controlled, so brave—and we even had times for laughter. Only the day before we were to arrive did I see that she was becoming increasingly anxious as she prepared for the terrible ordeal of returning alone to face families and friends. In this small rural farming community her husband was a hero, and his death an almost unbearable defeat.

I found myself reflecting on the way the War had brought together a great hodgepodge of people from wildly assorted areas—people from humble Midwestern farm communities, favored New York City members of the Four Hundred, the vast middle-class from coast to coast—and molded them into a single force where all faced the same uncertainties and hardships and risks. The War had unified us as a country.

To the Pacific

Dan continued his training at Long Beach until he was ordered into combat duty in the Pacific area as a bomber pilot. Just before Thanksgiving in 1944, I saw him off from San Francisco; then I went back to my home in Garden City—to wait. Our baby was due in January 1945. But who knew when Dan would be back?

As it turned out, he arrived only six weeks after Leslie, our daughter, was born. After several months of active combat duty, he had been ordered to Hawaii for reassignment, most likely as a combat replacement. But—destiny again?—Dan was directed to return to stateside duty. He called from California to tell me that he was on his way home on leave.

Communications being imperfect, though, I had no further word until he unexpectedly showed up in person—in the middle of a bitter cold night early in spring. He had just come in on the Long Island Railroad and found no means of predawn transportation to my home—not even an off-duty taxi. But he was absolutely determined to see his new daughter without losing another minute. Undeterred by rain, and sleet, and gloom of night, wearing his lightweight summer uniform in the freezing weather, he *ran* the remaining six miles from the station at top speed.

And it cost him nothing more than a severe bout of pneumonia later on. Small price!

For now, he was through with combat service. When the atomic bombs fell on Hiroshima and Nagasaki and the Japanese surrendered on board the battleship *USS Missouri* in the late summer of 1945, the young Wells family was living in Hollywood, Florida, while Dan remained stationed at the U.S. Naval Air Training Command at Opa Locka airfield as an instructor.

Soon after the War, Dan retired with the rank of Commander, though he continued in the Reserves for many years and was recalled to active duty in 1951 during the Korean War.

Then our traveling years began, from Italy to the Philippines, where he pointed out to me the various places he had been stationed and areas where his squadron had dropped bombs. It was upsetting to be told.

War is a dirty game, went the saying. But we were among the lucky ones. Even though Dan had witnessed many horrors at first hand during his engagement in the Pacific arena, he himself came home unscathed. We were a typical young wartime family struggling as best we could to live lives as near normal as possible. Fate was especially generous to us through these war years. We were grateful, too, for a happy, fulfilled married life which lasted almost another half century.

After the War, Dan finished up his interrupted college degree. He and Connie brought up three children while moving around a good deal as Dan's work and continuing service in the Naval Air Reserves took them worldwide, from Italy to the Philippines to various U.S. naval air bases in between times. Finally, in 1991, after a ten-year residence in their converted ski lodge in New London, New Hampshire, they moved into Kendal at Hanover. Dan died in 1995.

Post-War Service

FROM KP TO BLAIR HOUSE

~

Jean Wiley Beard

M Y ONLY EXPERIENCE WITH WORLD WAR II, until rather late, was indirect. I was the youngest of five sisters; two of them were married to servicemen, and a third had joined the Army Nurse Corps. Meanwhile, I had graduated from the University of Delaware in Newark in 1943, with a major in Physical Education, and gone on to teach Phys Ed in a small-town public school, grades 1-12.

During this time, I learned that the U.S. Army was offering a course in Physical Therapy for those with a background in physical education or chemistry. Jumping at the chance to prepare myself for a second career, I applied and was accepted.

On April 12, 1945—a day of deep national mourning for the death of President Roosevelt—I embarked on my first ever overnight train trip headed for Fort Des Moines, Iowa, to begin basic training as a private in the Women's Army Corps.

WAC privates were paid "21 dollars a day, once a month." Basic training consisted of the usual: marching drills, formal parades, calisthenics, military courtesy, and KP duty. This latter in the WAC was assigned not as a punishment for misconduct but as a regular duty, and my turn came around only twice. My first KP assignment was to undertake the regular chores connected with preparing the meals for the day; the second time, I was to "scrub the bottom eight inches of the table and chair legs in the Mess Hall."

We spent Friday nights preparing for Saturday inspections. Our bed sheets and blankets had to be sufficiently taut to bounce a quarter; our shoes—including the soles—had to be polished; our hair had to be tucked up from the back of our collars.

The three months of basic training ended with a gas-mask drill. Preparing for the two-week leave before our next assignment, we asked what we should do with the gas masks. "Take them with you," we were told, "and turn them in at your next station." We found this puzzling in view of the secrecy that surrounded the gas masks when they had been issued to us: we were strictly forbidden even to take our pictures in them.

Walter Reed

My next assignment was Walter Reed General Hospital in Washington, D.C. There I was promoted to corporal T/5, with a pay raise to $39 a month, ready to embark on the course in physical therapy which had been my goal when I signed up. Walter Reed was, indeed, a special place. It was the Army's largest center for the treatment of amputees; moreover, being there gave me the opportunity to be right in the midst of the excitement on the political scene. Only two months earlier our country had celebrated the end of the War in Europe. On May 8, 1945, the Allies had formally accepted the unconditional surrender of the armed forces of Nazi Germany.

But World War II was not yet over. Our nine-month course had barely begun, and we were highly motivated to study. Failure to pass meant the obligation to remain in the WAC for three years in whatever assignment was needed at the time, and we couldn't see ourselves assigned to Cooks and Bakers School, say, or the Motor Corps.

After just a few more weeks, during which things went along smoothly, the War finally did end—with V-J Day, on August 15, 1945. There was great excitement in our barracks and we were soon on our way down town to join in the celebration.

At last, in March 1946, after the final months of training, graduation day came. We were discharged from the WAC and inducted into the Womens Medical Specialists Corps, which was created during World War II as a branch of the Army complementary to the Army Nurse Corps and was composed of physical therapists, occupational therapists, and dieticians. We entered the WMSC with the rank of Second Lieutenant and the title Registered Physical Therapist.

The Glen

As Army officers, we lived at Walter Reed's rehabilitation center at The Glen (originally Forest Brook Glen, a private school for girls) just over the Maryland line. This cluster of buildings was architecturally unusual: each was of a different style. Ours was an Italian Villa, one of the officers' quarters was The Pagoda, another was The Windmill. The Castle was our recreational space, where we held parties, sometimes in celebration of promotions, sometimes to bid farewell to friends and colleagues.

Working assignments were divided between patients at the Hospital in town and patients at the therapy department at The Glen. All were soldiers recovering from war wounds, and most were amputees.

As we gave them their physical therapy treatments, at their bedsides or in the clinics, warm relationships often developed, several times resulting in marriages between therapist and patient. We shared many other pleasant experiences with the patients. They often invited us to come back after working hours to play cards, or see a movie, or go with them to special programs. (To this day, whenever I hear "Chestnuts Roasting on an Open Fire," I associate it with one such occasion when I heard it on a patient's radio.) Famous entertainers and notable public figures often showed their compassion for these wounded veterans by coming to the Hospital or The Glen to visit and to entertain them.

Aside from our active social life at our Villa and our Castle, we took part in other events in the D.C. area. On many Saturday nights, we were invited to enjoy dancing at the Officers Club at Andrews Air Force Base nearby, and on Sunday afternoons in the summer we often went picnicking on the western shore of Chesapeake Bay. Officers whose amputations permitted were able to participate in these good times.

On one especially memorable occasion, I was invited to go to the

McLean Mansion on Tenleytown Road, NW, to enjoy the hospitality of Mrs. Evalyn Walsh McLean, the American mining heiress and socialite, who—like so many other well-known personalities—took pleasure in extending generosity toward the wounded soldiers. Mrs. McLean was famous for, among other things, being the last private owner of the 45-carat Hope Diamond, and the highlight of the evening came when she brought out the Diamond for us to see, admire, and actually hold in our hands.

One of my final assignments at Walter Reed was the responsibility for treating officers on Ward One. I became particularly interested in a certain captain who was waiting for an exceptionally difficult bone graft for his left femur, which, if it were successful, would be the largest bone graft ever done at Walter Reed. In preparation, I treated him with massage at the site of the prospective graft along with weight-bearing exercise to stimulate circulation and bone growth.

As it turned out, unfortunately, the graft did not take. But the captain, provided with a full leg brace, was at least able to get around—and even to dance acceptably!

To Anchorage

Two final events, one anticipated as pleasure and the other as duty, were of very special significance.

The first took place during the last two-week leave before my discharge in August 1949. Millie, my roommate, was determined that she and I should take advantage of our privilege of hopping a free flight with the Army Air Force for a trip from D.C. to Anchorage, Alaska, to visit a mutual Physical Therapist pal. And we did!

Arrangements were made, and early one July morning we showed up at Andrews Air Force Base. There, they issued us parachutes, instructed us on how to use them, and then told us to throw them into the back of a B-25 bomber. When we climbed in ourselves, between our luggage and the parachutes there was barely room for the two of us.

The trip proved to be somewhat different from the straightforward D.C.-to-Alaska hop that we had anticipated. After a stopover in Omaha, we finally landed in Great Falls, Montana, where we had to cool our heels for three whole days before taking off again. This time—on my birthday, as it happened—we flew on an Army cargo plane that was delivering parts and equipment to various bases. We took our seats on benches across from several other passengers who were traveling on Army business, confidently expecting that our next stop would be Anchorage.

The captain had told us we could go forward during the trip if we were interested in a pilot's-eye view, and I did. But I had no sooner gone through the door when the crew became aware that one of the four engines had stopped.

"Perhaps you'd better go back to your seat," the captain suggested. I did so, determined not to alarm the others by mentioning the dead engine.

"What's going on up there?" asked the man sitting next to me.

"Oh, nothing." I shrugged.

"Then why," he asked, "is that propeller standing still?"

It then occurred to me to wonder what was going to happen next.

What happened next was that we managed to land at Edmonton, Canada, where an engine we were delivering was unloaded from our cargo and installed on our own plane.

And so, after yet another long wait, we took off once more—and finally landed at Anchorage.

With four days already gone from our two-week leave, we were prepared to make the most of the remaining time happily visiting our friend. But when we checked in on arrival, we were told that we must be ready in *three days* to return to the "mainland" (as the rest of the United States was known to them before Alaska joined the Union in 1959). They were adamant, though, and remained deaf to our pleas for a longer stay.

There was nothing to do but resign ourselves to going back early (this time on a less eventful trip) and finishing up our leave time at home.

Blair House

When I reported back for my final two weeks of duty at the hospital, I learned that one of my major assignments was to treat Mrs. Wallace, Bess Truman's mother. At the time, the First Family was living at Blair House while the White House, across the street, underwent major structural repairs. After I was taken to Blair House for a preliminary introductory visit, the time came for me to go by myself.

I entered and went right up to Mrs. Wallace's room, only to find the door closed. I knocked. There was no answer. Nobody was around. I didn't want to open the door, fearing that something might have happened to Mrs. Wallace. What to do? I finally uttered a timid "Yoo-hoo!" No answer. I tried it again. This time, Mrs. Truman heard me from somewhere and came down the hall. She received me very graciously and went into the room herself. It turned out that Mrs. Wallace had been in the bathroom!

I proceeded to give her the first of her series of treatments, a general body massage, and continued my visits three times a week until the date of my discharge. Each time I left from these visits, Mrs. Wallace generously insisted that I take along some of the bounty of her beautiful flowers and fruit, to share with "the girls."

On one of these occasions, I met Margaret Truman, too. She was visiting her grandmother and had been taking a sunbath in the back yard. And now, she said, she was about to give herself a home permanent!

And so, this aspect of my wartime experiences ended in a tenuous connection with some illustrious people—if not the President of the United States himself, at least with three female generations of his family.

I had journeyed from Private to First Lieutenant—from KP to Blair House.

After her discharge from the Army as 1st Lieutenant, Jean Wiley continued as a physical therapist, working with the physically handicapped. For 20 years she was principal of The John G. Leach School in New Castle, Delaware, a public school for children with physical handicaps, also serving on numerous boards of directors of health and education agencies in Delaware and Pennsylvania. In 1958 she married Eugene Beard, and in 1991 they moved into Kendal at Hanover. Eugene died in 1995. Jean is interested in the Enfield Shaker Museum and has supported their volunteer activities. She is an active member of St. Thomas Episcopal Church in Hanover.

Bouncing Along with Zhukov

Janine Daudon Hawkes

Janie with her husband Herbert Hawkes

My FATHER'S WW I HISTORY in France, Russia, Algeria, and later during WW II with the United States Army, led to a complicated national identity for me. So my father's story—and my mother's—is interwoven with my own WW II experience and is thus worth recounting.

Dad—Col. René Jean Daudon—was born in the Champagne area of France. He was in Russia, where he had lived and was educated for 12 years, on vacation from an engineering university in Frankfurt, Germany. When WW I broke out, he rushed back to France by way of Murmansk and the Low Countries so that he could enlist in the French army before the War was over. At the enlistment center, the officer in charge asked, "What kind of a damn fool are you to come all this way to be killed?" He served in the French army and survived the battle of Verdun.

Following the Russian Revolution, the Allies were worried that a token Russian brigade would contaminate their soldiers with revolutionary ideas. Because Dad spoke Russian, he was ordered to accompany these Russians to Algeria to work in a vineyard far from Europe.

They, and he, remained there until the War ended, whereupon my father accompanied them on the trip back to Russia, by then the Soviet Union. He watched as "the poor devils" (as he put it) were conscripted into the White Russian army. For this service to the Tsarist government he received two medals, the Order of St. Stanislaus and the Order of Ste. Anne.

But my father's story was only half of my complicated national identity. My mother, an American citizen, went to school in Switzerland and met my father on a ship; they had a whirlwind romance and were married in France. I was born in Nice, my brother Dan in Paris. But because life was difficult in France after WW I, my parents came to the United States, where my father continued his education. He said he had almost received a Ph.D. from the University of Pennsylvania— "almost" because he had chosen to write a bibliography of the works of Rabelais, and the effort became more than daunting. I think he was glad to give it up to join the U.S. Army, where he gained an officer's commission.

Early in WW II, American war matériel was sent to Russia by way of Persia (now Iran) because of the devastating impact Germany's "wolf-pack" submarine attacks were having on convoys traversing the North Atlantic and the Baltic Sea. The convoy that my Dad had been assigned to was routed into the Pacific Ocean, a longer but safer route that ended up in Persia. While in Tehran, he was invited to many Russian army parties and said that he often had to cry for mercy while trying to keep up with the alcohol consumption of his hosts. The Russians encouraged him to wear his WW I Russian medals because "they are part of our history!"

Because of his multilinguistic skills, he became extremely valuable to the Army as a translator and was one of the translators at the Tehran conference involving Franklin D. Roosevelt, Winston Churchill, and Josef Stalin. After WW II ended, he was stationed in Berlin, which by then had been divided into four parts by the Allies. Again he served as a translator and, as he later admitted, also functioned as a spy. Initially after the division of the city, one could easily travel between the American, French, British, and Russian sectors. But the Russians later sealed off their sector, which was the poorest part of Berlin: the Soviets did not want their soldiers to see how well the people in the West lived.

*Col. René Jean Daudon,
Janie's Father*

My college years at Bryn Mawr were interrupted when my family moved to Berlin in June 1946, the first American dependents to arrive there. On the ship were two other American girls my age, and we became close friends, forming a nucleus of young ladies of many nationalities who could play bridge, ride horses, and play golf together. Life was very gay for the occupation forces. We lived in a house in Dahlem, which, supposedly, was spared by our Air Corps so Americans would have a place to live. There was a large garden with several fruit trees, and I recall gorging myself on fresh cherries. The British sector included the Wansee, a large lake where there were sailboat races twice a week. My dad was an excellent skipper, and we won a few of those races.

A black market was flourishing in Berlin when we arrived. One soldier bought a Steinway grand piano for 30 cartons of cigarettes, and the Army shipped it to the United States. We could buy Meissen and Dresden china, jewelry, and furniture for a few cigarettes. From his days in Russia, my father knew a Russian noblewoman who had married a German count. After the War, she went by train to Jena in the Russian zone to dig up the family cache of jewels buried during the War—a very dangerous undertaking. She brought them back hidden under her clothes and sold them, so they had white bread, real butter, coffee, and other scarce items. We were invited to see the jewels: emeralds, rubies, and diamonds, quite amazing to this American girl. My Dad bought two ruby rings and some diamonds to put around the central ruby and gave one to me and one to my sister-in-law. When General Clay arrived, his wife found the system to be unfair, and she started a legal market where Germans could get a decent price.

Instead of embassies, Allied governments from Scandinavia to South Africa to India established diplomatic missions. Almost every night, one mission or another had a party—a girl's dream. At one party I danced with the Crown Prince of Luxembourg, who was not only handsome but also a good dancer.

The Soviet parties were lavish: bowls of caviar, both black and red, tables just groaning with food and liquor, including Russian champagne (a contradiction in terms).

At one Russian party, I danced with Marshall Zhukov. Later I discovered that he was a Russian career officer in the Red army who, during World War II, had played a pivotal role in leading the Red army through much of Eastern Europe, to liberate the Soviet Union and other nations from the Axis Powers' occupation and conquer Berlin; he was the most decorated general in the history of both Russia and the Soviet Union. He was about my size and did not speak English; also, he was not a good dancer, so we just bounced along!

I was totally amazed that so soon after the War had ended, two opera companies were giving performances. The first one we attended was *Madame Butterfly*. Having been a fan of the Metropolitan Opera in New York, I was accustomed to hearing opera sung in the language of the composer, but here was an opera written by an Italian about a love affair between an American and a Japanese being sung in German!

The most exciting performance I attended in Berlin, never to be forgotten, was given by Moiseyev Russian singers and dancers. When they sang a beautiful haunting song called *Evening Bells*, the audience went wild, and the song had to be repeated three times. For years I searched for a recording of it, to no avail; then in 2009, in Rutland, Vermont, the Russian Boys Choir sang it—and was selling it on CDs!

There is so much to say about that experience, one hardly knows where to stop.

One of the more interesting outcomes of the War was that my brother Dan and I were discovered to be "illegal aliens," in the language of today. My mother had two passports, American and French. To go to the United States for her brother's wedding, she used the French one, with a visiting visa, and our names were not mentioned: we were listed simply as *deux enfants*. After the wedding, my mother did not return to France, and Dad joined us in the United States. When he was naturalized, he asked about the status of his two children and was assured that since he was now a citizen, so were we. However, someone in the bureaucracy overlooked the fact that we were still "visitors": we learned this only when Dan tried to get into the V-12 program, and neither the Army nor the Navy would take him. But the Marines were not so picky, and he earned his citizenship through his service as a United States Marine. During wartime, I actually drove a jeep for the Navy—until it was discovered that I was not an American citizen.

For me, getting into the United States was not hard, but the means of achieving it seemed ridiculous: I had to go to Niagara Falls, New York, go across the Rainbow Bridge to Canada, then walk back and enter the United States on the 1946 French immigration quota. It wasn't all bad, though; the trip was exciting and memorable. The Falls had not lost some of its rocks, and an excursion aboard The *Maid of the Mist* below the Falls was thrilling.

In less than five years after that, I became an American citizen through my marriage to an American. At the naturalization ceremony I was the only one who could speak English! I am now a citizen, my children are citizens, and I am living happily at Kendal in Hanover with my many memories.

At age four Janie attended an experimental "open-air" school—it was open even in the winter, when students wore boots and wool coats. This was followed by seven years at Haverford Friends School, where she learned to love learning for its own sake. After marrying a New Orleanian, she had four great children. Working as a Library Aide in a black school in New Orleans was a time when she felt she was really contributing to the opening of children's eyes to the world of literature. She has been active in peace efforts in all parts of the world. Janie came to Kendal at Hanover in 1991.

Epilogue

HAWKS

Robert Christie

(This poem was inspired by reading Andrew Carroll's book War Letters.*)*

Hawks,
read the letters,
the war letters.
How can you read them
and not cringe or weep?

Choose a war,
any war,
but then focus on ours, WW II…

Do you want to read of the carnage at
the water's edge?
Try a Marine's letter home
about the first wave at Iwo Jima
where he lost an eye and part of his face.
Do you want to know the view
from a B-24 over Ploesti?
Savor Bubba Young's letter
before he died
describing sudden death in the skies
and devastation on the ground.
Or let nurse
June Wandrey describe
death
in a field hospital.

Hawks, have you forgotten,
or maybe never knew…
of the GIs' terror during the shelling
at Monte Cassino.

And the agony at Anzio?
Read about Nagasaki:
once again you can hear the silences
of the dead in a dead city
penned in a letter by
Fireman First-Class Keith Lynch.

Enough of their letters have been saved
to tell the anguished stories:
the notes to Mom;
to Susie; a wife about to bear a child;
the last letter home,
scratched out in a blessed interval
in a battle's fury.

Words penciled and penned by
an infantryman, lonely, terrified of death,
in a foxhole laden with his own excrement;
courageous words of phony optimism
to calm the fears of those at home;
misspelled words
from one who knew
he was about to die
and didn't...,
but lived
to see his buddy
dropped by a sniper's bullet
through the head.

Read, Hawks, the letters of death and dying;
death,
so merciful when sudden and total;
or death of a man,
his belly ripped open by shrapnel,
trying to hold in his spilling guts
plaintively sobbing to anyone,
asking if he's going to die.

And read, Hawks, accounts of the agony
of a not-yet-dead GI,
lying on the battlefield
calling for his mother.

Read the tales of men starving
and rotting in a prison camp
or a Japanese "hell ship"
dying of thirst, dehydration,
and cholera.
Read about the men
wantonly bayoneted or beheaded
on a death march.

How many good and precious lives
need be traded
for the death of one madman,
of one Hitler,
of one Mussolini,
of one Hideki Tojo,
of one Saddam Hussein?
Consider the cynical words of a Joseph Stalin,
that one death is a tragedy,
a million deaths only a statistic.

Read the letters.
Listen to the cautions of the
generals
who have been there and through it all.
They know.
But you will only get the answer you asked for:
the numbers.

You want another war, O kings, presidents,
prime ministers, dictators,
secretaries of defense (*sic*),
senators, congressmen?

Then stand up, O Hawks,
you super-patriots, you,
who some have called chicken-hawks,
so sure that you will never have to see battle!

Hawks!
Stand up!
Enlist!
Be the first to enter into harm's way.
Offer your own blood
as did the kings of old,
leading their armies into battle.

Take your turn.
Have your chance to write a letter
from some far-off land
lying to your best friend's mother
about how courageously
her son or daughter died,
suffering no pain.

But Hawks, first read the war letters;
perhaps then you can think of another way.
A way other than
the shedding
of someone else's blood.

LIST OF CONTRIBUTORS